The People of South Africa

The People

OF

SOUTH AFRICA

by *Sarah Gertrude Millin*

ALFRED A. KNOPF   NEW YORK
1954

L. C. catalog card number: 53–6853

THIS IS A BORZOI BOOK,
PUBLISHED BY ALFRED A. KNOPF, INC.

FIRST AMERICAN EDITION

TO
MY HUSBAND
PHILIP MILLIN

PREFACE

This book is based on a book, called THE SOUTH AFRICANS, which first appeared in 1926, and then, revised and enlarged, in 1934. "South Africa," said the Preface to the second edition, "with all the world, has changed." How little one knew in 1934 what change meant!

The book of 1954 is half again as long as the book of 1926. Four fifths of it is new. Not many pages are unaltered.

For the sake of continuity, however, the system of the book remains the same and the beginning and end are more or less as in 1934.

S.G.M.

CONTENTS

Part One

CHAPTER   PAGE

I   THE BEGINNINGS OF SOUTH AFRICA   3

II   SOUTH AFRICA AND THE DIAMOND ADVEN-
           TURERS   48

III   SOUTH AFRICA AND THE GOLD ADVENTURERS   75

IV   LIVING IN SOUTH AFRICA   102

V   POLITICS IN SOUTH AFRICA   122

Part Two

VI   THE AFRIKANERS (Dutchmen, Boers)   203

VII   THE ENGLISH   225

VIII   THE JEWS   231

IX   THE INDIANS   239

X   THE HALF-CASTES (Coloureds, Kleurlinge,
        Mixed Breeds, Cape People, Bastaards) 262

XI   THE AFRICANS (Bantus, Natives, Kaffirs)   274

INDEX   *follows page* 337

Part

ONE

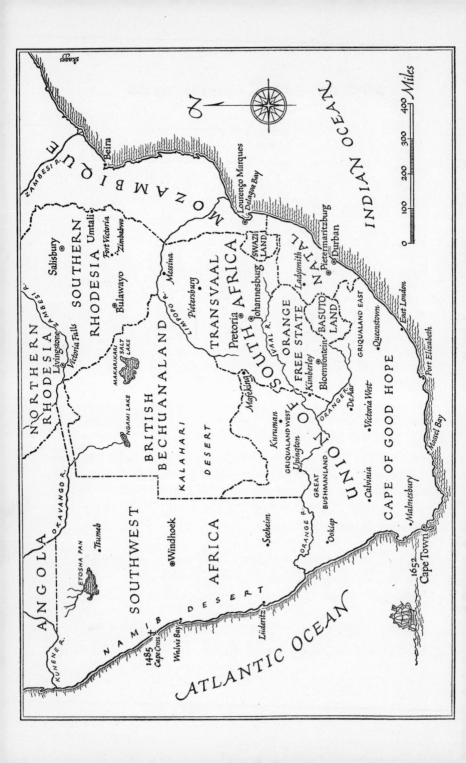

CHAPTER ONE

The Beginnings of South Africa

I

Are we a great and independent South Africa?" Rhodes asked in his maiden speech in the old Cape Parliament. "No, we are only the population of a third-class English city set in a great continent."

He said it in the year 1881. That was seven decades back. He meant, when he spoke of the population of South Africa (and most do today), the white population of South Africa. He did not include in the population of South Africa those black ones who, in calling themselves Bantu, declare that they are people too—Bantu: people, not dumb things —and he did not mean the other people who are not white.

The white South Africans are today more than the population of a third-class English city: they are a fourth of the population of greater London. All the Union's inhabitants together—black, coloured, and white—are somewhat more than the population of greater London.

The Union is that association of the two Boer republics and the two British colonies Rhodes always spoke of, but did not live to see.

In 1894, again, Rhodes spoke of a separation of black and white and he called it a Bill for Africa.

He called it a Bill for Africa because he meant it to set a way of life for his All-Red route from the Cape to Cairo.

Rhodes's Bill for Africa—this separate way of life for black and white throughout Africa—is the model followed by every Prime Minister since Union: Generals Botha and Smuts; General Hertzog and Dr. Malan too.

Only General Hertzog and Dr. Malan said Apartheid, instead of Separation. Their Nationalist followers supported them on the word Apartheid.

The word Apartheid means Apart-hood. It exactly means Separation.

The word Red, however, has now a different meaning from what Rhodes meant in 1894. It stands for Russia, and not Britain. Therefore, Dr. Malan, like Rhodes, wants a Bill for Africa.

Between the Union and Egypt are 250,000 white people and 150,000,000 black people.

And though, from the beginning of his public life, Rhodes feared the Germans, he did not foresee that, only twelve years after his death, they would begin that assault on the world which has led to the upsurge of all those previously held down; the decline, the defeat, the departure of their lords; a congress of nations in which two thirds of the delegates represent the dark-skinned peoples of the world.

When Anthony Trollope came to South Africa in the year 1877, he went through it—its provinces and problems—swiftly and imperturbably and thoroughly, as was his way. He dined with governors; slept in Boer farmhouses; inspected mission-schools; talked with Kaffirs, Hottentots, poor whites, Dutchmen, Englishmen. One used then the word Kaffirs. Until a generation ago, the word Kaffirs, which is now thought offensive, was used by officials, missionaries, and all other people in South Africa, including the natives themselves.

Trollope was sixty-two, but he bought himself a cart and a team of horses, and travelled across land as yet untracked by railways. He entered a Transvaal recently annexed by Sir Theophilus Shepstone, his eight civil servants, and twenty-five policemen. He chronicled, as he went on his way, a new revolt by Kreli and his Galekas. He saw the importance of the diamond fields, but not the greater importance of the gold fields. And standing thus at the exact point in history where the old Africa ended and the new Africa began—looking, listening, recording—he said: "I shall write my book and not yours"; and, in the Bay of Biscay, as he was going home, he wrote his conclusion: "South Africa," he wrote, "is a country of black men—and not of white men. It has been so; it is so; and it will be so."

Every now and then, from her dreams of glory, South Africa sits up suddenly, as one awakened by the clapping of his own heart, and asks if that is true; if it is really possible that this land may not be the land of the white man and the heritage of his children; if South Africa is, indeed, as Anthony Trollope said, a land, not of white men, but of black men.

There is in South Africa a river called the Vaal River. It is not a wonder of the world like the Victoria Falls. It has not the grandeur of the great mountains of the Cape of Storms against which two oceans battle. It has not the terrible, primeval beauty of the naked and desolate ranges of the Transvaal. But yet it is this Vaal River, this dun-coloured river, which most truly symbolizes South Africa.

That is what its Afrikaans name means—dun-coloured. In olden days the Hottentots called it, applying to it the adjective that described their own skins, the Gij Gariep, the Yellow River.

One bathes in this Vaal River, and there is a fine layer of mud settled on one's chin. In winter, when in the north it does not rain, it trickles apologetically among great black shiny defiant stones; and in summer, swollen by the rains of the Transvaal, it rushes down in a thundering wall of water, thick and overbearing and dangerous and arrogant, like a whining beggar who has been left a fortune overnight. Boers, escaping from the pressure of humanity—looking for some place where they might not see the smoke from the next man's habitation—sought for loneliness beside it and across it. The half-caste Griquas and Bastaards, trying to make nations of themselves, settled along it in little defensive groups, and with them came missionaries. The black queen Mantatisi trained her soldiers in frightfulness along its banks. All flying from the wrath of God and man came to it for refuge. . . .

Under the hot sun it shines, when it is not in flood, like molten metal. It runs through the lands of diamonds and gold. In the very bed of it there are diamonds, and the adventurous and the careless and the outcast seek in it for sudden wealth. From its strength the land gets power, from its surplus, food. Its water is drunk in three provinces.

And along its banks are trees called Wag-'n-bietjie trees —Wait-a-bit, that Afrikaans name means, because there are thorns on the trees which catch at one and make one stop . . . wait-a-bit.

Wag-'n-bietjie has for long been the mood of South Africa. It has said the words thoughtfully, menacingly, alluringly, hopefully. In the old days, when the question of the black man rose before South Africa, it said: "Yes, yes. One day. When we have time. Wait-a-bit."

But the two German wars came, and all was different in the world. The thorn of the Wag-'n-bietjie was in the flesh, the wound was festering, and there was no more time for anyone to wait-a-bit.

Even for South Africa there is no more time to wait-a-bit.

II

So now a feeling begins to run through the land like the feeling that is communicated from one to another in a crowd until suddenly there rises up a common cry. Today all understand that South Africa can no longer ignore its native question, can no longer depend on it to solve itself. The black man and the white man are irking one another; the Indian is troubling both; and whether it is to be eventually a black man's country or a white man's country or an Asian's country is not the only question. There is the question of the present as well as the future.

Here we all are, a heterogeneous collection of Europeans; an imported and established population of Indians; a man-rather than a God-created nation of half-castes; a ghost-hood of yellow aboriginals and a flood—a strong and spreading flood—of dark-skinned peoples. And, since we are not alone on the planet, and, so small as we are, cannot control our own destinies, the problem that chiefly concerns us is how, being here together, we may live and grow with the least unhappiness and enmity.

Now a distinction has just been made between the South African aboriginals and the spreading flood of other African peoples. These, in the United States, would be called Negroes. In the word Bantu they simply declare themselves to be people, which is to say, human beings—not dumb animals. In the book named *The South Africans*, the predecessor of this book which was written twenty-three years ago, the word Kaffir was used for them — Kaffir being to the East African Arabs, whose blood is in them, an infidel, a non-believer in Mahomet; Kaffir being the name officials, missionaries, and others called them; Kaffirland—the Kaffraria of today—being the land where Europeans first met them; the Kaffir Wars being in origin their own civil wars;

Kaffir being what they called themselves. A hundred years
ago the Fengu, Tiyo Soga, the first Christian minister
among the South African natives, said: "If you wish to
gain credit for yourselves—if you do not wish to feel the
taint of men which you sometimes may be made to feel—
take your place in the world as coloured, not as white, as
Kaffirs, not as Englishmen. . . . You, my children, belong
to a primitive race of men . . . second to none in nobility
of character."

He said these words in a testament he left to his family
which he called: "The Inheritance of My Children." But
there was a particular reason why he told his children rather
to be Kaffirs than Englishmen. He went overseas and married a British woman, and so did all but one of his sons.
Most of his grandchildren, therefore, could only to a quarter claim to belong to this race of men he justly thought second to no other primitive race in nobility of character, even
though in the United States they would impartially be described as coloured or Negro. For all his attempt and the
attempts of his children to join the white race, in the end
it was his discovery that, for their own good, his children
had better "take their place in the world" as what he called
Kaffirs.

A new *South Africans* came out in the thirties. And by
then it seemed better to use the word Native, instead of
Kaffir, for many thought the term Kaffir—infidel—unpleas-
ing, and Native is what they are now generally and officially
called: even though history cannot change the name of
the Kaffir Wars; Kaffraria still stands; the South African
gold share-market is referred to, anywhere in the world, as
Kaffirs.

We are now in the nineteen-fifties. And now the term
Native is being disliked. Native remains the official term;
most natives call themselves natives; their own college in the

Cape is the Fort Hare Native College; but Negrophilists use the word African; the intellectuals among themselves also use the word African; the South African Broadcasting Corporation has instructed its broadcasters to say African.

Well, African. Geographically and racially they are certainly African, but so are all their kind on the continent of Africa. The term African therefore does not associate them with South Africa, it gives them no nationhood in their own country.

Again, in the Union of South Africa, there are two white peoples with two different languages. Though an African in English is a black man, an Afrikaner in Afrikaans is a white man of Boer descent, and if he translated the word African into his own language he changes a black into a white man.

Further, the English form of Afrikaner is Afrikander, and this is also a breed of cattle. And then a South African, in either Afrikaans or English, is a white citizen of any European descent whose land is South Africa; and no black man, however long his ancestors have lived in the land, can be a South African; and no white man, born of the land, is its native; and anyhow South Africa has to be distinguished from Southern Africa since South Africa is only a piece of Southern Africa.

There is a further complication. The Hottentots the first Dutch settlers found at the Cape were called the Cape Men and now the mixed breeds of Hottentot, Negro, Asiatic, and European descent are called the Cape People; so Europeans living in the Cape are not Cape people, but the Afrikaners often refer to the Cape People as simply Hottentots, for, after all, the Hottentots were the original Cape People.

In this book the terms Bantu, Kaffir, Native, African, Black Man will be used, as seems suitable at the moment, for those dark invaders who arrived in South Africa no sooner than the Europeans; whom the Europeans met as

they were escaping east from other Europeans; who, like
the Europeans, overcame the little yellow men they found
there—the first inhabitants of the land—the Bushmen and
the Hottentots.

The Bushmen and the Hottentots are no doubt the real
South Africans. But they will not compete for the title;
they are all dead.

III

South Africa was discovered at the same time, upon the
same quest, as America.

It was towards the end of the fifteenth century. The
overland trade of the East had given Venice the title of
Queen of the Adriatic. Other nations desired this trade
with the East. The Portuguese had a monopoly from the
Pope, not only over the natives of South Africa, but over
the seas to the Indies round the Cape of Storms. Henry the
Navigator had already got as far as Sierra Leone when he
died. While the Portuguese continued their quest eastward
round the coast of Africa (carrying religion and trade together like their overland rivals, the Crusaders), the Span-
iards, respecting the Pope's decree, sought the Indies to
the west.

Columbus reached America four years after Batholomew
Diaz discovered South Africa, and five years before Vasco
da Gama rounded the Cape and saw land on Christmas Day
which he called (as it is still called) Natal, and sailed on
to an East Coast Arab colony which is now Portuguese
East Africa, and, arriving at Calicut in India, dethroned
the Queen of the Adriatic and ended the Mediterranean's
title to be the centre of the earth.

The Portuguese settled in the east and west of Southern
Africa. They found, in the east, yellow and black men,
Arabs, and a confusion of Arabs with black men. They

entered the land Monomotapa that was called after the
title of the Chiefs of the Makalanga tribe. The Makalangas rejected their Christianity and live, an unimportant
people, in Rhodesia today.

In Abyssinia there was now the magical kingdom of
Prester (Presbyter) John. For the last three or four centuries this kingdom had been situated in India; but here
it was in Abyssinia, where the Greek Gods (Homer said)
banqueted with the kings and the sun set in the east.

And not only had Prester John a stone that gave light
and another that gave sight and a third that made men
invisible and a mirror that showed the world's happen-
ings and a fountain of youth and a stream whose bed was
full of precious stones and a sea of sand—not only had
he these material things and kings and dukes for servants,
he had also archbishops and bishops and a high priest and
a patriarch because he was a Christian, and he went to
war with thirteen great crosses made of gold before him
but, to show his Christian humility, he called himself
Presbyter John, which was the smallest of clerical titles.

Nor could there be any doubt of these things. He himself had communicated them to prelates and popes and
in a letter to the Byzantine Emperor, Manuel, the friend
of Crusaders, and the letter began: "Presbyter Joannes, by
the power and virtue of God and of the Lord Jesus Christ,
Lord of Lords."

Naturally, then, Vasco da Gama also went to Abyssinia
to look for Preste Joham. The thing he did not do was to
settle his Portuguese at the southernmost tip of Africa,
behind which there were at least seas of sand and streams
whose beds had precious stones and more gold than was
needed for thirteen crosses, however large they might be.
It fell to others to take South Africa.

In 1601, ships of the English East India Company began to stop now and then at the Cape; and, in 1620, two

English captains thought they might as well plant the flag of King James I at the Cape.

But there it ended. The English, too, failed in good time to take South Africa.

It was the Dutch who, in 1652, established at the Cape a fort, a vegetable garden, a cattlefold, and a trading-station. It was the Dutch East India Company that found those Bushmen and Hottentots of whom van Riebeeck, the Company's first Governor, wrote: "They have been trying vainly to get at our cattle, and we have been trying vainly to get at their persons."

Now to Monomotapa, at about the same time as the Portuguese, there had come those Xosa-Zulu tribes that, travelling east and southeast, had brought with them to the land da Gama had called Natal, and also to the land whither the Dutch were already trekking, the blood of the Arab and Phœnician traders of Sofala and, together with their own laws, certain laws about purification, circumcision, and sacrifice customary among the Jews.

The Zulus settled in Natal. The Xosas came further south, adding to their already mixed blood the blood of Hottentots and to their language the Hottentot click. The Hottentots too, natives of South Africa, had somehow got a few Semitic laws. They would not eat pork, or fish without scales.

When Dutch sailors, wrecked at Delagoa Bay in Portuguese East Africa, told of a new people they had met who were different from the Hottentots—darker and able to grow beards, yet not as black or thick-faced as the West African slaves nor as aquiline as the convicts and slaves from Java, Malacca, and the Spice Islands—when they returned to the Cape with this tale, it was the Zulus they meant. But it was not the Zulus the Dutchmen came upon when they began trekking east, away from the controls

and impositions of the Dutch East India Company. These
people they met, who were trekking west as they were
trekking east, were the companion nation of the Zulus,
the Xosas.

Boers and Xosas alike, as they went along, destroyed the
aboriginals of the land, the Hottentots and Bushmen.

The tiny yellow Bushmen—with their hollow backs;
their hollow cheeks; their little Mongol faces; their wrin-
kled loose-skinned bodies; their women, so big behind that
they seemed on the way to becoming centaurs; their bows
and arrows and unguents and poisons; their language of
clicks and croaks—lived in clefts of the valleys, in holes of
the earth and of the rocks. They had no rulers and no
possessions except the ornaments round their arms and
legs; the skins over their shoulders and between their legs;
the poisoned arrows they carried like a halo in a snake
band round their heads, the quiver of arrows slung beside
the bow across their backs.

But they knew the things of the earth and the ways of
the wild and spoke to birds and beasts in their own language. They knew the bulbs and roots with which to poison the wells of their enemies. They took the poison for
their arrows from the sacs of the snakes they ate. They
also ate locusts and lizards and roots and berries and honey
and raw game dripping with blood. In hunger or revenge
they cut the living flesh of the cattle of their enemies.
They mutilated the people they killed and, in bad times,
ate them. They killed their own children if they were ill
begotten or starving. They could eat for days on end and
starve for days on end.

And it was they, the Bushmen, who were the actors, the
dancers, the story-tellers, the music-makers, the painters, the
instinctive artists among the aborigines of Southern Africa.
It is their paintings scientists and artists seek and copy in

the caves where they lived and starved and were driven out
by smoke and perished by the spear. It is their paintings, in
the caves of Rhodesia and South-West Africa, that tell a
tale of men too light in colour ever to have been aboriginals of South Africa: in short, the "Red Men" of the
Greeks: the Phœnicians. So far they came down Africa,
in their hunt for gold—for ivory, apes, and peacocks—that
the Bushmen saw them and, on their rocks, said so.

Now all but a few slightly bastaard Bushmen, tended like
animals to preserve the last of a species, are gone from South
Africa.

The Hottentots, bigger than the Bushmen (though, as to
their women, hardly less big behind), with clicks but no
croaks in their language, died in great numbers from the
white men's drinks and diseases, but still they did not vanish, like the Bushmen, from South Africa. One may call
many Namaqua and South-West tribes by the name of Hottentot, though they are not pure Hottentot. More than the
Bushmen, they are preserved in the bodies of the Bantus.
Through the bodies of Eastern slaves; of passing white men;
of masters, careless of the fruits of their passions, they are
preserved in the bodies of those people called, after themselves, the Cape People. . . .

There was an old widower from Holland—in his young
days a rake, and later a mystic—who heard the call of the
London Missionary Society for men to preach the gospel
among the heathen of Africa.

He failed among the Xosas and turned to the Hottentots.
Passion struck his heart for a dark slave-child. He freed and
married her and began to preach the doctrine that, all men
being alike in the eyes of God, it was the Christian duty of
the holiest to marry without regard to the colour of the skin.
His name was Johannes Theodorus van der Kemp. Other
missionaries followed him. He praised his chief associate
for not corrupting himself by marrying a rich woman, but

fixing his choice, by the Grace of God, on a young Hottentot girl whose only possessions were two sheepskins and a string of beads and greater riches, he believed, in God.

The Hottentots finally vanished as a race from the land of South Africa when there was an end made to slavery and a servitude like slavery. The missionaries did what they could for them; but, indeed, they were no more able to fend for themselves than cage-birds or circus-trained animals. They became free, as it turned out, to die.

Thus the tale of the Bushmen and Hottentots is soon told.

But the day the virile black man and the virile white man came face to face there began a struggle in South Africa that is not yet ended and whose end none knows.

IV

South Africa—this union of four provinces which we loosely call South Africa—is primarily a land of racial problems. It has, in the last generation, become a country—a national entity—as one might speak of Canada or Australia or even the United States. But consider, for one moment, its composition. The people who first discovered South Africa, the Portuguese, are not a part of it. But for the rest this is, taken chronologically, the mixture that the Vaal River typifies:

The Dutch, stationed here by the East India Company, the "free burghers"—nine to begin with—they permitted and restricted.

The Hottentots—the Cape Men—that they found. The Bushmen.

The Negro slaves they imported.

The Madagascar slaves. The East Indian convicts, made slaves.

The banished Indian political offenders of standing who brought their families and servants and continued coming for over a century.

The small parties of young women from Dutch orphan-
ages sent out for the bachelor settlers to marry.

The two-hundred-odd French Huguenot refugees who,
following the revocation of the Edict of Nantes, came to
seek religious freedom and had to struggle anew to get it.

More Dutch settlers, but of a higher class than the early
ones.

Some Low-Germans: no woman among them.

The British colonists, principally the settlers of 1820,
brought out, in part, to help maintain order against the
blacks.

North Germans who, having fought beside the British in
the Crimea, were now accommodated near them in the
Cape Colony: one woman among them.

The Indians imported to Natal, from 1860 onward, as
indentured labourers to the sugar planters, and today challenging in numbers Natal's white population.

The diamond and gold adventurers—the settlers of 1870.

The Jews, flying from the pales and pogroms of Russia
and Poland, as later from the horrors of the Nazis.

The British immigrants of 1946 and 1947, escaping from
the socialism in England, unlike the world's previous emigrants in this: that they were not escaping from an old way
of life to seek a new, but that they were escaping from a
new way of life to maintain the old.

The Bastaards and the Cape People (no longer simply
Hottentots)—the results of the human permutations and
combinations of the early Cape days, living their self-con-
tained lives apart from the whites, intermarrying and estab-
lishing a new race on the earth.

The outweighing, overbalancing millions of black people. . . .

Of these the Dutch and French combined soonest. But,
indeed, the two had to combine because the government of
the day insisted upon it. The Huguenots found little more

freedom in South Africa than they had found in France. In fifty years their French language was lost; they themselves were merged in the Dutch; a new people—a people, as one might expect, self-centred and impatient of restraint —was being evolved, whose descendants, with their names as likely as not French or derived from French, are the Afrikaners of today.

It was this passion for freedom, so strong that it was almost an abhorrence of social life, which first, indirectly, brought the white man into conflict with the black.

It must be remembered that the original white possessors of the Cape were not a nation, but a trading-company. What the Company's directors—the Lords Seventeen in Holland —wanted, what their thousands of Dutch shareholders wanted, were not national assets but commercial profits. What they meant to make of the Cape was not a colony but a depot. They ruled to that purpose, and they ruled harshly.

And those French-Dutch settlers, with the blood in them of men who had escaped from persecution in Europe, were not the people to submit to persecution in Africa. . . . Only five years after the Dutch East India Company began its rule at the Cape, Boer farmers were proclaiming themselves Free Burghers "want zij gheen compagnie's slaven willen wezen"—since they wished to be no Company's slaves. But there must have been good trek-blood through the French too. While the original Dutch at the Cape, from Governors to sailors, began as servants of the Company, the French were, every one of them, pilgrims of freedom. For only three years—the years of the Batavian Republic's rule at the Cape—was there a Dutch government that based itself on the liberty of the individual; and that government followed the lead of the French Revolution.

By this time, however, the blood of those first two hundred and twenty Frenchmen was well mixed with that of the first Dutchmen; and, though it meant more in the small population of the Cape than the blood of the hundred and one voyagers of the *Mayflower* could mean in America, who can say now whence it most fiercely came, the desire of the Boer to get away—to get away?

Well, the Boers trekked. They began the system which they followed generation after generation, and compared with the Exodus of the persecuted children of Israel. And it was as they were trekking along—escaping further and further from the Company's pursuing borders—that they came upon the Kaffirs, arrived southeast from Monomotapa, and advancing to the west.

Thus white and black at last met in South Africa, and soon they were at war.

But, however high each individual in South Africa held himself, however insistent upon his freedom, he was not, in those days, the master of his own destiny. There were conflicts going on in Europe which involved South Africa: that is, the Cape. While the trekkers were evading authority and struggling, by treaties and force of arms, to ward off the Kaffirs, the French Revolutionaries had overrun Holland; the Patriots of Holland had helped them conquer Holland; they had cast out the detested Princes of Orange with their domineering German wives, and installed the Batavian Republic.

Upon this, the Patriots of two eastern districts in the Cape, sporting the revolutionary Cockade and raising the Voice of the People, had also proclaimed republics and called upon their brothers, the free men of France, Holland, and America, to come to their aid.

A French warship was already on its way from the Indies when there sailed into Cape Town harbour, to guard the Cape (as Ceylon) for the House of Orange and defend the world against Napoleon, the Redcoats and Bluecoats of England, and on Cape Town's fortress, called the Castle, ran up the British flag. The year was 1795.

The Patriots of the Cape asked for terms. "What terms?" replied the English colonel. "You are subjects of King George the Third of England."

A century later Alfred Milner, Governor of the Cape, answered the assurances of Cape Boers that they were loyal: "Of course you are loyal. It would be monstrous if you were not."

Such insensibility caused General Smuts himself, in the shadow of the looming Boer War, to write a book called *A Century of Wrong*, which told of the grievances suffered by the Boers at the hands of the English in the nineteenth century. And a half century later the Boers have not yet ceased to brood over their wrongs. Even with Union, when none but a Boer has ever used the house left by Rhodes to the Prime Ministers of a united people, and all the endeavours of the English, both in England and in South Africa, have been to placate the Boers, the Boers, like the Irish (three hundred years after Cromwell fell upon Ireland) cannot forget the past and want to be alone.

Yet it was not the English who sowed the seed of this Century of Wrong—they only had the misfortune to inherit its rank ineradicable growth. All began with the fury of the Boers against the Dutch East India Company. How were the English to understand it when their minds, in coming to the Cape at the call of the House of Orange, were set on nothing but the menace of Napoleon, his threat to Egypt and India?

But then they formed a regiment of Hottentots—of those people concerning whom the burghers of the Cape had decreed that "every Bushman or Hottentot . . . shall for life be the lawful property of such burghers as may possess them, and serve in bondage from generation to generation."

And it also seemed to them that the Boers, rather than the Xosas, were to blame for the cattle-raiding—the burning and fighting—that ruined the Boers. And they brought out missionaries who blamed any but their black and yellow charges, not only for their sufferings, but even for their wrongdoings.

The English stayed for eight years. There followed the Treaty of Amiens under which the English gave up everything that had come to them through Napoleon, except Ceylon and Trinidad. They handed the Cape back to the Dutch—the new Dutch, the Batavian Republic, that based themselves on the new French.

Napoleon had said: "If we cannot dislodge England from the Cape, we must take Egypt." There was Trafalgar, and now he had to say: "On the Elbe and on the Oder, we have won our India, our Spanish colonies and our Cape of Good Hope."

The English came back to the Cape.

Resisting them, the Batavian Republic assembled an army of two thousand. The army had Dutch regulars; French sailors, by chance in the port they called Little Paris; the Hottentot corps created by the English; a Malay corps; a group of Mozambique slaves; some German mercenaries.

There were sixty-one English ships with four thousand soldiers, six hundred sailors, guns that had seen the wars of Napoleon.

The Battle of Blaauwberg was fought and soon lost. Once more the English flag flew from the Castle; and there it continued to fly when, after the Congress of Vienna in 1814, the Cape Colony was formally and finally ceded by Holland to the British Crown for the sum of six million pounds.

That meant renewed reasons for trekking. The land was big enough. If one was dissatisfied with anything, if one resented being shuffled backwards and forwards according to what was going on six thousand miles away and belonging, without reference to one's wishes, now to this distant ruler and now to that, one moved and sought to belong to oneself.

One took one's waggons and one's spans of oxen, and one's horses and herds and household goods and Hottentots and slaves, and one journeyed with one's family, under clear skies, across great mountains and empty lands, at the rate of a few miles a day, until one came to a spring, sheltered by a hill. There one outspanned for the last time, built a house and thatched it; made furniture of the hardwoods of the country; strung beds and chairs with strips of hide; kraaled the cattle within fences of thorns but by day let them wander about the veld; planted grain and fruit and vegetables. . . .

And the world was one's own, the earth and the sky, and, as far as the eye could reach, all the universe. . . .

One rose in the morning, strong and unused as the day. The pale sun climbed the pale sky and swiftly fired and blazed and drained the earth and all; weary, in the short twilight, one walked the veld, and little thin scents gave memories and pains; a small wind rose; night came and one went within; the candles were soon out and through little holes in the dark blue tent of the sky there were the lights of other worlds. . . .

There would be no communication with the life left behind, and none would be wanted. There would be no tradition but the tradition of freedom, there would be fleeting hospitalities of loneliness. The only culture, the only teaching, would come from the Book. As one demanded little of life and there were all the days of the generations in which to get it, one went slowly. One's ten sons and the slaves and Hottentots tended the beasts and scratched the earth. . . .

But it had needed deep resolution and a perilous journey

to find this peace; a new soil had had to be broken to maintain it; and, since the world did not in fact end where one's eye could reach, and who knew what was beyond the reach of the eye, the trigger was ever ready.

Wild beasts might come, and Kaffirs; fighting and again fighting.

The date of the first Kaffir War is 1779, and it began a century of Kaffir Wars. But the first Kaffir War was not a war between Kaffirs and Europeans. It was a war between Kaffirs and Kaffirs.

In 1779, a Xosa Chief, Rarabe, was killed fighting for his honour against the Chief of another branch of the Xosas, the Tembus. The question of honour had to do with the offer by the other Chief of only a hundred cattle as lobola for Rarabe's daughter. Therefore the two Royal Houses, with all their followers, fought; and Rarabe was killed, and also his eldest son.

This left the son's infant child as heir. The second son of Rarabe became his Regent. When the child, Gaika, grew to manhood, his uncle, the Regent, Ndlambe, still desired to rule; a part of the contention was that the young heir had taken his uncle's wife; here began a war that never ceased while they lived, and was carried on by their successors, friends, rivals, enemies; in this war Dutch, English and even Hottentots joined; it was in the year of the French Revolution that the whites got mixed up in this confusion of women, honour, power and death among black men.

On the side of the whites, the matter had, at first, to do with cattle.

In these days the boundary between blacks and whites in the east of the Cape Colony was moved from the Bushman River to the Great Fish River. Nobody was supposed to cross the Great Fish River, but the Kaffirs crossed it to take the

Boers' cattle and the Boers crossed it for reparation and revenge.

There exists a letter written to the Colony's great rebel, Coenraad de Buys, whose first ancestor in the Cape had been one of the Huguenots, and who was seldom without a price on his head.

This is the letter:

> *Respected Cousin Coenraad de Buys,*
> *I have to inform you that Langa lets you know he requires payment from you for beating his Kaffir, otherwise he will immediately come again, for this is a challenge to him, and the Christians must not think he is afraid to make war.*
> *With compliments from us all,*
> *I am your uncle,*
> *Petrus de Buys.*

Langa was the high Xosa Chief to whom it had fallen to set round the neck of Gaika the royal necklace of kingship and to say:

"Grandson of Rarabe: This day you become King of your nation. May you rule with decorum, wisdom and justice. These are your people. Be a father to them. Let your hand rest gently on them. Raise it not up in anger."

Gaika has been described by white observers as one of the most proper monarchs, in his person and royal attributes, there could be in the world. It was Gaika the whites, in later years, chose to support against his uncle Ndlambe and above all other Xosas. Thus they entered the Kaffir Wars and in 1819 finally defeated Ndlambe, though the Kaffir Wars went on so long that Trollope, in 1877, was able to chronicle the last of them.

After the war of 1819, which the English helped Gaika to win, there came out to those fighting parts of the Colony an organised body of 3,500 British settlers.

One of the reasons for their coming was that white men were needed to replace, in some measure, an expensive standing army.

They came, artisans, farm labourers, sailors, "a large portion of them" (wrote Thomas Pringle, poet and champion of a free press) "squalid . . . slovenly, discontented and uncourteous"; but among them were also men of breeding and high officers ruined by the Napoleonic wars.

At their first service, regarding the desolation of their new home, they spoke the words of the Bible: "By the waters of Babylon, we sat down and wept"; but ten years were not past before they were rooted in the new soil, contented and prosperous. Their home remained the eastern district of the Cape Colony.

V

When the Cape became finally England's, she left the Common Law—the Roman-Dutch Law—which remains in South Africa today, although in Holland it is no longer followed. But she made the land more English through those British settlers. She established the English language. She encouraged British missionaries.

Of these British things, the Dutch disliked most the missionaries. They disliked it because the missionaries blamed them, rather than the Kaffirs, for the miseries of both. They said the Hottentot mission stations were no more than a sanctuary for Hottentot thieves and deserters. There began, about 1811, a wandering Court, called by the Boers the Black Circuit, that was chiefly inspired by the missionaries van der Kemp and Read, who had married coloured girls. And here came Hottentots to lay complaints against their masters—some justly founded; some impossibly presented; some dating from the time in 1806 when the British returned to the Cape and presently gave the Hottentots their charter of freedom, so that henceforth

no master might deal out justice to his own servants. Here
came, to support the Hottentots, missionaries preaching
that, since all people were the children of God, white men
might, like themselves, marry Hottentot girls.

The Boers knew well enough that the half-caste population of Cape Town was almost double the white. But for
this they blamed the original settlers very much less than
the passing soldiers and sailors and the German mercenaries the Batavian authorities had used to help them
against the English. For these were now, many of them,
settled in Cape Town, and they found the coloured girls
simpler to live with than the more demanding white girls.

No Boer, moreover, defended the frailty of men who
went to dark-skinned women. No Boer went about calling Hottentots the equals of white people. This, they clam-
oured, was left for the British men of God to do in direct
contradiction of the Word of God:

"Cursed be Canaan. A servant of servants shall he be
to his brethren. . . . God shall enlarge Japheth, and he
shall dwell in the tents of Shem, and Canaan shall be his
servant."

While his fellow missionaries so exalted Dr. van der
Kemp that the best of them, Thomas Moffat, thought him
"little behind the chiefest Apostle of our Lord," the Boers
wrote his name upon their tablets for their children of the
future to revile.

There was a Hottentot who laid a complaint against his
owner, a man called Bezuidenhout. It was not the sort of
thing a Bezuidenhout was prepared to yield to, and he refused to obey a summons to answer the charge.

A party that included Hottentots was sent to arrest him
and, in resisting arrest, he was killed.

The Boers got together for rebellion. The rebellion did
not take place because the five ringleaders were publicly

hanged on the spot—Slachter's Nek (Butcher's Neck)—
where they had sworn to drive out the foreign tyrant. Since
the scaffolding broke under their combined weight, and
the first hanging was therefore unsuccessful, a second gal-
lows was erected that they might be hanged again, one
by one, in the presence of their friends and relations. To
them this was more than an outrage against humanity, it
was a smiting down of the very hand of God. And when,
in 1874, Froude was sent by the British government to report on the situation of the South African natives, he
found the memory of that hanging still green in the land;
and so it is today.

The farmers trekked. They continued trekking. There
was such a thing as a surfeit of human right.

It was not alone the English who were responsible for
this surfeit. If the Boers had not liked the Dutch East India Company, if they did not now like the English, the
Batavian government had hardly pleased them more. For
one of the things Abraham de Mist, the Batavian Com-
missary-General, had contrived to do in his short three
years at the Cape was to proclaim a liberty of conscience
that gave to people of all religions, Christian or pagan,
equal protection under the law; and this liberty (one
might call it libertinism) applied to schools too. . . .

They did not yet know, while they trekked for this and
that, the liberty of liberties which was impending.

In 1833, a month before he died, Wilberforce won the
battle he had fought for forty-six years. Britain abolished
slavery throughout the British world.

The news reached the Cape in 1834.

The Cape had thirty-six thousand slaves, and their owners valued them at exactly what Britain had paid for the
Cape—six million pounds. The official valuation was three
million pounds. The owners of the slaves were to get, in

compensation for releasing them, a *pro rata* share of the twenty million pounds that was being divided among the nineteen slave colonies. But, as it turned out, the Cape colonists received little of the compensation assigned to them. It was whittled down and whittled down. It was made payable in London. London! How should one get to London? Agents went about offering to negotiate, speculating in claims. Many slave-owners were ruined. Some were too incensed to accept their depreciated bounty. Others were too ignorant to understand the transaction. They gave up their claims to the speculators for whatever they could get. Farmers were left without labourers. Crops remained ungarnered. A gentleman, who later became a judge, has left on record his indignation at receiving less than fifty pounds for a slave for whom he had refused five hundred.

If this does not rouse one's sympathy as it was meant to do, since a slave worth over five hundred pounds must have had qualities that deserved freedom, it does remain that the affair was managed with more enthusiasm than sense. The Boers had been born and bred, as aristocrats until yesterday, in the tradition of their fundamental rights over certain inferior beings. They had inherited their slaves as any other kind of property is inherited. The charity of England was bankruptcy to them. They rejected the ideals of England, and they rejected England.

And they trekked. Some of their aforetime slaves trekked with them, and also Hottentots freed under their Charter.

The other Hottentots, most of them, died.

Perhaps having, in Emerson's words, guano in their destiny, they would not, in any event, have been able to face a changing world. Still, this is certain: they were freed, and they are not here today.

Their blood, however, with that of the actual slaves, survives, as does the Negro blood in the old Slave States of

America. Opponents of black blood passed it on to their children.

The trekking of the Boers this time was a formidable affair, and it received a further impetus from the fact that, not only were they not fairly compensated for the loss of their slaves, but they were also not compensated for the loss of their cattle at the hands of raiding Kaffirs; the missionaries blamed them for the continual Kaffir Wars in which they became involved when Ndlambe and his people crossed to their side of the Great Fish River and his enemies pursued them and the burnings and raidings were indiscriminate; they were made to return to the Kaffirs the lands they had gained from them.

There was a missionary called Dr. Philip speaking very hotly on behalf of the dark races, saying they would be exterminated if they were exposed to intercourse with the white people; that the only remedy against this was to establish Bantu states ruled over by chiefs under the guidance of missionaries; and that such Europeans as the missionaries considered undesirable should be excluded from these states. . . .

Today there is again talk of Bantu states—meaning not the Swazi, Basuto, Bechuana states under British protection, but reserves that one might choose to call states. The talk is also not by people who love the natives after the manner of Dr. Philip. The reason is not that they are in danger of being exterminated. Dr. Philip, as time has proved, was wrong there. No, on the contrary. The talk is now of Bantu—one might say states—because they are so dangerously increasing. . . .

But in the eighteen-thirties the Boers when they were displeased could do what they cannot do today and need not do today: they could trek.

They issued a Manifesto saying they were weary of the

plunderings of the dark peoples; their losses over emancipated slaves; the odium cast on them, under the cloak of religion, by missionaries. They despaired, they said, of saving the Colony from these evils. And since (they said) they were assured the English were as little eager to keep them as they to remain, they were now going to leave the fruitful land of their birth to enter a wild and dangerous territory: with only the wish to live quietly and justly; molesting none unless molested; at peace with all; under God and their own laws.

British settlers of 1820 gave them a Bible "as a farewell token of their esteem and a heartfelt regret at their departure."

The Boers brought out, as their fathers had done, their white-tilted waggons that could hold a family; they assembled their kine and their kindred; once more an exodus began, but an exodus now in thousands. Between 1836 and 1840, six thousand trekkers left the Cape for the unknown east and north. The very Trek of Treks was on—the Great Trek.

Perhaps the Boers were not less free under English rule than under the rule of the Dutch East India Company; perhaps they had, but for the slave business, prospered. They had trekked, however, in the old days, before ever the English came to the Cape, because each man wanted to do as he chose and not as others chose for him; because, in fact, those early Dutchmen had so learnt to hate any kind of government that, even on the Trek of Treks, they trekked away from one another.

They must have been a difficult people indeed to manage.

Yet their pride in their achievements—the increasing pride of their descendants—is not unjustified.

They had prepared to face dangers, known and unknown, in the cause of independence, and they had greatly met them. They called themselves, they are called today, the Voortrekkers: those who went before.

Among the Voortrekkers, a boy of ten, was Paul Kruger.

VI

While the Voortrekkers were moving away and the 1820 settlers were digging themselves in, the Kaffirs opposed both.

Now the Kaffir of those days must not be confused with that one who is still called Kaffir by people whose sentiments are the sentiments of their ancestors. Today the black man, brought low by his brother Bantu, is subjugated and bewildered. The white man is his lord, his tyrant, his friend, his teacher, yet fears one day to become his victim.

In the early days of the nineteenth century, the Kaffir was principally a warrior. His great business was to raid cattle and fight.

The most famous warrior of Southern Africa was the Zulu Chaka.

Chaka was born in 1783. His name meant Beetle. And the reason why Chaka had a name meaning Beetle was that when his unmarried mother began to swell with child, the court wizard of the Zulu tribe of the Zulu nation diagnosed the swelling as a growth caused by a beetle in her bowels. The reason for this, again, was that his father Senzagakone, the heir to the tribal throne, was not yet through his initiation. Chaka could not therefore be his son. When Chaka was born, his mother, Unandi, fled with him from tribe to tribe (rejected by one after another for the disruptions she caused) until they arrived in the land of another Zulu tribe, the Tetwa.

The ruler of the Tetwa was one who called himself

Dingiswayo, the Outcast, because he, too, had in his time fled from the wrath of his father. He therefore had sympathy with Chaka and greatly promoted him.

Dingiswayo was the ablest of the Zulu monarchs. It is said a white man taught him how to drill his men in regiments. He also devised the long shield to cover the whole body and the short spear (besides the long hurling spear) for closer fighting. He taught his people to make things. He engaged in barter with the Portuguese.

Dingiswayo needed to do little besides show his strength for tribe after tribe to submit to him: upon which he treated his new subjects with fatherly domination.

In the service of Dingiswayo, Chaka learnt his ways; became a notable soldier; returned to the land of the Zulus; was welcomed by his father, whose Great Wife had brought him no heir; killed his father; killed two rival half-brothers; killed Dingiswayo; became thus king, not only of the Zulu tribe, but also of Tetwa; killed and conquered; killed and conquered; killed and killed until a million—some say two million—were killed; killed until men became cannibals; killed until whole tribes and leading generals fled from him across the Drakensberg Mountains and there killed for themselves as Chaka had taught them. Kaffir Wars that lost the Xosas their strength were not comparable with the wars of the Zulus that lost all Africans of South Africa their strength. One might call the Bechuana-Basuto people, who did a little neighbourly killing but whose chief sport was rather Bushman-hunting than war, a mild and gentle people beside the Xosa-Zulu people.

Chaka soldiers got no pay—not even food; they had to ravage or scavenge for themselves. Their rewards from Chaka were honours: the honour of belonging to crack regiments; the honour of wearing necklaces made of little horns or roots—a horn, a root, for each man killed; higher still, the honour of wearing armbands or neckbands of copper or brass; highest of all, to die like men, and let the sun "draw their honours reeking up to heaven."

To make his soldiers fiercer in battle, Chaka forbade them to take a woman except in conquest. That a son might not do to him what he had done to his father, he took no wife, and if one of his twelve hundred concubines bore him a living child, she was killed with the child. He gave his discarded concubines to his officers, and took new ones from his conquered.

The punishment for less than high courage in battle was death. For less than such courage a whole regiment might meet its death. Singers were blinded the better to dream battle-songs. At his word regiments, crying Zulu Pezulu—Heaven of Heavens, King of Kings, walked over cliffs or into the sea.

When Chaka's mother died, the ten most beautiful girls in Zululand went into her grave; and soldiers with their shields and spears, and sixty thousand people from kraals near and far, came to the place of mourning to shout and dance and sing; and a hundred thousand bellowing cattle were brought to add to the tumult; and in the midst of it all stood Chaka, having the gall of living calves poured over his head to strengthen him in his suffering.

Shouting, chanting, dancing without pause, seven thousand mourners died of thirst or were killed in frenzy. Three thousand old women were killed that their sons might share the grief of Chaka; three thousand cows were killed that even kine might know what it was to lose a mother; for a year all milk was spilled on the earth and none might work, fight, sing, dance or conceive.

On the place where Chaka one day killed a number of useless old men, he built his Royal Kraal which he called Bulawayo, the Place of Killing.

And when, in time, his greatest general, Moselikatze,

took half the nation away with him over the Drakensbergen and fought his way to the land that is now Rhodesia, he called his capital, after Chaka's, Bulawayo, the Place of Killing; and so it is called today.

Moselikatze's own name meant Pathway of Blood. But yet his path was less Chaka's than Dingiswayo's. For he killed not only to destroy; he absorbed under a paternal wing his conquered enemies together with their cattle, so that these conquered enemies were proud to follow him and call themselves, with his own people, by the new name Matabele—AmaNdabele: Ama, meaning People; Matabele or AmaNdabele, meaning the People with the Long Shields —those long shields that Chaka had copied from Dingiswayo and Moselikatze from Chaka.

Other Zulus too fled from Chaka—the people that, fused with others, became the Swazis and Shangaans; those that sought sanctuary among the Xosas, crying "Fenguzi-la"— "We are in want," and were henceforth in contempt called Fengus by the Xosas they joined; also a part of the tribe that once sheltered Dingiswayo as he had theretofore sheltered Chaka.

These came to a nation across the Drakenberg, the Batlokwa, that gave them refuge. Among the fugitives, though not of their tribe, was one who engaged the fancy of Mantatisi, wife of Mokotsho, the Batlokwa Chief. The Chief died. She called to her the fugitive, Motsholi. He rejected her with the words: "Shall I eat Mokotsho's food?"— meaning: "Shall I take the place of her husband only to be poisoned too?"

Mantatisi said to her son: "I want Motsholi's collar"— the brass badge of his rank and honour, so moulded about his neck that it could not be removed.

With twenty friends of his initiation class, her son re-

moved the collar: he brought it to his mother with Motsholi's head.

Now the fugitives fell on the Batlokwa who, led by their
queen, had to fly. When, at last, they came to rest on the
Vaal River, she taught them what she had learnt of Chaka
from the fugitives. She bettered Chaka's ways. Not only
did her warriors, like Chaka's, fight naked. Their bodies
were polished black. Upon them shone collars and waist-
bands and armlets and anklets of copper and brass (for
the Batlokwa were metal-workers). On their heads were
great plumes of black ostrich feathers. She trained them
to grimace and clamour like devils.

She herself, it was said, had a single eye in the middle
of her forehead, but she lived now in the parts where,
forty years later, great diamonds were found: the single eye
was possibly a diamond. It was said she fed her warriors
from the milk of her breasts: one may take it she put her
heart into them.

Her followers, henceforth called the Mantati, destroyed,
like Chaka's, tribe after tribe; taking only the strong and
beautiful to join them, killing the old and very young.
Mantatisi's armies grew greater and greater. They went on
conquering until there was nothing left to conquer. . . .

Also until there was nothing left to destroy. Also until
there was nothing left for them to eat. The grain was gone.
The cattle were gone. They ate one another.

They were already in this state when they fell upon the
Griquas on the Vaal, the charges of Thomas Moffat. The
Mantati were 15,000 and the Griquas 150. But the Griquas
had guns. Their bullets could reach the Mantati where
the spears of the Mantati could not reach the Griquas.
So the Mantati were at last beaten in battle.

When, utterly broken, Mantati warriors were brought
before Moshesh, King of the Basutos, charged with having
eaten dead Basutos, he said merely: "Let them go."

"But they have eaten your own father."

Moshesh said: "Shall I desecrate the grave of my father? Let them go."

There was another warrior queen of whom it was sung:

> *At Gubela's kraal there are no gates.*
> *The kraal is shut with the heads of men.*

The missionary Thomas Moffat had, as charges on the Vaal, not so much Griquas as Batlapis, a weak and cruel Bechuana tribe. Numerous Batlapis were also in the fight between the Mantati and Griquas, but they did not come to the battleground until any were left but the dead and wounded. These they stoned and speared and killed; they killed women and children; they cut off heads and kicked them about; they cut off arms and legs for the ornaments they carried.

The Batlapis, however, were the only Bechuanas spared by Moselikatze when he arrived to sweep away the remnants left by the Mantati so that finally the Bechuana and Basuto peoples were as devastated as the Xosa and Zulu peoples.

And the reason Moselikatze spared the Batlapis was that he had a love for Thomas Moffat so deep that he called him to work among his Matabele and in all the years they were together refused him only one thing—a belief in his God.

It was in the parts where Pretoria now stands, the capital of the Transvaal, that Moselikatze thought he would at last settle his nation. There he built his Royal Kraal and there he held, in many kraals, his teeming cattle.

But, as he had driven along the pathway of blood that had brought him his name, so he was destined to be driven.

When the Voortrekkers left the Cape they went, under different leaders, in different directions. The greatest of

them, Andries Pretorius, came in the end to the new home
of Moselikatze and made it a new home for the Boers.

Moselikatze drove forth again. There was again a pathway of blood. He found his final home in the land he
called Matabeleland, which Rhodes then took from his
son so that it became Rhodesia.

Rhodes was called one day to see the desecrated tomb
of Moselikatze in the Matoppo Hills. There Moselikatze
sat, on a chair of rock, overlooking forever a great waste
as of dead planets.

Rhodes stood muttering: "What a poet the man was!"
And it came into his mind then to rest in death on the hill
of Moselikatze; to face with him that eternal desolation:
"Here lie the remains of Cecil John Rhodes."

VII

It fell to the Voortrekkers who went east to meet historic
tragedy, so that theirs is the compensation of death, the
great legend.

In Zululand now the ruler was Dingani (Dingaan), the
Vulture, the Eater of Other Birds, Chaka's half-brother
and murderer. As Chaka had killed two of his half-brothers, so two of his half-brothers fell on him. He cried, as a
servant stabbed him—clear in his conscience, like Hitler, he
cried: "My brothers! My brothers! There is no wrong!"

The grief of his people may one day be matched by the
grief of Hitler's people for Hitler; it is as the passion of the
French people for Napoleon.

The Zulus cried: "He gave us victory! He gave us greatness! Follow him in death as in life!' They killed one another and themselves to go with him; and, after his death,
many saw him visiting his kraal in the form of a big green
snake—they saw, indeed, the snake.

· · ·

The only white people in Natal, at this time, were a few Englishmen, who were allowed to live there because one of them had successfully treated a sickness of Chaka, and who had, in vain, begged England to take over the country. When the leader of the eastward trekkers, Pieter Retief, came with some others in advance of his main party, these Englishmen offered to establish, with the Boers, a joint republic.

The Boers, however, wanted a Boer Republic. There were enough of them here to make a republic of their own. They decided to ask Dingaan for some of the land laid waste by Chaka. The land was Natal.

They went to Dingaan and found him willing to bargain. Mantatisi's son Sikonyela, that one who had brought her Motsholi's head with the collar of brass, had robbed Dingaan of a great many cattle. If the Boers got back these cattle for him, they might have the land they wanted.

The cattle were duly retrieved. A thousand white-hooded waggons, the families and goods of the Boers, their cattle, sheep, and horses, crossed the Drakensbergen into Zululand.

The Zulus had never seen horses—hornless cattle—before. They had never seen walking houses—these tented waggons—before. They were terrified by the guns—the shooting sticks, the entire mystery of so many white people entering their land.

When Retief, bringing the cattle, came to Dingaan's kraal to collect the reward—this land of Natal—mutual compliments were paid. The Boers fired a volley—in salute, one might say, or one might say in threat; the Zulus danced a great war dance (in salute too, or in threat?); a feast was prepared within Dingaan's kraal.

The Boers, as was the courteous way, left their guns in charge of their Hottentots outside the kraal, and went in. . . . They were seized; dragged to the hill of execu-

tion; beaten to death with knobkerries; and, towards the
unprotected camp they had left behind them, at this place
that is now called Weenen (Weeping), ten thousand
warriors swept and slaughtered the men, women, and
children.

So the Zulus, it seemed to Dingaan, had taught the
white people, with all their demands and magic, a lesson.

It was, however, the Boers who ended the tale, and the
power, too, of the Zulus in Zululand.

There was a battle scene. Thirty-six regiments of Zulus
advanced, close-packed, with proud plumes, with shields
and assegais, with great roaring, upon the Boers. Against
a riverbank the Boers had their laager surrounded by pro-
tecting waggons. Inside were the huddling cattle; the little
children; the women loading for their men; the men shooting bitterly straight while other men crept out of the camp
to attack from behind. The Zulus—crying: "If we go on,
we die. If we go back, we die. Go on!"—were routed and
driven into the river which is now called Blood River.

Here began the end of Dingaan. No longer was he (the
Boers had proved) the eater of other birds. As Dingaan
had turned on Chaka, another brother, Panda, helped by
the Boers, turned on Dingaan, and, carrying with him half
of Dingaan's followers, broke him. Dingaan fell into the
hands of Swazis and was by them done to death.

And, as Dingaan had murdered Chaka, as Panda had
betrayed Dingaan, so, presently, another brother, Clu-Clu,
killed Panda.

That was the end of black power in Natal. . . .

Yet there is something to be said, even for Dingaan.

Except in fighting, it was seldom black men killed white
men. The Englishmen in Natal were not disturbed by
Chaka. Missionaries lived with tribes of savages and, even
when they were not venerated, they suffered no harm.
Moffat lived among the cruel Batlapi; he lived for years

with Moselikatze, the Pathway of Blood; his son-in-law,
Livingstone, went unguarded into what was called Dark-
est Africa. All remained unhurt.

When Dingaan saw the Boers coming with their thousand waggons to take Natal; when he saw those walking
houses, the hornless cattle, the shooting sticks, what did he
think?

It is known what he thought. He shouted to his men
when they fell upon Retief and his followers: "Bulala
Matagati"—"Kill the Wizards." He feared the Wizards,
that asked so much. . . .

On December 16 the South Africans celebrate Dingaan's
Day.

On December 16, 1949, there was opened a monument
to the Voortrekkers. A quarter of a million people came.

Fortified by a new creed that, though the Monument
celebrated (first) the Boers' escape from the British, the
British too were somehow Voortrekkers, a few British
came. Unwitting that it celebrated (second) the Boers'
triumph over the blacks, the Boers' black servants came,
as they had come on the Great Trek itself.

And all went sweetly at the Monument.

The only dissonance was at an African Congress where
Africans said Dingaan was the black people's hero; the
Battle of Blood River, his fight for their freedom; the
Great Trek, "a gigantic plunder expedition, besmirched
with the blood of innocent natives."

One might call it a higher tribute to freedom than Monument Hill that they could speak thus and none hinder.

The Boers stayed in Natal, established a republic, and,
in direct opposition to the idea, advocated by the missionary, Dr. Philip, of setting up friendly Bantu states, made
fugitives of the tribes already ruined by their own rulers.

One might think it, in the circumstances, not unnatural; but the British, after much hesitation, decided they could not tolerate it. These Dutchmen, they argued, were, after all British subjects. They might follow their offensive and disparaging policy of running away from British rule, but bound by that rule (the British claimed) they still were. The independence the Dutch required was not granted. England declared Natal a British colony and, after opposition from the Dutch, occupied it. British immigrants began to come. The black people were allowed to return. Today Natal is the most British of the Union Provinces. But the Dutch made their inevitable retort. They trekked.

Here is how Trollope imagined their thoughts:

"We first took and cultivated and civilised the Cape Colony. But as you want it in God's name take it and use it, and do with it as you list. And let us go and do as we list elsewhere. You don't like slavery. We do. Let us go and have our slaves in a new land. We must encounter endless troubles and probably death in the attempt. But anything will be better than your laws and your philanthropy."

They had had these endless troubles, they had met death. They had won Natal past the jaws of the Drakensbergen—the mountains of the dragons; they had sown their tears at Weenen; they had made a river run red with the blood of their killers; they had reaped peace of their sacrifice. But here the British were again with their laws and philanthropy.

They sought in vain to lay their grievances before the Governor of Cape Colony; again said: "As you want it, in God's name take it"; again abandoned their homes; under the leadership of Andries Pretorius, went towards the Vaal.

Bands of Boers were wiped out by the men of Moselikatze; guns took revenge; a land passed to the Boers even bigger than Natal—a land that included most of what became the Transvaal, half of the Free State, the whole of Southern Bechuanaland as far as the Kalahari Desert. . . .

And then, as ever, the waving, seeking tentacles of the British government; a rebellion, a renewed wrenching away from the British embrace.

There were some who were content to remain in a land which called itself the Orange River Sovereignty. There were others who were not. The story of Andries Pretorius, the avenger of Pieter Retief, the leader to the Boers who trekked away from British rule in Natal, and of his son after him, became now a story of crossing and recrossing the Vaal; of diplomacy and fighting; but a story at last that seemed to have an end.

These Boers were too determined. There was no staying them. They would go on trekking. They would trek to the Limpopo as they had trekked to the Fish River, the Blood River, the Vaal River. They would trek, as Trollope said, across the Zambesi if they were pursued across the Limpopo, and across the Equator if they were hindered at the Zambesi. This Africa was too big. Better leave these ungovernable farmers. Let them cross the Vaal if they chose. Let them consider themselves a republic. Let them call it the South African Republic if they wanted to be as proud as all that. . . .

The foster children of England were at last in a home of their own. Indeed, in two homes. There was not only the South African Republic across the Vaal, there was also, presently, the Orange Free State to take the place of the Orange River Sovereignty. With a sigh of weary abandonment, Great Britain gave up her claim to this land that lay between the Orange River and the Vaal. The Orange Free State stood, rather nervous of its new dignity and the responsibilities it involved, a separate nation, before the world.

The internal independence of the Boers living beyond

the Vaal was recognized by the Sand River Convention of 1852; that of the Boers between the Orange River and the Vaal, in the Bloemfontein Convention of 1854.

In this year, too, the Cape Colony acquired its Constitution, and in 1854 Natal, having hitherto been a dependency of the Cape, became a separate colony.

Here, then, marked and divided, were the four states that today make the Union of South Africa: the Cape, the Transvaal, the Orange Free State, and Natal.

Each might now develop, unhindered, its own national consciousness.

VIII

But not only were the white people of South Africa in those days concerned with their national importance. The Hottentots were making their final protest against white domination. The Basutos, under Moshesh, were struggling against the Free State Boers. The half-caste Bastaards and Griquas, settled under missionaries along the Vaal, had their aspirations. Moselikatze was making a new nation of his fugitive, fighting Zulus, now the Matabele. In those parts where the 1820 settlers had come to make their home, the Xosas, having already struggled against each other and the whites for eighty years, staked whatever they had and stood for on one of the wildest gambles in history.

At the beginning of the century, Gaika, King of the Xosas, and Ndlambe, his uncle, regent, and rival, had each a holy man. Gaika's was called Ntsikana. He was one of the few Kaffirs Dr. van der Kemp converted to Christianity, and he composed what is called the Great Hymn "Ulo Tixo 'Mkulu"—Tixo being the Kaffir name for God; Tixo being the name of the praying mantis, first worshipped by the Hottentots as God; Tixo standing for the

Giver of Pain, and thus to be conciliated. It is to be assumed that among the things Ntsikana learnt from van der Kemp was a belief in the Resurrection.

Ndlambe's holy man and chief adviser was called Makana. He had attended services of van der Kemp after van der Kemp had been thrown out by Gaika, and, though one could not strictly say he had been converted, he had gone even further than believe in the Resurrection: he had declared himself to be the Son of God, able to raise the dead.

With the help of the white men Gaika had defeated Ndlambe. Makana was sent to a little island off the African coast and, about the time Napoleon died on another island off the African coast, he had tried to escape in a small boat and been drowned.

The followers of Ndlambe would not believe in his death. For many years longer they expected him to come back to them and, according to his word, raise them up again. It was only when all was lost for the Kaffirs that they began to say (as one might speak of the Ides of March): "Kukusa Kuku Nxele"—"You are looking for Nxele"—you are expecting the impossible. They called Makana Nxele, the Left-Handed One, because the name of Makana was too sacred to pronounce.

Meanwhile there was this belief in a resurrection among the Xosas which caused them, in the end, to destroy themselves.

At least, so one might imagine. Historians do not find, in van der Kemp's teaching of the Resurrection, the reason why the Xosas destroyed themselves.

In the year Natal parted from the Cape Colony there arose among the Xosas a prophetess called Nongkwase who, going one day to a stream to draw water, saw a vision. The spirits of the great dead appeared before her and told her that the Xosas would rise once more. On a day, near at hand, the world would change. The fields would teem with more cattle than a person could count. There would spring up mealies, ripe for eating. Sorrow would vanish from the land, and sickness; not again would age or ugliness affront the Xosas.

And there would come to them, in all their vigour and battle-pomp, the departed leaders of the old mighty days; and, at the head of invincible Xosa armies, they would hurl themselves with shields and spears and battle-cries upon the white man and drive him into the sea. The black man would rule South Africa.

One thing alone was needed: a faith in this resurrection so strong that, in proof of it, one was willing to destroy one's all.

There are historians who believe that all this was inspired by chiefs who saw no hope for Kaffirs against white men except in despair: when all was gone, the Kaffirs would fall on the whites as hungry locusts on a green land. There are some who think that Moshesh, desiring to trouble the white people, gave them the idea. . . .

Nongkwase stood on the bank of the river crying the message of the spirits: "Kill! Destroy! Have faith!" If faith was not absolute, if there was a doubting of the spirits, they would turn away and the promise would remain unfulfilled. Let no man, therefore, dare to make his usual puny efforts against the future: storing grain, herding cattle. Plant no more. Eat the beasts and grain. A new world is coming. Let nothing be done but the preparing of great kraals to hold the glorious new herds, the skins to hold the milk.

Sandile, their Chief, said:

"Obey the spirits!"

Believers obeyed the spirits. Unbelievers obeyed their Chief. The Xosas ate up their cattle and their mealies, they destroyed their possessions, they lay in the sun awaiting the millennium.

The great day arrived. It came, and it went, like any other day. The Kaffirs stood on the hills, their bellies lean, waiting for the fields to wave with corn and the kraals to seethe with cattle. Perhaps they did not so urgently wait for their dead leaders.

If Sandile had indeed expected them, in their despair, to fall on the white people, he had made a mistake in neglecting to assemble them for the resurrection. The Xosas were scattered over a broad country in famishing groups. They could not be called together to attack the whites. The final throw was lost.

There was blustering talk of a Day still to come—if only one believed.

But belief was gone, and gone too were the mealies and cattle. The Amaxosa had passed beyond anguish to exhaustion. They died in their tens of thousands. Those white men they were to drive into the sea helped whom they could, and their were Xosas who ate their dead. Seventy thousand died or disappeared. The Xosas were finished.

Sixty-five years later, not far from the scene of this Great Amaxosa Delusion, as it is called, there arose at the place called Bullhoek another black prophet who commanded his people to have faith. They were to believe—he did not say in their savage spirits, but in the God of the Bible. They believed, and gave their blood to prove it. . . .

In the lands, desolated by faith, two thousand German Legionaries, who had fought beside the British in the Crimea, were offered a home that Swiss mountaineers had refused. Not all the German legionaries came, and none had families: so that wives, mainly Irish, had to be brought out for them. Then, against the wishes of the British government, four thousand German peasants were sent by a German emigration firm.

The story of the South African native after that is a story of black controlled by white. In the north, in the Orange River settlements, Moshesh was conducting a long campaign with the Boers which ended in his begging the English to "let me and my people rest under the large folds of the flag of England, before I am no more"; from time to time other black tribes rose in rebellion; but there was no longer any question about who owned South Africa. It might be, as Trollope said, a black man's country, ever had been and always would be; but the immediate fact was that the white man had possession of it.

Into corners, across rivers, over mountains, he was pushing the black man, forever making new boundaries. In the big land he was spreading himself. Across the same mountains he himself had overcome in search of freedom, he sent the Griquas of the Vaal River out of Griqualand West to Griqualand East. On a pass in the Drakensbergen they perished in their hundreds.

Griquas one might call them, after a Cape Griqualand where once Hottentots had lived (the missionaries preferred that); but one might also call them Bastaards, which they themselves preferred. They did not think it an indelicate name for a nation; they wished to declare that they had white blood in their veins. The Griquas and Bastaards alike were descended from the association of white men with Hottentot women, but they also had a little Malay blood in them, some Bushman and Kaffir blood. The Coenraad de Buys who, sixty years before, had got into trouble with the Xosas along the Great Fish River—a spectacular creature seven feet in height, a constant rebel with a price on his head, an adviser of black Chiefs—begot a whole clan of Bastaards that live still, under his name, in the Northern Transvaal. He was indeed, this man who could not bear white women, the first white settler in the Transvaal.

The Griquas were led by dynasties called Kok and Waterboer, the Bastaards by a succession of Barends. There were also, in the lands of the Vaal and Orange rivers, Griquand Namaquas under a clan of slightly bastardized Hottentots, originally from the Cape, whose surname was Afrikaner. There were Koranna—very Hottentot, but with Bushman, Bantu and a little white blood in them. There were the bandits of the bergs—the Bergenaars—living like Bushmen and baboons in caves among the rocks of the hills, enemies of mankind. There were the Bushmen themselves, the prey of all. There were fugitive Basutos, Bechuanas, Xosas, and Zulus.

The yellow men had fuzzy hair, high cheekbones, protruding mouths and, quite often, grey eyes. They were bigger than Hottentots and slimmer than white people. There was something in them which urged a man to go wandering and wandering that he might escape restraint. . . .

The Griqua Chief who was forced to sell his land to the Free State and who founded a national home for the Griquas beyond the Drakensbergen was Adam Kok III; and he became a formal ally of Queen Victoria. Still, it was another Griqua leader, Nicolaas Waterboer, who had assigned to him the more prominent role in the pageant of South African history. It was Waterboer who played the part so important in any procession: he was the lay figure, the effigy, the dummy, the man of straw. . . .

For it happened that Waterboer and his followers were, somehow or other, connected with Griqualand West when the first diamond was found there in the year 1867; when, three years later, the dry diggings of the Diamond Fields thrust themselves before the world.

CHAPTER TWO

South Africa and the Diamond Adventurers

I

THE DISCOVERY of diamonds meant the passing of the old
South Africa and the birth of the new. And this was the old
South Africa:

A great bare land, sharply picked out in gold and black
by the sun, and thinly inhabited by white folk; a land from
which its oldest known children—the Bushmen and the
Hottentots—had gone and were going. From the north
there had come to it savage, but virile and courageous,
black tribes; and from the south, Dutchmen and Frenchmen and Germans and Englishmen, and their dependants.

That these people were in Africa at all proved them to
be of adventurous stock. An emigrant is obviously, for better or worse, an exceptional man. If he were not, he would
be at home with others of his kind. He is likely, in fact, to
be an unsuccessful sort of man (why should he leave home
if he were successful?) with enough character to try a new
life.

The Frenchman, who had been urged to South Africa
that he might practise the religion he chose, was probably
the best of all the settlers, since he had come as a servant
of the ideal rather than the material. Now, however, he was
merged in the Dutchman, had clipped the Dutch language

and raised the Dutch temper. Something of German blood and German speech had also unobtrusively crept into the mixture. This new type of person, then, this person standing away from the Europe that had begotten his fathers—from its restraints, but from its culture, too—was the Dutchman, the Boer, South Africa had evolved.

The Englishmen were descendants of the people who had come out to govern the Cape Colony, of their servants; of soldiers and squires ruined by the wars of Napoleon; of missionaries; of artisans and farmhands and souls, lost at home, come to find themselves in a new land.

But between the Englishman and the Boer there was this fundamental difference. The Englishman remembered his old home and felt himself to be but an exiled son from it. The Boer had forgotten his beginnings. South Africa was his home. He had no other home. He wanted no other home. He was not a South African colonist. He was a South African.

That was, for long, the barrier between the Englishman and the Boer—the quality of the feeling each had for South Africa. As that quality varied, as the Englishman was prepared, or not, to substitute South Africa for England, so was the barrier lowered or raised.

It has been the Englishman's effort, within the last generation, to prove himself as completely South African as any. It is the Englishman who today strives to lower the barrier.

But it is now eighty years since diamonds were found in South Africa.

In those days the position was still that the Boers wanted to belong to South Africa and wanted South Africa to belong to them, while the English wanted to belong to England and wanted South Africa to belong to England. For the time, however, there was a slackening in England's pursuit of South Africa and, with it, the Boers. The English

had their two colonies and the Boers had their two republics and the Hottentots and Bushmen were fading from the
land and the Kaffirs were broken, dazed, no longer warriors:
serfs.

They came now, in their tens of thousands, to work for
the white men on the diamond fields, as later they were to
come in their hundreds of thousands to work for them on
the gold fields.

II

Up to the year 1870 South Africa had been chiefly a land of
refuge. The only people it had rejected were the convicts
England had once tried to settle there.

Now, suddenly, it became the Mecca of fortune-hunters.
No more was it a fleeing from the next man's smoke. No
more was it a question of wanting twenty thousand acres
on which to run a few hundred cattle. No more was it a
standstill meditative life on a stoep, with coffee and a pipe
and the Bible on a table in the voorhuis—the front room.
No more was it an affair of a clearing away of the wild
beasts and wild men of the land that one might settle near
a stream and beget enormous families of giant children, se-
cure from civilization.

Now it was a new life. Old man du Toit and old man De
Beer, who owned the ground on which the diamonds were
found, received, respectively, six thousand six hundred
pounds and six thousand guineas for their land. They
turned their bewildered backs on this urgent, rushing, pushing, struggling, delving madness, and continued the ances-
tral tradition. They packed their waggons, and they trekked
into the veld.

In after years De Beer complained to his wife that he
ought to have had not six thousand but six million guineas
for his land.

"But what would we have done with all that money?"

asked Mevrouw De Beer. "There are only the two of us, and this house is big enough. We have our front room, and our bedroom, and our kitchen. What more do we want?"

"We could have had a new waggon."

"We have enough to buy twenty new waggons."

"And a new Cape Cart to go to service—to Nachtmaal."

"That, too, we can afford. . . . Ach, my little heart, be easy. What have we to trouble about? We have enough."

But old De Beer could never again feel easy. He could not imagine what there was in the world one might do with six million guineas (fifty years ago the whole of the Cape had been bought by the English for a little less), but he felt it should have been his, and he wanted it.

The men, however, who came to own De Beer's mines knew what to do with money. That was why they were in Africa.

What sort of a town do people outside Africa imagine Kimberley to be—this Aladdin place where the biggest hole in the world supplies the diamonds for most of the engagement rings of four continents? . . . That was how Rhodes calculated his chances in diamonds—why, the engagement rings alone! . . . But how, then, ought Kimberley to look?

Farcical films and books have been made about the gay wild life of Kimberley in the seventies and eighties—a Bret Harte life of prostitutes and diggers, of drinking and dancing, of the making and spending of fortunes, of a softness under all the hardness. The best-loved stories of Harte and Kipling are probably nothing like the truth: there were surely never any outcasts like those of Poker Flat; nor any little Indian girls and their English lovers saying to each other: "My love, dost thou truly love me as well as ever, though I am faint and sick and worn?" "Yes, I love as I have loved, with all my soul. Lie still, pearl, and rest."

There is no doubt that men, winning money suddenly,

drink and gamble more than others. But Kimberley had quite soon a decorous little social life, with families and churches and hospitals; and it must have been then as it is now, and this is how it is now: Sandy veld, with here and there a few thorn-bearing trees. No water. Grey-green dumps. Suddenly a little town, with haphazard streets and iron-roofed buildings and, on the outskirts, a disreputable location of Kaffir huts—hives made, as often as not, of paraffin tins and old sacking; a little town, hot and dusty, where gardens grow under protest because the soil is the kind that prefers diamonds to green growth. It is indeed a mutual love. If there is a thing diamonds adore to live in, it is desert. . . .

Yet Kimberley it was that began the civilization of South Africa. As Trollope said: "The work of civilising as it has been carried out by simple philanthropy or by religion is terribly slow. One is tempted to say that nothing is done by religion and very little by philanthropy. But love of money works very fast."

And he said it, looking at Kimberley, where Kaffirs were brought, "not by the spasmodic energy of missionaries or by the unalluring attraction of schools, but by the certainty of earning wages. . . . Who can doubt that work is the great civiliser of the world—work, and the growing desire for those good things which work only will bring. . . . Because of this" (said Trollope) "I regard Kimberley as one of the most interesting places on the face of the earth."

And not only was civilization brought to South Africa by the ten shillings a week the Kaffirs earned on the mines. It was brought by the millions of pounds white men took out of the mines. Men who wrote their names across the brooding, patient continent of Africa came, like genii, from a hole under Kimberley.

The greatest of these, of course, was Cecil John Rhodes.

.   .   .

At just about the time Rhodes, with his weak chest and flaming imagination, arrived in Kimberley, England suddenly again resumed her pursuit of the Boers. And, although one may explain how England took the Cape, how England took Natal, how England took the Free State and Transvaal, because—well, because the Boers had been British subjects and where they went was consequently England, one can only say she took the diamond fields as booty that falls to the strongest.

It is hard, really, to establish anybody's right to Griqualand West. The Orange Free State claimed it as part of her purchase from an Adam Kok who was supposed to have inherited it from another Adam Kok. England claimed it on a cession from Nicolaas Waterboer. Even the Transvaal, thinking there was no harm in making the attempt, laid a sort of claim to it. If anyone can imagine the rabble all these mixed breeds were—from the Bastaards to the Bergenaars, from those that called themselves Afrikaner to those whose names meant Tough-bush and Jacket, from the Koks who came to run a comic opera state in Griqualand East to the all but Hottentot-Bushmen, Chudeep and Chudoo—if one has ever seen such people one can imagine the farce this business was of their owning and selling whole kingdoms of land. There is, indeed, only one right people have to a land; and that has nothing to do with their being spawned on it: it is the use they make of it.

But then that has always been a farce in South Africa—the way its great lands have gone from one to another. People with no right to sell have sold to people who knew they had no right to buy. A group of black or brown or white men would find themselves on a piece of empty Africa, and it was theirs. If another group wanted that piece of Africa they would (if they could) force the others out, and then calm their consciences and entrench their positions by paying them something which might well be classed with the peppercorn of English legal tradition. For all the country the Griquas were supposed to own north of the Orange, the Dutch paid them (but they had not much to pay with) four thousand pounds. They also acquired from the Swazis, for a hundred head of cattle, the whole rich district of Lydenburg that was not only gold-bearing, but in the year 1925 became also the centre of great platinum dealings.

The year 1925 saw another of those booms on the Johannesburg Stock Exchange; the flotation of sixty platinum companies with a valuation of ten million pounds; a coming to earth when the stuff was found all but impossible to win and, on top of his, Russian competition brought the price of platinum down from thirty to five pounds ten an ounce. . . .

Still, a hundred head of breeding-cattle!

And then there is Rhodesia. In 1888, the champagne-loving Lobengula, son of Moselikatzè, "having been much molested of late by divers persons seeking and desiring to obtain grants and cessions of land and mining rights in his territories," was saved from his predicament by Rhodes. Rhodes relieved him of his harassing possessions and gave for them a hundred pounds a month, a thousand rifles, a hundred thousand cartridges, and a steamboat on the Zambesi. He similarly, for two thousand and a hundred pounds a year respectively, acquired Barotseland and Manicaland.

The London missionary who was Lobengula's adviser favoured the giving of rifles "because," as he said, "the substitution of long-range rifles for the stabbing assegai would tend to diminish the loss of life in the Matabele cattle raids and thus prove a distinct gain to the cause of humanity." The Deputy Commissioner of Bechuanaland agreed with him. "The use of firearms in modern warfare has," he said, "notoriously diminished the loss of life." And besides, he told the Colonial Office, one could also give arms and ammunition to the Bechuana Chief who was Lobengula's rival, and "the relative position of the chiefs would thus remain unchanged."

For all these humanitarian projects Rhodes needed money, so it was well the English managed to get Griqualand West.

The only superior right the Dutch actually had to Griqualand West was that some Boers were living there who paid taxes to the Orange Free State. How they came to be there —how anybody ever came to be anywhere in South Africa— is not the point. Nor is the talk of cessions from Kok or Waterboer anything but confusion. If Kok or Waterboer had anything to cede, they did not know what they were ceding or why they were ceding it—they knew only that somehow or other they had to go.

Now, having taken Griqualand West, England put herself in the wrong—admitted a debt—by offering the Free State ninety thousand pounds in compensation. And the Free State, having denied England's justification, put herself in the wrong by accepting payment of the debt.

So Griqualand West was English. Presently, too, the Transvaal was English. In 1877, in the year following the ninety-thousand-pound episode, Sir Theophilus Shepstone, the Secretary for Native Affairs in Natal, with eight Civil Servants (one of whom was Rider Haggard) and twenty-five policemen, rode into Pretoria and annexed the South African Republic. It made him impatient, he said, to see the way the Boers were mismanaging their affairs. And when England sent him along to enquire politely of the republic how it was getting on, and could she do anything for it—as a Trust might approach a small distracted shopkeeper on the verge of bankruptcy—when he saw how the republic was harassed and unable to meet its liabilities, he used the discretion that had been given him, asked for no further instructions from head office, said: "We are ab-

sorbing you," and the little shop, without opposition, wea-
rily succumbed.

Sir Theophilus Shepstone is the greatest native administrator South Africa has had. After England took Natal
from the Dutch, he settled eighty thousand black refugees
in homes of their own—savages brought up in the shadow
of Chaka and Dingaan—and did not lose a life, black or
white. The Zulus called him Somtseu, the mighty hunter,
and he was the sort of man who could sit under a tree and
listen while they told him, in their own tongue, without
the use of interpreters who "ate up the people's words,"
what was in their hearts. . . . But that it was right of him
to annex Transvaal is another matter. It only remains that
he did, and poor disillusioned President Burgers said. "I
would rather be a policeman under a strong government
than the president of such a state. . . ."

At this moment, then, England had both the diamonds
and the gold.

But on December 16, 1880, on the anniversary of that
day on which Dingaan's murder of Pieter Retief and his following was revenged at Blood River—on Dingaan's Day,
the Boers proclaimed again their republic, and opened up
hostilities against the British.

Two months after, there was the battle of Majuba, and
the Boers regained their independence under British suze-
rainty.

There were for long English people in South Africa who
spoke with passion of Gladstone and his Midlothian campaign which, they said, put this potency into Boer hearts;
and there were Englishmen in Pretoria who, when they
heard the news of the settlement, dragged their flag through
the dust.

III

In this same year in which the Transvaal went to war,
Rhodes founded the De Beers Company. He was then

twenty-seven. Next year he both entered the Cape Parliament and took a pass degree at Oxford. In 1887 he established his Goldfields Company on the Rand, which still exists as one of the biggest companies. And within the next three years he amalgamated all the diamond mines of Kimberley under his control; was granted a charter over Lobengula's dominions and another seven hundred thousand square miles for which he had concessions; and became Prime Minister of the Cape.

In the course of centuries there arises, now and then, a man who is accounted great because he has that within him which makes him conceive life on the grand scale.

Greatness is, after all, as much a matter of capacity as of performance. An artist is not made great only by a picture he has chanced to paint or a book he has chanced to write. He is a great artist or not in so far as his work is the expression of that which is himself.

There are people who have executed one splendid work, and there they ended. They could do no more. The greatness was out of them and they remained not great. Is a coward who performs one courageous deed a courageous man? Greatness, like courage, is an inherent quality. The people distinguished for one work are merely lucky people. They have struck treasure. They are not themselves compounded of treasure, so that whatever is dug out of them, although it may be compounded with dross, has value. On the Vaal River Diggings, one may stumble on a pocket of diamonds. All the surrounding ground is barren, and there, in a sudden hole, one comes upon a nest—diamond after diamond—as in a dream. And as suddenly as it began it ends. There is no more of it. It is not a Kimberley Mine or a De Beers Mine in which one can go on delving inexhaustibly for a century. It is not a mine at all. One calls it a pocket.

Rhodes. with enough vice in him to keep his virtues

earthbound, was a big man. That was his quality. His body, his passions, his desires, his schemes, his successes, and his failures were all big. He expressed what he was himself when he defined his future home: "I want the big and simple, barbaric, if you choose." And in that home he would have no little fragile objects, however rare or beautiful they might be. And he surrounded it with fifteen acres of ground, filled its valley with hydrangeas, and bought for its background a mountainside.

On his farms in the Cape he planted fruit trees in batches of fifty thousand. One of his farms in Rhodesia was of a hundred thousand acres. The dam on it held fifty million gallons of water. The avenue to his Government House in Bulawayo was three miles long. In his streets a span of oxen could turn.

He even coveted the valley of the Great Drakenstein Mountains for a farm. "How much do you want me to buy?" asked his agent. "Buy it all." "All! All the Drakenstein Valley! . . . It would cost a million!" "I don't ask your advice. I want you to buy it. Buy it!"

The agent bought what the owners would sell.

When Rhodes was concerned with diamonds he amalgamated all the diamond companies in Africa and paid for his control with the biggest check yet written. When he sought wealth he made a million a year. When he entered politics he became a Prime Minister. When he needed a jumping-off ground to raid the Transvaal he had part of Bechuanaland transferred from Imperial to Colonial control. When he went colonizing he added to his interests—and Britain's —a land larger than France, Germany, and the Low Countries combined. He planned an All-Red route from the Cape to Cairo. He set before Parliament his solution of the Native Problem in what he called—and meant to be—a Bill for Africa.

When he was besieged in Kimberley he wanted the course

of a war deflected to the purpose of his immediate release. When he needed solitude he sat on a ledge in his grounds from which he could see both the Atlantic and Indian Oceans. When he died he mingled his dust with the dust of a mountaintop. The writer he venerated was Gibbon. He believed he resembled the Emperor Titus. Like the greatest of the Cæsars, he left his possessions to the people. He gave his name to a country, and his life to "the extension of British rule throughout the world." He expected to be remembered four thousand years.

His manner was no less large, and his way with men royal. He met Herbert Baker, a young and unknown architect; decided immediately that here was the man to build his future home and his monuments; gave him a free hand with the first, and, for the second, a commission to see Thebes, Pæstum, Athens, and the tomb of Lars Porsena. Between them they established a taste which has not yet quite faded from South Africa. Of all South African leaders, Rhodes alone had taste.

He wanted an expedition led to Mashonaland. He chanced on a man of twenty-three who seemed to know what he was about. "How much will it cost?" he asked him. "Give me four hours," said the young man, and, after the four hours, came back: "£89,295/10s." . . . "I accept your offer, and you shall command the expedition."

He abandoned an opportunity for millions to go to the deathbed of a friend. . . . "Blood must flow," roared Groot (big) Adrian de la Rey to him when he came to settle the matter of Bechuanaland. "Give me my breakfast," Rhodes answered. "Then we can talk about blood."

His largest gesture of all—that he might hear the grievances of the embittered Matabele and bring peace to the country they were harassing—was to stake his life on the honour he himself had helped to reduce and, with three friends, to attend their council in the depths of the

Matoppo hills. "Is it peace then?" he asked finally. "How do we know it is peace?"

"You have the word of Somabulane—of Babiaan, of Dhliso, chiefs of the House of Kumalo."

The chiefs laid down their sticks as a symbol of surrendered arms.

"It is good, my children. Go in peace."

"Hamba gahle, Baba.

"Hamba gahle, Aminduna."

"Mehla 'mhlopi, Baba."

"Mehla 'mhlopi, Aminduna."

Go in peace, Father. Go in peace, Chieftains. The eyes are white, Father. The eyes are white.

But he was large too in his influence for evil. The means that to him justified the ends became to others the end itself. It was not for good alone that "when he stood upon the Cape Peninsula," as Mark Twain said, "his shadow fell on the Zambesi." "Every man has his price," he quoted Robert Walpole, and corrupted politics. "I object to the ballot *in toto*," he said, and compelled conscience.

He was boundlessly arrogant. If his amiability was the condescension of an emperor, his imperialism was the expression of an autocrat: "We must adopt a system of Indian despotism in our relations with the barbarians of South Africa." He impatiently threatened to "hoist his own rag," when the Union Jack seemed reluctant to support him. "He imagines himself," said the first Jan Hofmeyr after the Raid—that Hofmeyr who had once hoped to work with him for a greater South Africa—"he imagines himself a young king, the equal of the Almighty." . . . And so, like Lucifer, he fell too, destroying more than men—destroying the faith of men. "What am I to do?" he said to Hofmeyr after the Raid. "Live it down? How can I do it? Am I to get rid of myself?"

He could not live it down. He could not get rid of himself. He had aspired to emulate Shepstone, who had so casually taken the Transvaal not twenty years before. He had hoped to achieve his end, and then smooth over his means. "I am just beginning my career," he said with bravado. But he had ended his career, and he knew it.

He had come to South Africa at seventeen, with ten more years to live: so his doctor thought. In 1891 he had had an accident and an illness and forty-five was then the limit placed on his years. He died at forty-eight. All he did, he did under the imminence of death.

"Happy?" said Rhodes. "I happy? Good God, no!" He indicated General Booth. "I would give all I possess to believe what that old man believes."

He said to Rosebery: "Everything in the world is too short. Life and fame and achievement, everything is too short."

"From the cradle to the grave, what is it?" he told Stead. "Three days at the seaside."

He lay dying in a little cottage near Cape Town. "So little done. So much to do.". . .

But, as his body was being lowered into the rock of the Matoppos, the black men he had won and betrayed and won again and saved gave him their royal salute: they saluted him, alone among white men, as they saluted their kings:

"Bayete!"

IV

It was on the diamond diggings at Kimberley that tens of thousands of those natives, who had had their land taken from them and had lost their chief occupation of fighting, were given their first experience of modern industry.

They came from the conquered territories of Africa—they came hundreds of miles on their pale-soled feet, so flat that one could tell an African's footprint from a European's, so hard that they feared neither the hot earth nor the stones and thorns and burrs—they came to work for the white man's magic. Two or three pounds a month they were paid (and nothing has changed so little in South Africa as the black man's wages) and they were given food and lodging.

And they saved their money to buy rifles and ammunition. They had seen the assegai of the Kaffir vanquished by this magic of the European. It was the dearest treasure a man might have.

When they had bought their magic, they went home again. When they needed more money, they came back.

But not only for the Kaffir was it, in these days, a different life. It was a new life for all South Africa.

Suddenly, on the empty veld, there had sprung up a town second in white population only to Cape Town, which was already over two hundred years old. In the year Rhodes formed his De Beers Company—in 1880—the white population of Cape Town was 30,000, that of Kimberley 18,000, Johannesburg did not exist. Today Johannesburg has 800,-000 people of all colours, and Cape Town 500,000. Pretoria and Durban follow. Kimberley's white population has only doubled; but it has the biggest hole in the world, and the meaning of that hole is diamonds, and Kimberley remains the heart of all that concerns diamonds in the world.

It is not that Kimberley has still, as in its beginnings, nearly all the diamonds in the world. Far from it. More and more are found. There are diamond mines in the Free State, there is the diamond mine near Pretoria which produced the largest diamond ever known. There are diamond diggings in Namaqualand so prolific that a stone is shown under which once lay four hundred and fifty diamonds. There are still the alluvial diggings in the Cape. There are four thousand square miles of diggings in the Transvaal.

The desert along the sea of South-West Africa is full of

diamonds. There are diamonds in Belgian Congo, in Angola, in Sierra Leone, in the Gold Coast, in French Equatorial Africa, and, extraordinarily, in Tanganyika.

Diamonds are not at all the rarity their price would suggest. What gives them value is the control of De Beers. First Rhodes amalgamated all the diamond mines of Kimberley and formed his De Beers Consolidated Mines. Then a diamond syndicate was created to buy the products of De Beers Consolidated Mines.

Diamonds kept appearing in ruinous quantities. But now another artist with money, a subtle and imaginative mind, rose up for De Beers. Ernest Oppenheimer made a company to control the diamonds of South-West Africa, which has now entered De Beers. The Diamond Corporation was formed to deal with the diamonds discovered in Namaqualand and on the alluvial diggings of the Transvaal. The Diamond Producers Association came into being, the Diamond Trading Company. All had to do with the control of diamonds.

The diamonds they did not own, they had contracts to buy. Were too many diamonds produced, were there business recessions in the world, then diamonds were kept back. Were fugitives escaping from war-menaced countries; had they need to transpose their assets into small, universal, highly valuable shape; was the world flooded with money that had little outlet, the diamonds came forth. The world's diamond cutters, the world's jewelers, waited on the decisions of De Beers. Kimberley itself lived by the wisdom of Sir Ernest Oppenheimer. It could not always live well. But it lived.

The diamonds of the little men on the alluvial diggings remained a free enterprise. But they were bought only as they were needed, only as they did not interfere with the seeming rarity of diamonds, only when they would not calamitously reduce the price of diamonds. . . . Twenty miles from Kimberley is a little town called Barkly West, which was the centre of the river diggings before Kimberley became the centre of the dry diggings; which once hoisted a republican flag under President Stafford Parker, sometime an able seaman in the Royal Navy; which was represented by Rhodes in Parliament until he died. Its population is today five hundred.

The river diggings, the various proclaimed alluvial diggings, are, in South Africa, the final stronghold of personal adventure. There men come, as they came eighty years ago, with their capital of either hope or despair, to search for luck under the ground. But the best ground is worked out. Luck was always scarce. There is little left today.

At one time there were camps of diggers all along the banks of the Vaal. Some camps are older than Kimberley or Johannesburg, others are the derelicts of an old "rush," few are proclaimed today.

This is what a rush means:

Diamonds have been found on private property. Because the owner of the property is not also the owner of its minerals, the ground can, if the government so decrees, be thrown open to the public.

Then, on a day, comes the mining commissioner, and proclaims the ground a public alluvial diggings. A pistol is fired and the aspirants race, with pegs bearing their names and ready pointed for planting in the ground, to the claims of their choice. The man who first pegs off the ground which, according to varying provincial laws, constitutes a claim, owns it. He pays the government a licensing fee, and the owner of the ground a percentage. . . .

The alluvial diamonds are found only tens of feet below the surface, where mine diamonds are found steadily through thousands of feet, but they are worth, carat for carat, three times as much as the mine diamonds; and there have been times when, owing to the control of mine diamonds, alluvial diamonds have shown the larger annual turnover.

Nevertheless, no digger has ever made a fortune. To the rushes come men with the joy of adventure in them. They depart. But there also come men—and they ultimately form the digging population—for whom the workaday world holds no place: men who have not been trained to a regular trade; men who cannot, or will not, work; men not designed for civilization, who are in a condition of that declining shame which, reversing Shaw's axiom that "the more things a man is ashamed of, the more respectable he is," must mean the steady abandonment of respectability. They are not ashamed of anything. They are not ashamed to live in one room of corrugated iron. They are not ashamed to have no money. They are not ashamed to get drunk. They are not ashamed to take a black woman and beget a coloured family. They are indeed, in a way, supermen: above social law.

Yet, even on the diggings, life has changed. The poor whites manage as best they may, living their blighted lives on the diggings as they would anywhere else, scratching inexpertly, and with desperate hope, at the ground. Yet River digging is not always now a simple matter of owning a cradle-like sieve called a baby; of a few picks and shovels, and tubs of water; of a shaft in the ground, a windlass, a piece of tin for sorting gravel and two or three Kaffir boys, or no boys at all.

Today, on such ground as is left, diggers work in big open holes they call paddocks; with large gangs of "boys"; with complicated machinery; with buckets sailing up and down wires in the air; and, on the ground, trucks running on railways; with sometimes even an engine. There are big men who support little men. There are shopkeepers who advance money for the working expenses and receive in return, if they do not lose on the gamble, a share in the profits.

And, of course, a man may get a stone worth a thousand pounds. He may. But what generally happens is that months will pass, and the small digger, picking his futile path through the ground, will find nothing; and the big digger, with his big expenses, will find a few diamonds, but they will barely pay for his boys' wages. . . . Yet each will have just enough luck to delude hope. . . . And, after thirty or forty years, the young digger has become the old digger: so much ground has been worked out, he does not know where next to try or what next to do; and there he ends and the diggings too gradually end.

In locations, on the fringe of the diggings, their shameful hovels breaking out on the face of the hills like the disease from which most of them suffer, live the natives. They are the remnants of the remnants that a hundred years before fled to the Vaal River: the Bastaards and Griquas and Koranna; the Hottentots and Bushmen and Bergenaars; the fugitive Basutos, Bechuanas, Xosas and Zulus.

Upon these had fallen the soldiers of Mantatisi and Moselikatze; they had fought among themselves; their descendants had mingled and with them had mingled white men; they came to follow, in the end, the fortunes of the white diggers.

Now there they are, derelicts of a vanishing world: not at all like their virile, primitive ancestors, yet with virtues of their own.

They are law-abiding and honest. There was a time when the natives, coming to the towns from their own lands, were no less law-abiding and honest. They are not today.

It is true that a native on the diggings sometimes steals a diamond from the claim of the digger for whom he is working and sells it, at a small price, to another person. But the temptation is very great. His wages are small, he works from sunup to sundown, and his food is a lump of mealie-meal. The lump of meal makes his lean belly sick. His legs are like reeds; after work, in the summer, he sweats so that he is unapproachable—it is the sweat and dirt, not nature, that makes him smell; but also he makes little use of the river that flows past his work. In the twilight of winter he goes about, protected from the cold by a sack, with a hole for his head, his brown skin a frosted grey, looking for sticks or cattle-dung to make a fire. As there are few trees or cattle, sticks and cattle-dung are scarce. And at home there is a large family, and the derelicts too of other families. Mealie-meal, cotton blankets, and syphilis are equally shared.

It is surprising, it is almost beyond nature, how seldom a native does try to help himself by illicitly selling a diamond he has found on his master's claim. Yet this illicit selling of diamonds—its illicit buying (I.D.B.) is, like illicit gold buying (I.G.B.), one of the grave crimes in the South African calendar.

V

The reason why the hand of the law falls so heavily on the thief—the illicit seller—of gold or diamonds is that this sort of crime cannot be compared with ordinary crimes. One knows one's other possessions. If they disappear one can discover their absence and perhaps trace their course. One can identify them.

But here is a digger, working and working his claim (or, rather, paying and paying for the working of it), and he does not know what diamonds, if any, there may be in it, and he cannot tell whether they eventually come to him, or whether a native has picked up one or two during his work, and sold them to someone else. Who is to say in what claim those diamonds were found? Who can establish the elusive chicanery?

When there is a reasonable suspicion, when this suspicion grows towards certainty, a brutal, but inevitable, method is followed. A native in the employ of the police is sent to trap the Illicit Diamond Buyer. He offers him a trap stone, the buyer sometimes enters the trap and, upon conviction, is awarded the sort of sentence English law inflicts on a dangerous housebreaker. In the early days, indeed, the sentence might be anything up to seven years' hard labour on the new breakwater that was being built in Table Bay. And no less severely was illicit traffic in unwrought gold handled.

Now the mines have greater control over their diamonds and gold than the alluvial diggers. But yet there was a time, before Rhodes insisted on confining the native workers in compounds, when hundreds of thousands of pounds were annually lost through the theft of diamonds. In one year alone the loss was estimated at three quarters of a million. The natives secreted the diamonds between their toes, in their woolly hair, in their ears, in their mouths. They even swallowed them. Still today, before they leave the compounds to go home, is a strong purgative given them. "The Kaffirs," Anthony Trollope writes, "are not only most willing but most astute thieves, feeling a glory in their theft and thinking that every stone stolen from a white man is a duty done to their Chief and their tribe. . . . They come to the Fields instructed by their Chiefs to steal diamonds and they obey the orders like loyal subjects. Many of the Kaffir Chiefs are said to have large quantities of diamonds which have been brought to them by their men returning from the diggings. . . ."

For years, indeed, adventurers have been seeking these diamonds the chiefs were said to have. Lobengula, in particular, was believed to have bucketfuls of diamonds. The diamonds were never found. They were surely not bought. In the same way people are searching for Kruger's hidden gold. There is no Kruger's hidden gold. The gold Kruger's government had in 1899 was a half million pounds worth of bar gold, four hundreds pounds in cash, and twenty thousand pounds—war funds—standing to the personal credit of his commandant-general. This money General Smuts got, with the support of fifty policemen, out of the unwilling banks while Pretoria was being shelled by Roberts. It was used to pay for the Boer War, and when it ended the Boers lived on the country. There was no other gold. There was never any "Kruger gold."

It is now three quarters of a century since Trollope heard those tales about the diamonds and the Kaffir Chiefs. Fifteen years after Trollope was in Kimberley, Lobengula took, for all the mineral rights of Mashonaland (and this, in the end, was held to mean Mashonaland itself), a hundred pounds in gold a month, a thousand rifles and a steamboat. Two years later, when Rhodes wanted Matabeleland, Lobengula said to his people:

"Matabele! The white men will never cease following us while we have gold in our possession, for gold is what white men prize above all things. Collect now all my gold . . . and carry it to the white men. Tell them they have beaten my regiments, killed my people, burnt my kraals, captured my cattle, and that I want peace."

The gold Lobengula spoke of—"all my gold"—was a thousand sovereigns probably saved from the hundred pounds a month given him by Rhodes for Mashonaland.

When Lobengula, escaping from Rhodes's army, died, his sons worked for Rhodes. He had Lobengula's heir, Njubi, with him in Kimberley; and when, during the Boer War—three years after the Matabele war—there was trouble in Matabeleland (now called Rhodesia), Rhodes found a way to keep the Matabele heir safely with him in Kimberley.

For the boy loved a girl of low caste—one of the tribe called Fengu that had escaped from the Zulus to the Xosas:

A marriage with her would disqualify him from the chieftainship. Rhodes gave him fifty pounds and a house in Kimberley to marry the girl and telegraphed to his Administrator in Rhodesia:

> *Njubi was divided between lust and Empire. . . . It is better that he should settle down in Kimberley and be occupied in creating a family than plotting in Bulawayo to stab you in the stomach. . . .*

What emerges·from these incidents of a hundred pounds a month for a whole country; a thousand pounds—"all my gold"—for peace; fifty pounds to a boy (with the sort of house a native would get) to help him marry and thus give up his patrimony—what do the small amounts of money show but that Lobengula had no buckets of diamonds to sell or bequeath? Nor has any other native chief ever shown such signs of wealth as the possession of even half a bucket of diamonds—or even a cupful of diamonds—would bring him.

Probably not so many diamonds were stolen as was imagined; but still enough must have been stolen to add to the desirability, in Rhodes's eyes, of compounds.

The other good things about compounds were that the white people of Kimberley were safe from the tens of thousands of savages, and also that they had to buy from De Beers.

One can live in Kimberley for twenty-five years and never, unless one makes the deliberate effort, see a native mine-labourer.

This compound business and many other things became possible when all the mines in Kimberley were consolidated under one control.

This was in 1888. In the year before that Rhodes had bought out all the shares in the mine called De Beers. Barney Barnato, the vivid young adventurer who, as Barnett Isaacs, had come to Kimberley a few years after Rhodes to sell to the excited and overflowing fortune-hunters his stock-in-trade of sixty boxes of cigars, was trying to do the same at the Kimberley Mine. To this, in little more than a decade, the young Whitechapel Jew had come—to the handling of millions.

Now they each said, Rhodes and Barnato, that the holdings in the mines had to be amalgamated, and others agreed with them. It was becoming impossible for men to work side by side, sometimes on only a few feet of ground at the bottom and on the sides of these largest holes in the world, without intolerable difficulty and dangerous dispute.

In the beginning the dry diggings had been worked like the River diggings. On a claim thirty-one feet square one laboured with a few tools and a few natives. As more and more diamonds were found, the price of claims rose from a hundred to four thousand pounds or even five thousand pounds and five thousand five hundred pounds—though, naturally, there were claims that had no diamonds at all and were therefore worthless.

The claims that cost so much began to be divided and further divided. The delvings descended deeper and deeper. They were presently two or three or four hundred feet deep. They had shafts and tunnels. They were past the soft yellow ground to the hard blue ground, the real ground— no longer the ground diggings are made of, but the ground mines are made of.

Men worked their claims as near the edges as they dared. The space between the claims grew so narrow that men, black and white, carts and mules, carrying soil, could hardly move. Men, mules, carts, the precious earth itself fell down the sides. . . .

In due time, the diggings became quarries, supported by timber. Roads and carts were no more. Instead, from the surface to the depth of the quarries, iron ropes were stretched on which ran buckets bringing the blue ground to the surface, there to be delivered to boxlike erections, thence to be taken to a place for sorting. The buckets ran up one set of ropes to bring the ground to the top, they ran down another set to be loaded with more ground. On the floor of the quarry worked thousands of black men and their white masters, each group separately at its own bit of ground.

The earth continued to tumble. It had to be moved for the buckets to take the good blue ground. It became impossible for men to dig without encroaching on each other's holdings. The rain that falls so seldom in Kimberley could, nevertheless, at times fall with such force, in such quantities, that shafts were filled with water and then the water could not be pumped from the shafts. The earth fell more and more—there was one fall of millions of cubic feet of reef that entombed a great number of claims. Men were killed by the falls of earth.

A Mining Board had been set up to deal with all these difficulties. Within a few years it had spent over two million pounds trying to keep the mines safe, it was in debt and could not get an overdraft.

It became clear that the day of the small digger, the individual digger, was gone.

It was in these circumstances that Rhodes and Barnato and others of their kind went about buying claims. But there was still a further stage. There was the question of controlling the whole system of diamond production; the engineering of output and prices. Rhodes wanted to be the man to do that. So did Barnato. It became a rivalry in the buying up of claims.

The final scene was staged in Dr. Jameson's cottage in Kimberley between the Briton, Rhodes, and three Jews.

One, Beit, was on Rhodes's side. Barnato had with him his nephew, Woolf Joel.

It was Rhodes who won. He might now do what he liked with diamonds. Those great holes might now be systematically exploited: with labour-saving machines; with plans for the working of millions of tons of earth; with great plates of vaseline to catch the diamonds; with trays bearing oily-faced, glittering fortunes; with a peremptory holding-back from a market not eager enough; with an equally potent releasing for a market willing once more; with a standing-up in Parliament to speak from one mouth concerning a whole industry. . . .

More striking than all, Rhodes might do, with the surplus profits of De Beers, what his dream and his passion inspired him to do; he might use those profits to an end that had no connection at all with mining. Who could stop Rhodes if he was determined to carry the Union Jack from the Cape to Cairo? . . .

De Beers Consolidated Mines meant all the diamond mines of Kimberley, and an outstretched, closing hand towards diamond mines wherever they might be found. Here was the most complete trust on earth. Here it was in the land where men had come to escape control, and had gone on and on to escape control. So it was that the old South Africa died and the new South Africa was born. . . .

It had died, indeed, the day old du Toit sat in bewilderment on his little dung-smeared stoep and watched the overrunning of his ground by a wild concourse of adventurers, coming on horseback, on foot, by Cape cart and by ox-waggon—coming with pick and shovel and shout and argument and the firm offer of seven and sixpence for the perpetual freehold of a claim whose value was beyond computation. . . .

And now it was not only diamonds, it was gold too. Those same men who had lain sprawling with snatching hands over the Diamond Fields were now on the Gold Fields. There was in particular a man called Robinson, whose destiny in the declining years of a too long life was the fighting of lawsuits relating to events of a generation back, and he was beating even Rhodes at the gold game.

About three hundred miles from Kimberley, nearly a thousand miles from Cape Town, lay the Witwatersrand—the Ridge of the White Waters.

CHAPTER THREE

South Africa and the Gold Adventurers

I

JOHANNESBURG, as everyone knows, is the heart of the gold industry. Right through Johannesburg City runs the gold reef on whose product is largely based the economic system of the world. The tarnished-silver mine-dumps form part of the skyline of Johannesburg. And, on still nights, in some parts of the town, when the wind is blowing a certain way, it is possible to hear a distant murmur, like the faraway beating of waves against a shore; and that murmur is the crushing, crushing, crushing of the ore by the battery stamps, the whispering end of that noise in whose immediate presence the ears grow tight and the voice falls dead. But it is a noise no louder in the life of Johannesburg City than the beating of a heart in the body it inhabits. Those battery stamps *are* the heart of the Rand, and as secret. One does not hear their throbbing except when the blare of living is hushed.

Johannesburg was born in the year 1886. Then Rhodes, describing "its wonderful climate, its facilities for work, its enormous auriferous deposits," quoted the spreading view that "the Rand is the biggest thing the world has seen."

Did Rhodes really think that, so strangely and rapidly as Johannesburg had risen—with its gold, its climate, its passion—did he think it was, or absolutely could become, "the biggest thing the world has seen," or did he mean simply the biggest thing of its kind?

Johannesburg, six thousand feet above sea level, dry in winter, rain-fresh in summer, has an electric air which gives men ardour in thought, in act, and competition, and creates in them the vitality from which spring the excitements of South Africa.

But this ardour apart, the treasure under its soil apart, Johannesburg cannot match, and now never will match, the big things of the Old World or even of the New World of the two Americas. It has missed its chance of being a noble city.

There it stands, so high; on its ridges that face such distances; with space unlimited for growth; with its miraculous air—and, its dwelling-houses apart, what is it? A few square miles of narrow streets, flanked by undistinguished tall buildings; and the streets are lined with cars, and cars and buses and people are all trying to pass one another, and it is for no pleasure one walks in the streets of the City of Johannesburg.

It began because nobody cared how Johannesburg looked or thought of it as a place for any purpose but the making of money. It continued its frustrated way because it lacked public men of imagination.

Of the three men who gave Johannesburg their name, one was Kruger, and he not only did not care how it looked, he hated it, he saw in it that which was to bring him disaster. The gold of Johannesburg, he always maintained, would cause blood to be shed; and though it was only thirty-five miles from his house in Pretoria and it was his duty as President to visit the bigger towns at least once a year, he only thrice in his lifetime came to Johannesburg.

Even his State Secretary Reitz, once President of the Free

State, said of Johannesburg: "What has its wealth done for us? The money has only injured the noble character of our people. It would tend to our advantage" (he said after the Boer War) "to be rid of Johannesburg."

At the same time, it was for the sake of money Kruger had the streets of Johannesburg made so narrow, with so many crossings; for corner sites, he was informed, got the highest prices.

The Uitlanders, too—the Outlanders, the Foreigners— over whose franchise Milner said he had to go to war while Kruger cried: "It is not the franchise, it is my country that you want"—the Uitlanders had no interest in Johannesburg except for its gold.

In the beginning, indeed, the same mistake was made about the gold of Johannesburg as about the diamonds of Kimberley. People did not know that the real thing was below the surface thing. The Uitlanders thought they would scratch the gold from the top of the Rand and then go and live in the West End of London.

It was not until the early nineties that deep-level mining began in Johannesburg and one saw there was gold in the Rand mines—gold a mile down, two miles down, gold everywhere, gold enough for a lifetime and another lifetime— it was not until then that people began to think of Johannesburg as a possible home.

How gay, too, was life in Johannesburg. An English pro-Boer wrote: "Every luxury of life, every extravagance of behaviour, every form of private vice, flourished unchecked; every man and woman said and did what seemed good in their eyes."

But by then Johannesburg City was laid out as it was forever to be. The Raid came. The Boer War came. And although Herbert Baker came too, it never fell to him to design many buildings besides the houses of people now ready to live in Johannesburg. The buildings of Johannesburg City were designed by others. And this is the reason that the alluring parts of Johannesburg are its houses in their gardens on the ridges, and nowhere in its city.

On the rocky ridges of Johannesburg stand these houses, white or of stone, with roofs tiled or thatched or shingled. The ridges run so that a man may have a street at his front door and a valley at his back door—and, beyond the valley, a vision for his eyes of forty miles of country rimmed with mountains.

The rocky ground on which his house is built is blasted with dynamite so that grass and plants and trees may grow. Gardens are quickly made in Johannesburg. A forest is the work of only a few years' sunshine and rain.

In the old days the best parts of Johannesburg were wherever the mining lords chanced to live. Today not many of these are left in Johannesburg. Deputies represent them.

Yet, Baker house or not, cherished garden or not, people seldom stay long in one house. They want to be nearer the schools. They want more ground. They have made money in gold shares, so why not a larger house? They have lost money in gold shares, a smaller one will have to do. Only one reason does not, as in other parts of the world, make Johannesburg people move from large to small houses, or from either large or small houses to flats—and that is the question of servants. South Africa's Black Problem solves almost every other problem; and that, if nothing else, prevents the solving of the Black Problem. Who could bear to have it solved at the expense of all the other problems?

It is amusing—and morally, if not factually, instructive—to read in the 1911 edition of the *Encyclopædia Britannica* a list of Johannesburg's fashionable suburbs. Only one of the eight is still a fashionable suburb; and even that is no longer quite aristocratic. Of the others, one or two are far down the social scale; they are slums; they are being given up to coloured people.

Every few years, indeed, a new fashionable suburb arises —always further and further from Johannesburg City.

In one of the older suburbs there is a terrace from which may be seen the silver dumps of twenty mines and a great part of the city besides.

There are streets in Johannesburg called Gold Street, Quartz Street, Banket Street, Claim Street, Nugget Street.

Even though mining is now only the second industry in the Union, its gold remains what the world chiefly desires. The feeling has not yet departed from Johannesburg that gold mining is more a religion than an industry.

Well, there, on the ridges, among the gardens, facing the views, live the people who have made money. The business buildings grow higher and higher. In the narrow streets more people and vehicles find it ever harder to move. It is faintly what befell the Kimberley diggings when the earth became too precious to be spared for roads.

Under the city, a hundred miles east and west, wall to wall a mile or two miles deep, lie the forty-three gold mines of Johannesburg. Running out of the city, past signboards bearing Oriental names, past shops dwindling from wholesale to retail, past native eating-houses and Indian tailor-shops, in crazy sheds of discoloured corrugated iron, swarm the squalid beings, of all nations and colours, who have sunk to the bottom. At the moment there are not many white people unemployed, but, as a general rule, the Europeans who live there are poor whites—those people who cannot maintain a white standard. They have come to Johannesburg because there is no work for them on the land. In Johannesburg, they have heard, a man, without money, without training, without capacity, without moral purpose or the desire to work, can make a living.

When there is trouble, when growling hounds spring suddenly against an enemy, these poor whites come out of their hovels and join in the fight.

It probably happens in other parts of the world too that, when farmers put up their prices and shops put up their prices, tradesmen put up their prices in a way that is peculiar and has peculiar results.

In Johannesburg, for instance, white tradesmen get six shillings or less an hour and their native assistants six shillings a day. The employers, however, charge the customer from ten to fifteen shillings an hour for the white man and ten shillings a day for the native. Then the strange thing is that all this money the customer pays—its proliferation through slow work—seems to do neither tradesmen nor employers any good.

The building trade is considered the standard trade. It is also the first trade to suffer when times begin to get bad. Promptly tradesmen are in real trouble through lack of work, master builders go bankrupt, and the value of what they did (which seldom was good value) is also reduced.

Since the two German wars, again, the mine-owners—their shareholders—have their own particular trouble.

For wars create industries. These industries can charge what they hope to get for their products. They can pay the people they employ higher and still higher wages.

The product of the gold mines has a fixed price. While other commodities, after the last German war, rose fifty, a hundred, two hundred per cent, and the mines had to meet the new costs, gold itself rose only fifteen per cent. Therefore they could not pay either white or black workers what other industries paid them; they could not get the black and white workers they needed; they could not produce enough gold to make up for their smaller profits; the price of shares went down and down. . .

When people speak of this Mammoth, this Moloch, the *Mines* (that speak of themselves, again, in capitals, as THE INDUSTRY) they forget those mine-owners, the little shareholders, who have to sell their houses when their shares go down.

For naturally the most tempting investment in Johannesburg is gold shares. The centuries have not yet (our world being what it is) found a better investment than gold . . . as a general thing. . . .

But is there now a general thing? Is there anything one can go by? Is there anything one can depend on?

The two German wars have thrown into the *ewigkeit* the ballast of the world. Stability is gone. There is no general thing.

Yet, remarkably again, there is a general thing.

It is good old gold.

The world, swinging hither and thither, tumbling this way and that, returns tentatively, despairingly—it clings, as ever, to gold.

The mines, like other industries, live under the constant threat of workers' demands. They have to yield to their white workers. What of their black workers?

There the black men are, a mile, two miles, under the ground, along corridors a mile or two miles long, the hundreds of thousands of half-naked savages, grunting as they work, who have been recruited by agents from faraway kraals.

They are drilling holes into the rock for dynamite charges. Their naked black torsos are glistening with sweat. Water is dripping, naturally or artificially, washing down the mine-dust, the silica that does not now, as once, so hungrily eat up the life of the miner.

What is one to do about the black miner?

Between 1932 and 1946 the Rand mines paid the government in taxes and for leases (a capital tax really) two hundred and forty million pounds where, as ordinary companies, they would have paid a hundred and twenty-eight millions. They paid other taxes through the charges of the State-owned railways, and their shareholders, at the same time, paid taxes on the income they got from their shares.

Nevertheless, in the year before the war, the mines made thirty-two million pounds profit (of which the government got twelve) from the eighty-three million pounds earned by their gold. After the war, they made only twenty-one million pounds (of which the government got six) from an earning of ninety-three millions.

Because farmers, tradesmen, manufacturers, miners—even white-collar men—all wanted more money and, by world agreement, gold could not earn more money, mines began to give in . . . until four of Johannesburg's forty-three producing mines were in dissolution and twenty more feared dissolution and so did the Reef towns they supported.

Then, if they shut down (so the Chamber of Mines President told a Commission of Enquiry) eighteen thousand white miners and a hundred and twenty-seven thousand black miners would be thrown out of work on the mines and would not find it easy to get other work. Factories, in the midst of a depression, would not be able to take them. The Free State mines as yet required workers in thousands, not tens of thousands. Even the machinery of the Rand mines was not exactly suitable for the Free State mines. . . .

The government tried in desperate ways to get a higher price for the gold of the mines: to save the mines, to save the country, to save the government. It sold a little gold abroad for manufacturing purposes—with embarrassment, with explanations. It prepared to manufacture simple gold articles in South Africa—one always spoke of cigarette cases. It repeated and repeated (but who cared?) how high were the costs of production, how all things were dearer in the world, how gold alone, the world's staple, had barely increased in value in the last fifteen years. It even "reserved the right" to sell gold at its own price.

The country, as in 1932, before it went off gold, was on the verge of catastrophe when suddenly Sir Stafford Cripps, having sworn never to devalue ("and so decrease the price of our exports and increase the price of our imports"), in the very midst of swearing not to devalue—devalued; and with him all that stood on sterling.

The price of gold rose from £8 12s. 3d. to £12 10s. an ounce. The gold of 1949, expected to fetch a hundred million pounds, became worth a hundred and forty-four million pounds. The Reef too poor to work became payable. The position was not so splendid as it had been in 1933, when the United States too paid a higher price for gold, but who knew that the United States would not still have to do it, and was it not already good enough?

South Africa sat in the sun again. Where England had to battle to prove to the world the value of her goods at a cheaper pound, where America had to battle to maintain the value of her goods against the cheaper pound, all South Africa had to do was glow in the renewed effulgence of her heaven-sent gold.

The government would tax the mines up to nearly sixty per cent on the most profitable mines; it would tax the overwhelmed stockbrokers; the gold speculators; the higher-paid workers; the shopkeepers, the manufacturers, the builders, the importers—perhaps even the farmers—all the people who would make money because the gold mines were revivified.

A few weeks ago, how unhappy the government had been, how confident the Opposition!

There was the matter of luck. "Lucky Havenga!" the people called Dr. Malan's Minister of Finance who had also been General Hertzog's Minister of Finance last time gold was devalued. Things, they always were sure, must come right with Lucky Havenga! Again the country was saved. Again by gold.

It was three weeks short of fifty years since, for the sake of Johannesburg's gold mines there had come about (as all the Boers believed) the Boer War.

II

Johannesburg was not a decade old when its existence fired the Jameson Raid. Until the second German war, when Englishmen in South Africa were much embittered by sympathizers of the Germans, few justified it. They saw the mere truth that Rhodes wanted a united South Africa under the British flag; had arrived at that stage of unhindered success where a man regards it as his duty to the world to have what he wants; and did not find the Transvaal any the less desirable because of its gold.

In 1895, as in 1877, when Shepstone of Natal annexed the Transvaal, the country was unsettled. There were eighty thousand foreigners in the Transvaal; they outnumbered the burghers, Kruger said, by four to one; for that reason, with Rhodes at the back of them, they aspired, through a full franchise, to their share of the country's government; for that reason, and again with Rhodes as a background, Kruger dared not let them have it. "They have grown fat on my land; they are richer than our own people." What more did they want (Kruger asked De Villiers, Chief Justice of the Cape), what right had Britain to interfere with the British subjects in the Transvaal?

De Villiers spoke of their opening of the land, of their nine-tenths contribution to the State's revenue. Kruger said to Milner in the end: "It is not the franchise, it is my country—my country—that they want."

He was an old man, and he wept.

For it was not only the foreigners, the Uitlanders, that

plagued him—even among his own Boers men were plaguing him with their modernity. Why could he not go on ruling his country like a Biblical patriarch?

There he sat on the stoep of his little house that still stands in Pretoria, and the citizens came to take coffee with him and have a chat. And no one was so poor or so insignificant that he could not walk onto the stoep with his pipe and his veldskoene—his veld-shoes—spitting where he chose, and be the President's friend.

And the President himself—four times a President—of course he had his faults: he was an obstinate, reactionary old man; and of course he is ennobled in history by the tragedy of his final years.

Yet he was Oom Paul, the uncle of his nation. He was a burgher among his fellow burghers. He had come to the Transvaal with the Voortrekkers herding, at ten, his father's cattle. He had gone on commando against the Kaffirs when he was fourteen. He had taken up, at sixteen, two farms to which he was entitled and, a year later, had driven his horses across a torrential river to seek a bride. He was a widower before he was twenty-one and, on remarriage, the father of sixteen children. His Bible was his only education, except for three months under one Tielman Roos (whose namesake, in later years, brought about some strange events in South Africa). His life was the life of the Old Testament: he had the same kind of guile, the same kind of outlook.

Here, taken from his memoirs, is a discussion between him and Moshesh, the wily old Basuto chief. Is it not a conversation that goes back to Biblical days?

" 'Are you the man,' asked Moshesh, 'who brought Mapela down from the mountains?' [He meant the mountains in the Zoutpansberg which Kruger had vainly attacked.]

" 'Yes,' I said.

" 'Are you aware that two of my daughters are married to Mapela? . . . You need not think it was your courage that brought Mapela down from his mountains. It was the dispensation of God that punished Mapela.'

"Now, as Moshesh was at every moment speaking of the dispensation of God, and using pious words, I said to him:

" 'But if you are so devout, how do you come to have more than one wife?'

"Moshesh replied:

" 'Yes, I have just about two hundred. But that is not half so many as Solomon had.'

" 'Yes, but you surely know that, since Christ's time, and according to the New Testament, a man may have only one wife.'

"Moshesh reflected for a moment, and then said:

" 'Well, what shall I say to you? . . . It is just human nature.' "

Imagine such a conversation taking place in diplomatic Europe. Imagine the patriarch Abraham pitted, not against Chedorlaomer, King of Elam, or Tidal, King of Nations, but against Rhodes, against Milner, against Chamberlain. Imagine, on the other hand, any African Chief in the Union having a homely chat with any of its Prime Ministers; saying to him: "Are you the man who fetched Mapela down from the mountains? . . . Are you aware that two of my daughters are married to Mapela? . . . You need not think it was your courage that brought Mapela down from the mountains."

In modern days, the representatives of the natives' parliament, their Bunga, would be lurking about in some shadowy office or corridor in Parliament House; and they would be lucky if they found a pleasant secretary to tell them they could not be seen just now; they would be lucky if, in the end, they ever were seen. . . .

To Kruger, on his stoep, came men hunting for concessions. The government needed ready money, and he gave it. To Kruger, with his straggling chin-beard; and his little sore, pouched eyes; and his thumbless hand, on which he had himself operated; and his snapped-to mouth, came men wanting new systems of government, men talking and thinking and living gold. . . .

Gold! It was not that Kruger, any more than Abraham, despised wealth. But gold and gold-seekers, these he found to be the ruin of his Transvaal. "Every ounce of gold taken from the bowels of the earth will yet," he prophesied, "be weighed up with rivers of tears."

Jameson opened the year of 1896 by surrendering himself and his filibusters, as Kruger called them, to the Republic. The jumping-off ground in Bechuanaland that Rhodes had intrigued for; the arms sent through his De Beers and lying in a Johannesburg mine; the scheming in Johannesburg itself; the rising there in preparation of Jameson's assistance —they had all come to nothing. And Rhodes with them.

And then the last stage in the pursuit of the Voortrekkers, the climax of the Raid, the Boer War.

It was not, in the end, Rhodes who wanted the Boer War. He was dying, and he said of the Raid and the coming war: "I made a mistake. . . . I keep aloof from the whole Transvaal crisis so that no one will be able to say, if things go wrong: 'Rhodes is in it again.' "

It was also not Chamberlain who wanted it, though on the Continent they called the Boer War Chamberlain's War. Nor was it the British government that wanted it. The Headlam Papers—Milner's own words—show that one man alone brought the war about: Alfred Milner.

Chamberlain warned him that soon Kruger, old and against the times, must cease to rule; that to attack the Transvaal would arouse the Cape; that England was already compromised by the Raid; that "a war with the Transvaal, unless upon the clearest provocation, would be extremely unpopular in England; that it was better to endure a great deal than provoke a conflict" and "our greatest interest in South Africa is peace."

Milner could not tolerate the thought, in the midst of all his frustrations, of peace. He replied: "We must put our foot down and we must keep it there. . . . They will collapse if we go on steadily turning the screw. . . . There is no way out of the political troubles except reform in the Transvaal or war. . . . I should be inclined to work up to a crisis. . . ."

He brooded over "our impotence." He spoke of England's shame at "the spectacle of thousands of British subjects kept permanently in the position of helots, and the Boer intrigues for a republic embracing all Africa."

Kruger had indeed, after England's defeat at Majuba, triumphantly declared: "Then shall it be, from the Zambesi to Simon's Bay, Africa for the Afrikaner." General Smuts had quoted those words in his book *A Century of Wrong*.

It was, in the end, not at all a hopeless people that rose from Milner's rack. General Botha said, after the war: "When the war began, we had sixty thousand burghers, and we further relied upon help from the Cape Colony. . . . We also hoped that the Powers would intervene. We had provisions in abundance. Why, then, taking all things together, should that not happen which had happened in America, and the Boers be left to do as they liked in South Africa?" At that moment, indeed, the Transvaalers, as Deneys Reitz, author of *Commando*, came to say, were "spoiling for a fight."

General Smuts indeed has told that the Boers actually felt themselves better situated for a war against England than the Americans in the 1770's. Where the Americans were in chaos; with no money; with small and ill-trained forces, the Boers were a united nation, trained by a century of fighting, with arms acquired both before and after the

Raid. They also had plans to carry on the war in the British colonies—the Cape and Natal. They expected the Boers of the Cape to join them. There were dreams of taking, in the beginning, Durban, and, in the end, Cape Town. There were plans for destroying the very root of all the trouble, the whole cause of the war—the gold mines. What would the mine-owners say if they heard of that—they who wanted the war for the sake of the mines?

Throughout the war they talked of blowing up the mines. They did not do it because they could not do it—because, simply, they could not bring themselves to do it.

Nor did the war in any other particular go as they had expected. The Boers' hundred years of fighting was, but for Majuba, against Kaffirs or one another. Where the Americans had got their promised help from the French, the Boers did not get their promised help from the Germans. The Kaiser, who had congratulated Kruger on the outcome of the Raid, impartially gave Queen Victoria, his grandmother, a plan for winning the Boer War. He saw the English bringing four hundred thousand soldiers by sea from England to the Cape, and was led by that spectacle to build a great German navy; and here was planted the seed that grew into the first German war which led to the second German war which ruined the world. There it all began, in the Boer War. So the twentieth century began, with a shadow thrown over the civilization of so many other centuries by the Boer War.

When, indeed, Kruger himself during the war went to Germany to ask for the help promised him, he was refused admittance. "For us," said General Smuts when, all hope gone, the Boer commanders met to consider their future, "for us the foreign situation is and remains that we enjoy much sympathy for which we are of course heartily thankful. That is all we have got."

. . .

The Boer War ended. Since the Kaffirs would not work at wages lower than they had been promised, Chinese labourers were engaged to take their places. But, unlike the Indians brought in earlier days to Durban also because the Kaffirs could not be got to work, the Chinese were sent home again.

For, while in England the horrified talk was of Chinese slavery, and a government fell because of it, in Johannesburg one had learnt from the mistake of Durban: that of indentures there might be an end, but not of the begetting of children.

Even so, it was in Johannesburg that Gandhi's Passive Resistance was born. In Johannesburg, one might say—from which sprang the Boer War and Gandhi's lesson on how to make a passive war—the great British Empire first began to crack.

The new government which Chinese slavery had brought to England gave the Boers responsible government. The next step was the Union of the two Boer republics and the two British colonies. The Transvaal gold mines made good all deficits. The Union started clean. . . .

But now what did General Smuts mean when he spoke of men called Syndicalists, come to soil and spoil the new clean Union? The Union was only three years old when there they were, prodding the white workmen of Johannesburg, already hostile to Smuts because, in 1907, he had used force to stop a miners' strike.

In the middle of 1913, there broke out the first of a series of strikes which had to do, not only with labour and class, but with race, and which continued until in 1922 there was an actual revolution.

The miners began it when, on one of the mines, the Saturday working-hours of five mechanics were changed without what they regarded as proper compensation. The strike spread from that mine to other mines. A rabble of hooligans—poor whites and out-of-works—joined the miners. Firearms were looted from shops; the houses of strike-breakers were burnt down; casual bystanders in the streets were killed. Three thousand policemen; three thousand Imperial troops, still left from the Boer War; a force of special constables, guarded Johannesburg, the whole Reef, and the mines themselves. They came too late to stop the rioting. Johannesburg's station and the premises of a newspaper were attacked and partly burnt down. The strikers massed before the sacred Rand Club itself—the church, one might say, of the Gold Religion. They resisted the police and Imperial forces. They ignored a warning. . . . "Shoot!" cried one, opening his arms and offering his chest, and they shot. Twenty-one people were killed and forty-seven wounded, and some of them were not strikers.

And when Generals Botha and Smuts themselves met the strikers at an hotel to discuss terms, all carried revolvers except Botha and Smuts; Botha and Smuts were covered by strikers who had orders to shoot if the crowds outside the hotel were fired on by the guarding soldiers and policemen. They did not at the time know they were menaced, yet yielded to the strikers' terms in fear of what might happen to the town or mines. But when, driving away from the hotel, Botha, in his turn, cried "Shoot!" the strikers did not shoot. They had gained their end for the time being. They came out with further demands next year.

In January 1914 the General Strike Committee instructed the trade unions "to organize all their members into commandos for the greater efficiency of the Federation forces." It was said that the Commandant-General of the Union's defences, not long ago returned from Germany, was behind them.

Martial law was proclaimed along the Reef. General

Smuts gave an order to the soldiers: "Exercise greatest severity. Keep all strikers off railways lines or railway premises. Don't hesitate to shoot if any attempt to enter after warning, or on apparently malicious intent."

The strikers were told that their Trades Hall would be blown up unless they surrendered.

Among those who surrendered were nine leaders, not one born in the country. Smuts rushed them to jail, to a train, to a ship, to England. He told Parliament that "Syndicalism was a new development for which no legal provision had ever been made in South African law. . . . The syndicalists, who had already in six months made three attempts at industrial revolution, would have remained free to bring the Government to its knees by terrorism. . . ."

He was indemnified by Parliament for his illegal act. The deported strikers became heroes in England. "None of your six months' strike and go hungry," one of them told a gathering in London. "We don't believe in that in South Africa. We believe in a fight between organized labour and the ruling class, and the fight has to be short, sharp and to the point."

The deported men returned to South Africa. Some of them joined General Smuts's own party—one became a party secretary. "My whole life," said General Smuts afterwards, "was haunted by the deportation affair, but for them it was finished. So why not?"

Few knew at the time that the commandant-general who was behind the strikers had ideas of arresting General Botha, the Union's Prime Minister, and General Smuts, his leading associate.

One learnt more things about General Beyers when the first German war broke out in 1914. There was a revolution then. All the time until 1922 there were strikes, which were not only labour and class strikes, but racial strikes. One might say that from the time of Union ("a Union of Brothers," General Smuts had called it) there was a revolution underlying the life of South Africa that, every now and then, burst through the pretence of national amity. It came out as strikes, rebellions, revolutions, but it had always the same cause. Not all people could take back—could take to themselves—their greatest enemies, as General Smuts had taken back ("Why not?") the men he had deported. General Smuts might forget those things he had passionately set down in his book *A Century of Wrong*. He might think one could really have a Union of Brothers eight years after a long and bloody war. *He* could. Others could not.

What one called Syndicalism before the first German war one came to call Communism after the second German war. But in South Africa class and race have ever been confused—as they are under the Russians today.

After the white strikes of 1913 and 1914, after the war of 1914–18, the natives, who had been abroad in labour camps and had learnt (as was said) from foreign agitators, began to strike too. In 1919 there were native strikes in Bloemfontein, Pretoria, and Johannesburg. In 1920 the natives of Port Elizabeth demanded higher wages; their leader was arrested without a warrant; outside his jail several hundred natives, armed with sticks, demonstrated; a jet of water was used to disperse them and they threw stones; the inevitable first shot was fired by an unidentified person; there was a stampede; the police fired; six Europeans were killed and wounded and sixty-eight natives.

In the same year, seventy-one thousand natives in the Rand mines asked for more pay and downed tools.

In 1906, there had been a Zulu rebellion, but during the war the natives had learnt the new kind of warfare; and it is the warfare they threaten—and the half-breeds too—today. Nor could South Africa meet a challenge, of money, class, and race, so fiercely confused.

In 1922, the white men came out with talk of the Colour Bar, of keeping black men from white men's places; they came out carrying the banner of a White South Africa.

There were racial aspects most of the white men, struggling for their various reasons, did not understand. This revolution that was led by the sort of Englishmen General Smuts before the First World War had called Syndicalists was, in fact, part of the struggle of the Boer against the Briton: that had begun in 1795, when the British had taken over the Cape for the Prince of Orange and the hated Dutch East India Company; that had continued with the Great Trek, with quarrels wherever Boer and Briton met, with the Battle of Majuba, with the Jameson Raid and the Boer War; that had caused the Boers to veer towards the Germans in the war they knew was coming, and to rebel, as the Irish had later done, while the war was being fought. . . .

That is to say, the Boers who did not feel like General Smuts about a Union of Brothers. . . .

Now, while other men were away fighting, these men had their places; and, after the soldiers came back, both substitutes and returned soldiers wanted the same places; and though, when the 1922 strike began all workers seemed to be on the same side (the blacks excepted), here was also a white-and-white racial trouble that, in the end, ruined General Smuts.

Still, for the time being, it seemed to be the sort of revolution which attempts to divert property rights and change control.

III

There is no such thing as the power of the mass. It is always the power of the individual. And the mass is the instrument of the individual: powerful as a field-gun is powerful, as a steamroller is powerful, under a directing will.

What is the mass? It is a great ball gathering material and momentum as it is prodded along by a toe—sometimes in a hobnailed boot, sometimes in a patent-leather shoe.

Johannesburg has known the force of the hobnailed boot as well as the insidious manoeuvring of the patent-leather shoe.

At the municipal station which supplies Johannesburg with electric power there worked, thirty years ago, mechanics that received the wages of mechanics but were very important because, as they chose, the town could be left without light or locomotion and all its industries without electric power.

And so, more than once, it happened. It also happened that, on an occasion, these mechanics threw out the Mayor and Corporation and for some days ran the town themselves. But when a tramwayman was suspended for three days on account of insubordination, and the tramwaymen were all called out and for a fortnight Johannesburg (not, in those days, so full of motor cars) walked—then that was too much, and this strike was lost.

But there were other strikes. Periodically the householders of Johannesburg laid in large stocks of candles because the power station was making trouble. Sometimes they filled baths and utensils with water under the threat—never actually fulfilled—that the water supply would be cut off. Every now and then they overstocked their larders for fear of what the railwaymen might do. All kinds of meek workers, from housepainters to tea-room girls, went through their lives in a state of being "pulled out," and then laboriously pushed back again.

The town accustomed itself to walking on tiptoe; resigned itself to inconvenience and instability, to trouble and loss. After all, it was Johannesburg, and Johannesburg was like that: a place where things happened.

If only (the people whispered to one another), if only

one thing did not happen. If only the miners did not come out again.

And, in 1922, they did so. Though they came out to save (as they said) White South Africa, their strike was developed under the patronage of the power station.

When one speaks of miners in South Africa, one normally means the white gold-miners. The gold miners, the power station, were now threatening. But the strike, in fact, began well away from Johannesburg. It began (as strikes in many countries have the habit of beginning—and one may understand why) among the coal miners.

Of them General Smuts came to say: "Those men think they are on strike. They are not on strike. They are unemployed. They have destroyed their industry."

He said in Parliament, concerning the gold miners who followed them: "It is one of the most terrible facts that thousands of miners look upon their industry, not as a main interest in their lives, but as their enemy—as if they were anxious to destroy the industry that keeps them going."

He advised the gold miners to make their peace with the Chamber of Mines.

A Labour Member: "On what terms?"

Smuts: "On the Chamber's terms. On any terms."

He added: "I do not mind at all that I am called the paid agent of the Chamber of Mines. . . . I do my duty."

The strike of the gold miners grew while mines were picketed by armed strikers, and scabs were manhandled, and strikers were drilled and formed into commandos and led by "generals." Women joined the organized fury of the men. Natives, defending themselves with sticks and bottles, were attacked with firearms. Police stations were threatened. Policemen and civic guards went armed. Outside a jail where lawbreakers were lodged, comrades paraded singing "The Red Flag" and offering threats until the police fired and men were killed and wounded.

Then processions followed the dead men to their graves, and their banners said: "Remember 1913." "Remember our comrades murdered in 1913." The banner of the women's commandos said: "Our comrades murdered in cold blood by the police." After the revolution, certain people were to be executed. One heard of a red robe of justice and a black cap of death.

General Smuts told an alarmed House: "We shall let things develop. . . . We shall let the people see."

The Chamber of Mines wrote a terrible letter. It declined, it said, to "waste further time in endeavouring to convince persons of your mental calibre . . . slaughtermen and tramwaymen." And then the balloon went up.

A general strike was declared which a Judicial Commission of Enquiry later called a revolution. Since 1914, the Commission said, circulars had been issued to trade unions saying it was time this milk-and-water business was changed for something with fire in it, and it required the unions "to organize into commandos."

It found among other causes of the revolution the idea of Nationalist strikers that, through the strike, they could regain their old Republic, and also that three quarters of the miners and railwaymen (the two largest industrial groups) were Afrikaners.

There were among the revolutionaries twenty-two thousand gold miners; members of affiliated trade unions; railwaymen; the unemployed and unemployable of the slums of Johannesburg. The strikers also expected help from Nationalists in the Free State and the country districts of the Transvaal. One now called them, not strikers, but Reds, Rebels, Revolutionaries. They had a Council of Action and a General Staff. They carried rifles and revolvers and had

a few machine guns. They had commandos and commandants; cyclist, ambulance, and signalling corps; an intelligence system. There were drills and parades and bombing-
exercises.

The commandos were chiefly Nationalists, and so were
all the commandants. But there was also a commando of
returned soldiers, an Irish commando and commandos of
women. The organizers were English.

On the defence side there were four thousand regular
and special constables and three thousand civic guards. In
the beginning—in January—these had not been armed. In
February they carried rifles and there were continuous
clashes with the revolutionaries. In March—after the situation had, in the words and meaning of General Smuts, been
allowed to develop—martial law was proclaimed. It was proclaimed while along the whole Reef the revolutionaries
were attacking; after there had been heavy casualties and
the railways and essential services were at a standstill; and
the natives (as Smuts told the House) "from one end
of the Reef to another were in a state of wild turmoil."

Upon the declaration of martial law, the Defence Force
units on the Rand were mobilized and the burghers were
called out; Smuts himself came to Johannesburg; the revolutionaries, by this time, held all Johannesburg City except the chief railway station, the law courts, and a few
central streets. Their headquarters was a township a mile
from the heart of Johannesburg City.

Notice, in English, Afrikaans, Zulu, and Sesuto, was
given advising "all persons well-affected towards the Government" to leave this revolutionary stronghold within a
period of five hours. Then it was shelled, and, within an
hour, the Reds hoisted the white flag.

Six hundred people were killed and wounded; among
them three hundred of the government forces and a hundred and fifty natives.

But afterwards captured "Commandants" were photographed in a friendly group with Defence Force officers. "Red" Generals entered Parliament. Eleven men, reprieved from death, duly wrote to wish the Governor-General "the compliments of the season."

Still, the people, as General Smuts thought good, had seen; and, since 1922, there have been only a few strikes of any significance in Johannesburg.

That is to say, no white strikes.

For, in 1946, an unrecognized body calling itself the African Mine Workers' Union demanded an increase of nearly three hundred per cent a shift—in other words, ten shillings, instead of two and eightpence an eight-hour shift. And though one may think (by European standards) that ten shillings a shift is no great wage and two and eight a shift a small wage indeed, it can only be said that this two and eight is increased, by food, lodging, and many services, to five shillings a shift; and if the native miners were paid a three hundred per cent increase, or even a hundred per cent increase, most of the mines would have to close down.

As it did not recognize the African Mine Workers' Union, the Chamber of Mines made no reply to its letter; fifty thousand black miners downed tools; ten of the Rand's forty-three mines had to stop work entirely and another eleven had to stop partially; the strikers attacked the guardian police; the police used firearms; in the panic that followed, men were injured, crushed, or shot to death; the chief agitators were put in jail and their followers threatened with further force. An African leader, a doctor, said: "Africans who asked for bread, got lead."

For the strikes of 1913 and 1914, General Smuts had blamed what he called Syndicalists. He had warned the white strikers of a generation before that they were bent on destroying their industry and themselves.

For this strike of black men he blamed what he called

Communists; and he warned the agitators that they were inciting the natives to destroy their country.

But he did not now, as in 1922, let the situation develop —let the people see. One knew now how such situations developed. The people had seen enough. The world had seen enough. The strike was over in two days.

Afterwards fifty-two Europeans were charged with inciting, aiding, and abetting the strikers. Some pleaded, and were found, not guilty. Others admitted aiding and abetting, but not inciting, and were fined from fifteen to fifty pounds. In Cape Town various Communists, thought to be involved, were brought before the law; but court after court could find no tenable indictment against them, and what was in its mild way (compared with the ways of others) a Communist witch-hunt came to nothing.

It was during this affair of the native mine strike that the Native Representative Council, established by General Hertzog, demanded the repeal of all legal discrimination between black and white, and, being treated not very seriously, went into a retirement from which it has not yet emerged.

On May 1st of 1950 there was again an African strike which failed to develop. But black men threw stones, burnt buildings, and looted; and eighteen were killed and thirty-eight injured.

The men General Smuts chiefly praised in 1922 were the burghers: "We made the call. . . . Loyal burghers, we knew we could rely on you."

The loyal burghers, the men on whom General Smuts knew he could rely, were his old comrades of the Boer War. In the Boer War boys of fifteen had gone to fight. Smuts had been a commandant at twenty-nine. Some were not yet forty by the time of the Rand revolution. Most were not yet fifty. And, in later years, whenever he came to the countryside, there they were, his old followers, waiting for him on their horses; with a horse also waiting for him; and they rode together in a proud commando.

But, as the years grew further and further away from the Boer War, his comrades of those days grew fewer and fewer; and, in the end, only a small commando was left to meet him on their horses and ride with him as they had ridden with him against the English nearly fifty years before. It was strange that finally only those who had fought against the English were prepared to join him in his Union of Brothers—this union of English and Afrikaners in the Union of South Africa which was his making.

The new men were not. In the 1948 election General Smuts retained no seat at all—not even his own—in the Transvaal countryside.

CHAPTER FOUR

Living in South Africa

I

ONE stands before a violent and desolate landscape, thinking: "This is the world God contemplated when, on the seventh day, he rested and there was not a man to till the earth. I am Adam, the first man, and alone. This was made for me. In all the Universe there is not another soul. . . ."

One thinks: "It was not only made for me, but by me. As light creates colour, my eye has created all this. It did not exist before I saw it. . . ."

One is on the veld: A pale sun comes up a pale sky. It rises and blazes. It drains earth and body. One dies, but resurrection comes. The sun begins to go. A pageant of cloud crosses the sunset sky: cities and ships and sphinxes fire and redden as they pass along. The blue grows lighter. There comes a thin sharp green. A purple comes. A greyness. Black stands against the greyness. It is night and the air begins to breathe out little scents. Through a high dark-blue tent, the lights of other worlds stab holes. A veld fire runs, like a swift red animal, along the hills, eating up the land.

It is summertime in the Transvaal. The winter through there has been no rain and the rivers trickle weakly along. But the summer brings rain and the feeble river of winter is drowned in a flood of thick dark water, contemptuous of its bounds.

Against the hills lie lonely the native villages; and towards their huts walk the heavy-limbed, coarse-bodied women, singing in strident voices the wild songs of their people, vessels on their heads.

The earth trembles beneath the loud and syncopated stamping of black men, dancing as one to the rhythm of the land—monotonously, insistently, maddeningly—chanting their deep choruses with barely moving lips. Suddenly they are silent. Their pale-soled cracked feet do not leave the pale cracked earth; they stand spiked to the earth, their muscles quivering, writhing, running like frenzied snakes beneath their sweating black skins.

There is a mystery, a sense of slumbering fate about Africa that grows with life in the land. To live in South Africa should be a training in greatness. For it is not the habitation of lesser things: of brooklets and sown fields and singing birds; of spring and autumn; of intimate content. Brooks do not go on for ever in South Africa. As often as not they are dry. Rivers are dry. Birds do not merrily twitter. They creak before the dawn like rusty waggon-axles. There is no spring. There is no autumn. A dust-storm brings the rain, and it is winter. A dust-storm brings the rain, and it is summer. There are no stepping-stones. It is a leap across. Summer. Winter.

But plant trees, and in a few years there stands a forest. Let the rain come—not the gentle, creeping, insidious rain of Europe, but the bold, hard, beating rain, with its lightning and thunder like bagpipes and tom-toms: no, like waggons climbing over rocky mountains—and in two days the world that looked dead is green. Let it be winter and there is a desolation of naked grandeur that shames a clothed prettiness. Let it be summer and there is a passion of growth. And at night there is a clear, living warmth; and stars more than any other world can see stand stark in the sky. All through the year the sun shines unhindered, defining the shapes and colours of things, giving space and distance.

And then, underneath this brightness, also that darkness; the menace and mystery of a land that was the first continent and beheld the first man and may live to see the only man—if, as it bitterly amuses Arnold Toynbee to say, the Atom Bomb and all that end in man's beginning again with the Negrito. . . .

"Look," said General Smuts, "how old Africa is, how strangely made, how unaltered. What is there in it that baffles us? Why can it not go forward as other continents have done? Brilliant men come here to solve its problems and go away, defeated. But that is why it holds us: it has this mystery."

II

Whatever one knows well has a meaning. To its inhabitants probably every South African village has its secret quality. But, in fact, there is no peculiar town in South Africa except Johannesburg, which, for that strange living germ in it, has a special place in the world.

For in Johannesburg, because of its mines, there is the primitive unrestraint of Africa below the controlled civilization of Europe. That is why Johannesburg has its particular meaning: not because of what the eye can see; not because miners walk about its streets with gold nuggets in their pockets, though indeed the mine-dumps are a part of the city; not because (as was once said) it is a University of Crime and a Sodom and Gomorrah—not for these mere fictions, but because, for its germ of life, things happen in Johannesburg.

From their careful pockets people take money that Johannesburg may manipulate it. From the old settled towns of Africa, families uproot themselves and come to look for opportunities in Johannesburg. From the pogroms of Hitler, Jews, fleeing to South Africa, came chiefly to Johannesburg. The 1947 British Settlers came, if they could, to Johannesburg. The young men who qualify for professions do best if they put up their nameplates in Johannesburg.

The poor whites from the country hope vaguely that, in some inexplicable way, they will become in Johannesburg paid employees and useful citizens. The emancipated young Zulus and Shangaans leave their kraals to look for life and money in "Josaberg." The Rhodesian, Nyasa, and other foreign natives, who covet Johannesburg's better food and higher wages, may now only come to the Rand to work on farms or in the mines: that is where they are needed; there alone can they be housed, so that they do not wander about and commit crimes.

But they do not like to work on the farms or in the mines: the pay is not so good; the class of native is not so good. Therefore they either go on for years working in people's houses without passes (carrying a "special" when they go out); or they buy passes from Union natives and the Union natives tell their employers they have lost their passes and get new ones. It is all quite simple. The pass does not carry a photograph; what European official in a pass-office has the time (if he has the knowledge) to hunt out illegal natives according to their accents; what policeman casually examining a "special"?

The Rhodesian authorities also do not like their natives to go away when they ought to be working at starvation wages in Rhodesia. But the Rhodesian natives buy illegal permits, they jump trains, they walk a thousand miles to get to the Union. . . .

Socially, Johannesburg's chief quality is its English style. It is English in the sense in which one feels in South Africa: "This is an English town. . . . This is an Afrikaans town." For instance, in Pretoria, which is only thirty-five miles from Johannesburg, one would get an Afrikaans response on the telephone; in Johannesburg, an English response. Kruger correctly felt Johannesburg was no child of his, though it bore his name.

Cape Town itself, for so long the capital of a British colony, is not so English as Johannesburg, the heart of what fifty years ago was a Dutch republic. Even the English it speaks is not quite so English. But they are alike liberal—the most liberal in South Africa—about race.

Pietermaritzburg, called after a leading Voortrekker and now the capital of Natal, is English; and so are Durban, Natal's principal city, and the towns of the Cape's eastern province, which of course were settled in 1820 with British immigrants. The Witwatersrand apart, the towns in the Transvaal are more Afrikaans than English. Bloemfontein, the Free State's capital, which at one time was quite English in feeling, is now almost entirely Afrikaans. The whole of the Free State has only one United Party Member of Parliament—the son of the last President of the Free State.

Everywhere in the world towns differ strangely from their neighbours, but there can be few towns that differ so much from one another as Johannesburg and Pretoria.

Pretoria, cupped by hills, is semitropical. Johannesburg, standing on its ridges, has its strong and strengthening air.

Where Cape Town is the legislative capital of the Union, Pretoria is the administrative capital. This was arranged at Union when, in the arguments that preceded it, the Transvaalers wanted the capital to be Pretoria and the others wanted it to be Cape Town and General Smuts said that both towns had better be capitals since, "Without it," he said, "there will be no Union."

So now the Ministry travels backwards and forwards between Pretoria and Cape Town with what it calls its Zoo:

its secretaries, attendants, and families. The foreign representatives, now grandly known as the Diplomatic Corps, also divide themselves between Pretoria and Cape Town. The Governor-General goes back and forth and so does the British High Commissioner. Departmental heads go back and forth.

All this is very agreeable for the important people who have government houses, or houses bought or rented by their governments, in both places. But it is not so pleasant for the ordinary members, who have their affairs (and not the government's affairs) in the North; and it is not so pleasant for the secretaries and other officials. These have to let their homes or leave their families behind them and scramble for accommodation in Cape Town during the holiday season, when there is little accommodation to be got.

On the other hand, since it is the holiday season in Cape Town, the arrangement has its advantages.

In Cape Town the Prime Minister lives in the house that Rhodes, dying while Boers and British were still at war, left (such was his desire and prescience) to the Prime Ministers of a United South Africa, and that has never yet been lived in by any but a Boer. There is also a Government House in Durban where the Governor-General stays in the holiday season. Another Englishman has left a holiday house in Durban for the Prime Ministers of the Union.

So Pretoria has this advantage over Johannesburg. There all the High-Table people live, except that some of the Supreme Court judges have their homes in Johannesburg. In Johannesburg the mining lords and other big businessmen live. When important figures come to the Union, they dine with the High-Table people on a public platform and the mining lords and so on sit, as near their feet as possible, at tables on the floor.

But, afterwards, the important figures visit the Johannesburg big men in their homes.

What Cape Town has that Pretoria and Johannesburg have not is something of an aristocracy. It is not the sort of aristocracy there used to be in Europe, which always made one think of unicorns—of fabled creatures on emblazoned backgrounds. South Africa has no feudal landlords, or people idly rich by descent.

Still, there have been great-grandfathers in Cape Town; there remain some things they have left; Cape Town has a bit of what Oliver Wendell Holmes considered family: "Four or five generations of gentlemen and gentlewomen . . . Family portraits . . . Books. Original plates. Original editions . . . Some family silver . . . Claw-footed chairs. Black mahogany tables. Tall bevel-edged mirrors. Stately upright cabinets . . ."

And although these people round about Cape Town have not been the real makers of South African history, nor do they much affect its present and future, yet their ancestors had a feeling for architecture, a taste in furniture, a delight in beauty; and the sense of such things South Africa greatly needs.

They remind one also of Time—much wasted in South Africa. Eternity, that was before man became man and will remain after man ceases to be man, is a thing man need not trouble about. He holds it all in his hand at any moment, all that led to this moment—this Now of Spinoza—all that will come of it.

But Time—not the immemorial thing of the poets, but the measurable thing of life—that is his business. It is good for people to look on what is left of what has been and ponder their own accomplishments.

Two oceans meet at Cape Town, and great mountains

stand above them, and the background of the city itself is
that level and stately mountain over which mists settle—as
it is said—like a tablecloth. Travellers, from the time of
Drake, have thought its situation among the beauties of the
world.

The people who walk about the streets of Cape Town
are, nearly one out of two, the fruit of white men's possession of dark women.

In Durban there were, by 1932, 18,500 Indians. Today
there are 120,000 Indians and 128,000 Europeans. It is com-
puted that, in fifty years' time (assuming life goes on in
South Africa as it is going on now), there will be twice as
many Indians in Durban as there are Europeans.

This is what Durban thinks about, so bright and fresh as
it lies beside the Indian Ocean.

Durban is the best-arranged city in the Union, and, but
for Cape Town's magnificence of nature, the handsomest.
Its new harbour was the only one, from the Pacific to the
Atlantic oceans, where, during the war, ships could be restored. Right under anybody's eyes the great ships lay, and
from Lourenço Marques next door the tale of them went to
Germany, Italy, and Japan. In the middle of the year Johannesburg visits it on holiday, and its July Handicap is the
racing event of the year in South Africa.

East London and Port Elizabeth are South Africa's next
ports after Cape Town and Durban. They have many industries. There are some, indeed, who think they may surpass
Cape Town and Durban as industrial centres and as ports.

Bloemfontein, the capital of the Free State, was given, at
Union, the Appellate Division of the Supreme Court. It
was designed to be the meeting-place of political conferences. That was all one could think to do about Bloemfontein. Indeed, before the great slump that preceded South

Africa's going off gold in the early thirties, the Free State
was in effect bankrupt. The Union had to pay its provincial
expenses.

Then, not long ago, gold was found in the Free State, a
promise was seen of gold enough to match the gold of the
Rand mines.

Bloemfontein arose.

III

Even in an England under Socialism, there is more difference in the way poor and rich people live than in South
Africa. In South Africa, the poor people live above what
used to be called their station in life; and the rich people,
since there are not enough of them to form an exclusive
class, have to accommodate themselves to the standards of
less well-to-do associates. Whatever overseas folk may think,
there are not many millionaires in South Africa, and few
have inherited incomes. The fortunes that have been made
out of mining have generally been carried back to England.
And though, immediately after the war, English people, escaping from the austerities of England and fearing their
end under Socialism, in turn brought to South Africa English money, they presently feared still more to leave the
Commonwealth, and took it away again.

And so South Africa remains a land without a wide social
range, where the less well-placed person may, quite reason-
ably, be linked by a common friend to someone in better
circumstances. And in this way, as through the cinema, habits and traditions are passed from one to the other.

But what chiefly accounts for the interlacing of social
lines in South Africa is the fact of the black man. That immediately gives a certain station to the white man. The gulf
between black and white is so wide, so terrible and irreduci-
ble that, by contrast, no other division seems of fundamental consequence. To four fifths of South African humanity

the least white man is as much a lord as the greatest. And though things which are superior to the same thing are not necessarily equal to one another, yet between one lord and a second there can only be as much distinction as exists in a common peerage. Only an Old World aristocrat could ever have had the essential overlord feeling South Africans, all of them, inherit with their white skins.

Between individuals, of course, differences are exercised. But seen from the outside, all that is sharp and clear is the blocklike division of white from black.

The mixed breeds associate with neither black nor white, except when they are white enough to pass for purely white. Then, like the whites themselves, they keep away from their brethren with the less fortunate pigmentation. There are said to be a half million and more coloured people confused among the whites.

The whites stand by them. Even if skins are suspiciously dark, even if this or that is known about them, or said about them—as long as they "keep" themselves white, then white they are allowed to be.

The expressions are: "One tries for white." "One keeps oneself white."

And not only socially, but also economically, is life easier in South Africa than in England; and, while England struggles to stand again after the second World War (when she gave her greatness to prove her greatness), much easier.

South Africa has had controls too, but they were not controls under which people could get only tenpence worth of meat a week. They were controls which enabled natives on the mines to get about thrice the calories allowed in England. They amounted to not much more than a little less meat, sugar, butter, tea, and no white bread. But they did not keep the prices, and particularly of fruit and vegetables, from rising.

Potatoes, the stay of the poor, became two or three pounds for a shilling; other vegetables rose two or three hundred per cent. Fruit, the pride of South Africa, not only rose two or three hundred per cent, it became uneatable. While costly boards fussed, the tired grapes dropped from their withered stalks; the plums fermented; the peaches grew woolly; the pineapples, through the mere malignancy of nature, developed dead black chunks, and so joined the human scheme. Nobody admitted error—farmers, wholesalers, retailers, hawkers, control boards, governments and municipalities, they all did their duty for little gain; only the days of good, cheap fruit were gone: it was part of the world's blight.

One began to speak in South Africa of austerity. Long ago, in the Cape, when there was need to save money, one spoke of Sumptuary Laws. But still, for every person who pays taxes, four own motor cars. Shopgirls travel first class on trains and are taken, by their young men, to the best seats in a cinema. Coloured persons travel second class because they do not like to meet natives, travelling third class.

But there is no reason why a coloured person should not travel first class or a native second or, if he can afford it, first class—except that he must enter a station at a different entrance from whites, and travel in different compartments. He has long sat on separate seats on platforms and travelled in separate compartments, but the ostentation of the separate entrance sears his heart.

There is certainly a something called Society in South Africa, but it is a shifting, arbitrary group, including or excluding without any definite reason—except for the old families at the Cape, the mining leaders of Johannesburg, the sugar barons of Durban, the Ministers, the high officials, the diplomats of Pretoria and, nowadays, the high soldiery. Not much more is needed for some sort of invitation to

Government House than to write one's name in the Book. At Government House banquets, the diplomats, the Cabinet Ministers, the judiciary, the Members of Parliament, the clergy, mining people, social people are carefully graded, each with each, and more or less know whom, year after year, they are going to meet at dinner.

There are no idle rich in South Africa. There are no leisured classes. There are no upper classes. There are no lower classes. People may choose to make distinctions; but, on the whole, South Africa is a middle-class country whose complexities weave themselves about in the professions, the government services, the agricultural, commercial, and manual pursuits, and where money, as elsewhere, talks.

The fact that there are no leisured classes in South Africa prevents also the incidence of a deep culture, and so does the alluring climate. All the year round one may divert oneself in the open air. About the Cape coast it rains in winter; but in the north it rains only in swift, quick-drying bursts in summer; and on the east coast there is practically no cold weather.

So, although football and cricket follow the seasonal conventions, tennis and golf may be played all the year round. There is only this mystery: in effect, no Afrikaan's name occurs in first-class cricket and tennis; no English name occurs in first-class rugby, football. Has this to do with race? Is it a matter of temperament? Are Englishmen lither and Afrikaners bigger? Even in Rhodesia, where a third of the population is Afrikaans, they dominate the football.

Except at the Cape, walking is not regarded as an agreeable form of exercise.

In such a life then where men, if not women, all work, where the air and the sky offer hourly temptation, the forcing hand of ennui does little to encourage profound thought and passionate art. A South African, looking at London through its fog and drizzle, understands well why the mind is set going there. Something must move, if the body cannot, that existence may have its reason.

On the other hand, if there are not many people in South Africa whose lives are all ease, there are not many who are completely deprived of it. One has always the native. He does the hard and ugly work. So that if the mind is not so deeply engaged in South Africa as in England, it is also not so hampered. The greatest development may, accordingly, not be attained in South Africa, but a more general development is possible. It is likely that the average intellectual standard is as high in South Africa as anywhere else. And the South African, who has gone overseas with ideas about finding there a culture denied him in his own land, may return home feeling that he too knows his little things.

It is true that he can satisfy abroad social, intellectual, and artistic desires which are beyond fulfilment in South Africa. But, on the whole, the average South African loses by necessity only what the average European loses by choice.

One may meet cultivated people in London who do not enter the great art galleries once a year. That they go to see special exhibitions of pictures at Burlington House is evidence, not of their taste, but of the power of fashion and publicity. The same thing happens on the Continent and in America. There, too, the picture galleries are deserted but for tourists and students.

As for news, books, thought, one may get them in South Africa from anywhere by beam, air, or sea, within an hour, two days, or a month.

There was a time when one could also see the best English plays and even, if they were past their prime or needed a holiday or had had one or two London failures, the best English actors. But now it does not pay them to come. South Africans, like other peoples, prefer the cinema to the living theatre.

The cinema has all but the fleshly advantages. The public is to blame if those advantages are misused. The cinema can spend more because it need spend only once. It can get the best because it can spend more. It can get the best out of the best because it can try and try again. The best can be seen in the smallest village as in the greatest capital. Only the genius can beat the machine.

South Africa, like other countries, has its repertory theatres. These are run (as likely as not for charities) by a few passionate people, and precariously maintained by appeals to the higher natures of people not so passionate.

The government subsidizes what is called a National Theatre. This has separate companies acting in English and Afrikaans.

There is, besides, an Afrikaans theatre, but it has to use chiefly translated plays, for the language and its playwrights are new.

Could a board of twentieth-century bishops, could a panel of twentieth-century scholars, bring forth the Bible of King James? There may be something in a language that has not been soiled and spoiled, in phrases that have not become secondhand.

The Afrikaners have the use of a new language, grim, gay, and growing. Afrikaans grows by the simplest means. It takes a word from anywhere that it likes or needs; adapts it, through a few basic rules, to Afrikaans; and adds it to its language of the people.

But, though it is still fresh, there is now developing a sort of public-school Afrikaans, with a particular pronunciation of vowels and many high-sounding words, that Afrikaners of an older generation find a little strange and unhomely. The generation has now passed whose language of Church and State was what one called High Dutch.

The Afrikaans-writing South African has both an advantage and a disadvantage over the English-writing South African. His disadvantage is that he cannot match himself against competition, cannot enter world class. His advantage is that he need not. His works are the classics of home, church, school, and university. He has no rivals (like the English-writing South African) in the literature of centuries, in the writers among two hundred and fifty million Americans and Britons. His writings are *the* writings, the only writings. The Afrikaners, if they want to read their own language, must choose from the works of a few people of the day. They must buy them, and they do.

The English-writing South Africans, if they want fame or fortune, must go out into the wide world. Their writings are not at all the only ones South Africans need read.

So (until a few years ago) they published their books in England and America. They have been successful in England and America. Of all the Dominion writers, only Henry Handel Richardson has done better work than the South Africans. But then *The Fortunes of Richard Mahony* is the best English novel ever written. It may leave the South African writers untouched that they are not so good as Henry Handel Richardson.

English-writing South Africans, too, labour under a heavy imposition.

Before the second German war, they could, if they had an American success, do very well. But now the American tax is thirty per cent. After 1920, however, people living outside England had to pay a twenty-five per cent royalty tax on their books published in England. This tax was designed to catch English writers who could avoid paying income tax by living anywhere, though they published in England. During the war this royalty tax rose to fifty per cent. It is now forty-five per cent.

It fell, not only on Britons, but on writers living in the Dominions and paying their taxes there. These taxes too rose during the war. In South Africa the British tax on royalties was held not to be an expense incurred in the course of the author's work—it only happened after the work was finished. Therefore the South African writer had to pay South African tax on the whole of his English royalties (less, perhaps, his agent's fees of ten per cent); he had, on the same royalties, to pay the fifty—or forty-five—per cent tax required by the British Treasury. If his spouse had an income he had, in South Africa, to pay on their joint incomes —that is, on a higher scale. It could easily happen that the English-writing South African lost on his books.

Towards the end of its career, General Smuts's government thought of doing away with the double tax on authors. As to England, not America, Dr. Malan's government did so. The British government did nothing to keep its Commonwealth links through Commonwealth writers: it maintained its tax.

South African sculptors and painters have the good fortune that their works are sometimes bought at high prices to decorate public buildings. Also, when money is "hot"— when cash is paid to avoid income-tax declaration, when there is much money and the puzzle is how to use it—then works of art have a merry time. Any little framed thing fetches fifty guineas. A bigger framed thing fetches a hundred or two hundred guineas. But suddenly money gets cold again, and then even a good picture cannot sell.

South Africa's best artist is a sculptor, Moses Kottler.

No South African composers, singers, or instrumental players have risen to world stature; no South African architect can hope to do so. South African houses are often attractive, but the public buildings (except Baker's Union Buildings in Pretoria) must be among the worst in the world.

And there is this unfortunate fact about buildings. Unlike other forms of art, they cost so much that they are not easily obliterated. They can also not be avoided.

In the end, the art of a country is chiefly represented by its buildings. One can read a country's literature, one can see its paintings, or hear its music, in other places. One has to go to the country itself to see its buildings. People go to countries largely because of their buildings.

Such taste as is shown in the homes of South Africa (the old houses apart) is due to Rhodes.

It was actually Rhodes who made the South African thing—not the European or English thing—the fashionable thing.

Before his day of power, distrust adhered to all that was made in South Africa. The stern and honest furniture of the Voortrekkers, derived from the delicate forms of Europe, came to be despised, and tortured things came from Victorian England to warp and crack in the sun of Africa.

Rhodes set his style.

Now people demanded old Dutch houses and old Dutch furniture. Now they copied them. He died. Now they more than copied them: everything stood on claw and ball feet.

The age of the steel entrail arrived. Everything stood on steel. The iron age returned. All was wrought iron.

One day the government declared that, for two hundred years, no more stinkwood trees were to be cut down—the great hardwoods, hundreds of years old, that had made the waggons of the Voortrekkers and the furniture copied from the old Dutch furniture.

Now everyone had to have stinkwood.

It is possible for a South African to qualify for any profession in his own country. There are a number of universities at which he may attend courses in arts, science, law, commerce, music, education, divinity, agriculture, public health, public administration, economics, medicine, dentistry, veterinary science, engineering in half a dozen branches, African life, languages, and administration.

There are trade and mining schools.

The attractions of the Civil Service are limited by the poor pay. For teachers (since politics go through South African life from infancy to senility) there are factors, pay and language apart, which make teaching less agreeable to English people than to Afrikaners.

One white South African in two hundred attends a university, where in England, before Socialism, the proportion was one in a thousand. The universities of Cape Town and Johannesburg admit native students; the universities of Pretoria do not; four colleges have just been granted university status, of which Bloemfontein and Potchefstroom will follow Stellenbosch and Pretoria, Rhodes University in Grahamstown will follow the liberal tradition, Natal's university will continue to give non-Europeans the same teaching and chances as Europeans, only in separate buildings. There is, in the Cape, a purely native college. It describes itself as Native, and not, according to the new style, African.

Primary education is in the scheme, not of the government, but of the four provincial systems. In the towns there are too many children for the schools, in the country, not enough. At distances, thirty miles apart, live two or three farmers. On transport waggons there will be sitting a man, his wife, his children—with the household possessions—trekking in search of pasture for the beasts. Wandering over the country, slinking to the towns, are the poor whites. It is only because they cannot be reached that backveld children show, in the statistics, a backwardness.

Shortly before he died, J. H. Hofmeyr was studying the American plan of bringing isolated people to civilization instead of civilization to isolated people. It was thought a more practical idea.

Above all other considerations, there is today an insistence on Afrikaans which may be natural—because, to live, Afrikaans must be assertive—but which, at the same time, makes South Africa less a part of a world, so largely English-speaking, than it otherwise might be.

In truth, the time is not yet past when Afrikaners wanted their country for themselves alone so that every private, as General Smuts quoted the saying, might be a general. It is an aspect of this feeling that they wish to develop through the language which is intimately theirs. They are prepared even to reject the English literary heritage, claiming not unity but merely relationship with Holland and France; demanding to be regarded as their own ancestors.

An Englishman, knowing only English, will soon be as much a foreigner, if he wants a position under the government, as any other European. A barrister, an attorney, a businessman, any person who deals with the public, must essentially know Afrikaans. Nowhere does it, at the highest levels, matter what a man speaks as long as he speaks one language moderately well. If languages were the test, Swiss waiters would be at the highest levels. What matters is brains.

It is partly on account of the dual language position in South Africa that Rhodesia does not want to enter the Union. Even the Afrikaners in the Rhodesian Parliament have unanimously voted for one language alone—English. If Rhodesia—that is, Southern Rhodesia—did not dislike their poverty and British Negrophiles, she might unite or federate with Northern Rhodesia and Nyasaland. This union or federation could then extend to Kenya, Uganda, and the other British territories. A new Dominion might be born in Africa, excluding both the Union and Britain. For the Union, with five sixths of the white population in Africa, would be too dominating for such an affiliation. On the other hand, the whites in the British territories feel the same about the

Africans as the South African whites: they do not want Britain to be their natives' trustees; they do not want any Russian-type equality between black and white; they think in terms of what Rhodesia's Prime Minister calls a "benevolent aristocracy," and the South Africans plainly describe as the boss-ship of the whites.

CHAPTER   FIVE

Politics in South Africa

I

In 1906 England's Liberal Party won an election on what Dr. Jameson called "the pigtail question," and the Liberals called Chinese Slavery. Upon this, General Smuts went to England to ask the new government for Responsible Government for the conquered Boer republics; and though, as he wrote, he found in England a general fear of the Boers, he also found that "under the secret influence of this fear" they now wished to do them justice, and the end of it was that he got the Responsible Government he had gone for.

But he was already thirty-six; he referred to himself as one "of a later generation . . . growing old"; he felt there was no time to waste and he urgently wrote to Sir Henry De Villiers, Chief Justice of the Cape: "We who love South Africa as a whole, who have our ideal of her, who wish to substitute the idea of a United South Africa for our lost independence, who see in breadth of horizon, in a wider and more embracing statesmanship the cure of our ills and the only escape from the dreary pettiness and bickerings of the past—we are prepared to sacrifice much—not to Natal or the Cape, but to South Africa . . . the attainment of a United South Africa."

Two years later, a National Convention, presided over by

De Villiers, met, now here, now there. The South Africa Act of 1909—an Act of the British Parliament—was passed, and South Africa had what England had not: a written Constitution. The dream of many men was become fact— the Union of South Africa.

When the draft Constitution was published, General Smuts said: "The Constitution is not a man's work. It bears the impress of a Higher Hand." The high hand, however, was that of Smuts. There were arguments over Parliamentary representation; forms of government; the status of natives; the status of Dutch (then the Boers' official language and only in 1924 linked with Afrikaans, which presently supplanted it); the position of Natal; the place for a capital.

Smuts could, less than ever, wait. Greater Englanders were threatening the Liberals. Afrikaners were not reconciled. From Europe Steyn, ex-President of the Free State and vice-chairman of the Convention, had brought news that Germany was preparing to fight England. Though Lord Curzon, viewing the Convention, felt that "there was not one who, while loyal to his colony or his race or his following, was not more loyal to the wider cause of South African union within the sheltering embrace of the British Empire," Smuts knew better than to believe with him that "men who not long ago would have put each other to death" could so easily agree with one another.

There had to be compromises. Were there different claimants for the capital? Let there be two, said Smuts ("Without it there will be no Union"). Was Natal not anxious to join the Boers? Let there be a referendum. What of the two South African languages? Let both be equally used. How should the native question be settled? Let the natives and coloureds have, in each of the four provinces (the two colonies, the two republics) the status they had before Union.

Let each province, too, get something out of Union.

Pretoria became the administrative capital and Cape Town the legislative capital. Natal voted by three to one to enter the Union, and got some railway facilities she urgently needed. Bloemfontein got the Appeal Court. The natives and coloureds kept the full franchise they had in the Cape; an illusory franchise, which made it practically impossible for a native to vote, in Natal; no franchise in the Transvaal and Free State.

Their status could be changed only by a two-thirds majority vote in the two Houses of the Union Parliament, sitting as one. That, indeed, said Smuts, was among the chief reasons for Union. One needed, to deal with the native question, "a strong, central, unified Government." Women did not get the vote.

But where was the money to come from to run this new great enterprise? Every prospective province but the Transvaal was, in effect, bankrupt.

In the Transvaal, Smuts, upon Responsible Government, had let the leadership go to Botha. Yet Smuts was the man.

The Transvaal, he said, would maintain the Union.

He said to the nation:

"The Boer has fought for his independence, the Englishman has fought for his Empire, all have fought for what they considered highest. Now the highest is union. . . . Let us have a union, not of top-dog and under-dog, but of brothers."

On May 31, 1910, the Union of South Africa was formally established.

There was one great disappointment Smuts had over Union. He had taken it for granted that the three British Protectorates—Basutoland, Bechuanaland, Swaziland—would become part of the Union. For a hundred years the struggle has been going on about who should control these lands—

the British or the Boers. Here was a union of Britons *and* Boers. "Let us," said Smuts, "start a union here to rule the country from Table Bay to the Congo and even beyond that. Let us be the inventors of a great South Africa."

England would not make a present of the three protectorates to the Union of Brothers—it has not yet. "Let me and my people," the Basuto Chief Moshesh had said in 1868, "rest and live under the large folds of the flag of England," whereupon England had annexed Basutoland. Bechuanaland had fallen to her in 1885 and Swaziland had waveringly become hers within the first six years of the twentieth century.

When Smuts spoke of ruling the country from Table Bay to the Congo and beyond he had behind him the thoughts of his youth, of Kruger and Rhodes. He had dreamt of "a great African Dominion stretching unbroken throughout Africa." Kruger had more modestly prophesied, after the victory of Majuba, that now it would be "from the Zambesi to Simon's Bay, Africa for the Afrikaner." Rhodes had wanted to go from the Cape to Cairo; he feared the advance of Germany; he sometimes thought he would join Kruger in taking Bechuanaland ("We want to get rid of the Imperial factor in this question, and deal with it ourselves, jointly with the Transvaal"); at other times he would on no account have Kruger in it ("Don't part with an inch of territory to the Transvaal"). In short, if one wanted to go north, one had to have Bechuanaland.

What is Bechuanaland?

It is a piece of desert land, a quarter of a million square miles in size, four thousand feet above sea level, nowhere touching the sea, lying between the Union, Rhodesia, and South-West Africa.

Its native population, having lately increased, is now one to the square mile; it is a mixture of Bantu, Bushman, and

Hottentot; twenty per cent of the children go to school; there are a number of Christian sects; its revenue of two hundred thousand pounds is somewhat exceeded by its expenditure; the natives work well with furs, but cannot do much with sand. Many Europeans, however, think that under the sand is water. The European population, by grace and not (the officials apart) by right, is two thousand.

There was a time when the Bechuanas owned all the land—a third across Africa—between the Orange and Zambesi rivers. The Transvaal was once Bechuanaland. But, before the Boers had it, the Matabele had it.

Long ago the first men in the world stood up in the same parts—that is the latest thought. A few years ago they were said to have arisen in another part of Bechuanaland.

In modern times, Bechuanaland has been in the news for two reasons: both to do with colour and sex; both to do with power and pride.

For many years, Tshekedi, a Bamangwato Chief, was regent of that part of Bechuanaland which is under British protection. He ruled during the youth of his nephew, Seretse. Both are descendants of Khama, one of the great black Chiefs; both have the stuff of the Khamas in them, but Tshekedi has stuff of his own besides—better stuff than Seretse—and from neither his own people nor other people does he stand any nonsense.

In 1933, a white man, gone native in Bechuanaland, was found to be corrupting native women beyond the tolerance of their men. Tshekedi demanded his punishment at the hands of the British authorities, and when the British authorities did nothing, took it on himself to have the white man thrashed.

It was no doubt proper that the white man should be thrashed. But it is not considered proper in South Africa, where savages greatly outnumber Europeans, that white men should be thrashed by natives.

A spectacular business was made of teaching Tshekedi this lesson, which cost England four thousand pounds. The Navy came up from the British naval station at Simonstown; British panoply was displayed; a good time was had by all; Tshekedi was temporarily banished but was much strengthened by the publicity he got; the white man was permanently banished.

The black-white affair this time, in 1949–50, is on a different level and it has a different meaning.

Seretse is now grown up and ready to assume the chieftainship. He is well built but, if he were white, would be thought disfigured by his very big soft lips that belie his astute determined nature. He seems to agree and then goes his way.

Tshekedi, without such lips, is astute and determined too, and more experienced. Though he is not loved by his people because of his stern reforms, he had, in 1949, the subchiefs with him, and was looking for a chance to carry on his rule.

It looked like that chance when Seretse (educated in the Union and England) married an English girl and brought her to Bechuanaland.

The people themselves were at first delighted. The Paramount Chief of the Bamangwato naturally marries royalty and the Bechuanas, many of them, thought that Seretse's English wife came from the British royal family.

But in Rhodesia and the Union any white woman is royalty, and more, to any black man. One asked about Seretse's marriage if the English, who saw no racial fault in it, would have liked Princess Elizabeth to marry a Bechuana.

In the Union today black-white marriage is not only illegal, but criminal. The Union has never ceased to demand the territories which, even at Union, it expected to get. A triumph for Seretse, Chief of eighteen thousand Bechuanas, might have led to a position fatal to British power in south-

ern Africa. It was not wise to entice Seretse to England and
so make an opportunity to banish him from his tribal land
and cause the tribesmen to boycott the British High Commissioner. If Rhodes had had to deal with the matter, he
would have followed his practice with Njubi and, before
there were complications, have given Seretse a job in the
Colonial Office in England and some compensation.

This compensation might have come from Tshekedi,
who would gladly have paid it to become the authorized
Chief; the Bechuanas would have continued to benefit from
Tshekedi's rule, and the British would not have been prej-
udiced.

As to banishment, why the King of England, and not
Seretse? Why the King of the Belgians, and not Seretse?

In Basutoland too they have woman trouble. The heir
to the Chieftainship is a woman, the British Privy Council
confirms it, the tribe does not. Threat and fury.

The Basuto royal family is Catholic. Half the Christians
of Basutoland (and these are half the Basutos) are Catholics. There is a Roma in Basutoland. The teaching is largely
at mission schools.

The Basutos are the poorest people in South Africa.
They are so poor that, of their six hundred thousand people,
a hundred thousand men are working in the Union. The
soil has disappeared from their beautiful mountains, it can
bring a family no more than ten or twelve pounds a year.
The trouble is, as ever among the natives, the cattle they
keep that eat the plants down to the roots until the loosened
soil and water run away, and especially down the mountains.

Then, to build their huts and for other purposes, the
Basutos cut down their trees—millions of saplings recently
planted by the Administration have been cut down. Then
the manure of the cattle is not left to fertilize the soil: it

is used for fuel. Then the Basutos ride their famous little horses on the mountains, and they too have to eat.

One never, of course, knows what lies beneath the earth of Africa, but it is not for its possibilities of wealth that the Union wants Basutoland. It is because Basutoland, only twice the size of Wales (it once contained also the Free State) is entirely surrounded by the Union, entirely dependent on the Union (in times of drought, the Union has to send it maize); it is for prestige.

There are fifteen hundred Europeans in Basutoland—under the same terms as the Europeans in Bechuanaland. There is one mile of railway.

Swaziland is only half the size of Basutoland, but it is quite a different affair. If the Union wants Swaziland, it is not for sands, for mountains—it is because Swaziland is simply an Eden of a land, really a white man's land.

It lies in the fertile coast belt of Africa between the Transvaal and Portuguese East. Large rivers accept the homage of numberless small rivers. The Queen Mother has traditionally (won from a conquered tribe) the secret of the rain. There are no frosts. Everything grows. It has tin. It has a little gold. It has, in the lowlands, some malaria.

The hundred and eighty thousand Swazis are largely descended from people who came there when the other Bantu tribes arrived in southern Africa. They were then overcome by the conquering Zulus, so that Zulu blood is in them too. When, in 1843, the British took Zululand, they freed themselves from the Zulus, but some years later ceded land to the Transvaal to shield them further from the Zulus. They were friendly with the British. They were friendly with the Boers. Sometimes the Boers recognized their independence. Sometimes they did not. Sometimes the Swazis granted rights to the Boers. Sometimes they asked the Brit-

ish to free them from the results. Sometimes they were under British protection and sometimes under Boer protection. At all times they gave concessions too easily. Great
tracts of their land have been bought up by land companies
in the Union, and there is a Colonial Development Corporation, financed by the British government, that has acquired tens of thousands of acres to plant trees for the making of paper. In the nineteen-thirties the Japanese tried to
buy their land. It seems not unlikely that, one of these days,
it will be said the Swazis, like the Union natives, have not
enough land.

A generation ago, the Europeans of Swaziland, who—un-
restricted—are three thousand, thought of entering the Union. They were not content to be happy. They wished also
to be prosperous. They had dreams of a railway that would
make them the link between the Transvaal and Delagoa
Bay.

But, in the end, they stayed out because the Chiefs said
so, England said so, there were questions of the dual language and a reduced stature for both black and white in the
Union.

One did not, in those days, speak of Apartheid. Indeed,
Swaziland has its own Apartheid. Though, unlike the other
two Protectorates, it admits Europeans, like them, it re-
fuses Indians.

Six per cent of the Swazis go to school; twenty-five per
cent go to church; the country is happily fertilized with the
royal blood of King Sobuza, who has eighty wives in his
biggest kraal and other wives in lesser kraals.

In 1922, after the Chartered Company's rule was ended,
General Smuts went to Rhodesia to offer it the Union's
brotherhood. Already a quarter of Rhodesia's population
were Boers. There was his youthful dream of "a great African Federation of States . . . . members of a great African

Dominion stretching unbroken throughout Africa." He reminded the Rhodesians that it was also Rhodes's dream. He said to them: "The people of the Union will not look upon you in any way but as blood brothers. We shall help and support you as brothers."

He assured the Rhodesians that "this is not a political tour. This tour has nothing to do with politics." His opponents in the Union thought otherwise. They declared, for all the world to know, that what Smuts needed, after the passions of the war, the Boer Rebellion, the Rand Revolution, was voters no less than brothers. The Rhodesians heard them (and perhaps thought the same); they considered the matter of the two languages; the preponderance of Boers; the chance of losing the British connection; the certainty that they would become nobodies where they were now somebodies. They were not encouraged by the Rebellion and the Revolution. The dreams of Rhodes and Smuts were very well. But what were the facts? The fifteen thousand Rhodesians refused Smuts's offer of a brotherhood to dominate Africa.

In these days there is talk of Bechuanaland joining Rhodesia rather than the Union. Northern Rhodesia and Nyasaland would like to join Rhodesia. Tanganyika, Kenya, and Uganda could come in. Beyond them lies the Sudan. That could come in. Rhodes's plan of an All-Red route from the Cape to Cairo could happen (without, of course, the Cape and Cairo). Britain's plan of an African empire, in place of her Indian empire, could happen—were it not for two things. Rhodesia, approaching now a hundred thousand people, is trying to build herself up: she cannot build up other territories. The Africans are in a ferment throughout Africa.

There is one certainty: the Union will not be a part of Pan Africa.

. . .

On the other hand, the Union has got one thing which is not a dream.

There is an even larger waste than Bechuanaland lying on the Union's borders. It has no more than the same number of dark men than Bechuanaland, but it has forty thousand white men. In its desert sands of the south; in its belt of sand along the coast—the Skeleton Coast—lie those diamonds, those masses of diamonds, which are controlled by De Beers under the style of the Consolidated Diamond Mines of South-West Africa. There is also a substantial karakul industry. . . .

It was in 1883 German traders came to Angra Pequena, which the Portuguese had reached before rounding the Cape, and which the Germans later called Luderitzbucht.

In 1884, H. M. Stanley, famous since his finding of Livingstone, went to lecture in Germany and persuaded the Germans to take this land England did not want; and they also took what they called German East Africa. That was all, coming so late in the scramble, they could get out of Africa. At the Congo Conference, next year, they pledged themselves to preserve, protect, and develop the original races and their possessions. South-West Africa was, but for Walvis Bay, ratified. The first preserver, protector, and developer of German South-West Africa was the father of Hermann Goering.

After twenty-five years only thirty per cent of the population was left and the Chief of one Hottentot tribe wrote to the Chief of another who had accepted German protection: "You will have bitter remorse, you will have eternal remorse, for this handing over of your land and independence into the hands of the white people. . . . This thing you have done will become a burden to you as if you were carrying the sun on your back."

In 1905, the Governor of South-West Africa was General von Trotha. There were Hottentot rebellions. The cause of these rebellions was officially given as "systematic ill-treatment, flogging, appropriation of cattle, debauching of women . . . denial of justice." The means used to put the rebels down was extermination. Von Trotha's order was to "kill all, and take no prisoners."

The Germans too had their scheme for an African Union. They planned, before the First World War, a German Mittel-Afrika, starting from German East Africa and traversing the continent from the Indian to the Atlantic oceans. This could be linked by alliances—south, with South Africa, and north, through friendly Arab states with a Mittel-Europa and Turkey.

In Mittel-Afrika Germany would find her tropical material, a market for her industries, and an outlet for the German nation. A million black soldiers could be trained to defend it; it would have its own naval, U-boat, and air bases. It would command British lines of communication with Australia and the East. . . .

But this was nothing to the scheme Hitler revealed during the Second World War—the new German world of Allantropa. Two enormous dams, from Gibraltar to Tangier, from Italy to Tunisia, were to link Europe and Africa and provide power to drive trains from Berlin to Central Africa. There would be arterial roads from the Mediterranean to the Cape. Lakes and rivers of Africa would be dammed to form two inland seas—the Chad and Congo seas. Their overflow would create a river across the Sahara to flow through Tunisia into the Mediterranean, and another to enter the South Atlantic near Brazzaville. A German ship could cross Africa to Cape Town. Prisoners of war would create a new *Lebensraum* of two million square miles for the Herrenvolk.

But this, again, was nothing to the idea Rhodes had "for the bringing of the whole civilized world under British rule." The idea was to recover the United States; settle the continents of Africa and South America with Britons; also most of Asia; and thus create a power so overwhelming that never again would there be wars and thus there would arrive the millennium.

Well, he was in his twenties. He did get a great piece of Africa and it was called by his name. But, by the time he died, at forty-eight, all that plan of bringing the world under British rule had come down to the not very productive result of the Rhodes Scholarships. Hitler achieved less. In whose brain now lies the thought of bringing the whole world under one rule?

It was while the Kaiser was brooding over the notion of a Mittel-Afrika, joined with a Mittel-Europa, that ex-President Steyn warned the National Convention which led to the union of the four South African states that South Africa was "still a Naboth's vineyard" which Germany meant to take. "She wants our gold, our diamonds, our coal. Her plans are already made, her preparation even now nearly complete. Look at German West—which should have been ours. Acquired by fraud and force and held by brutal atrocities which no Christian people can think of without horror. . . . What else is German West but a jumping-off place to attack us from the north while their ships destroy our ports? Look at their railways! They are strategic railways—all directed at us. . . . I have means which you have not of knowing what is going on."

He had just been to Germany. The First World War was breeding there. It had hardly begun when the Germans of South-West crossed the Union border.

Then General Smuts told the House:

"All this German talk, all this rumour of German sympathies, has been spread by German commercial agents and German dealers, and I hope the people will realize that the Germans are placing a dagger into the heart of South Africa which they are eager to press home. . . . German South-West Africa is being used as a base for intrigue . . . for the undermining of our liberties and the seducing of our citizens. . . . We see how dangerous it is to have next door to us a neighbour such as the German Empire."

The Kaiser's most famous telegram is the one congratulating Kruger on the outcome of the Jameson Raid. He now sent one to South-West Africa: "Guarantee Boers existence Boer Republic if they attack immediately."

Among the citizens seduced by the Germans was the Commandant-General of the Union—that one who had been behind the Rand strikes. In the rebellion which followed his seduction by the Germans and the Union's entry into the First World War, he was drowned in swimming across the Vaal to join the Germans of South-West Africa.

When peace was arranged in South-West Africa (the first conquest in the World War) General Botha gave his men this order:

"All ranks of the Union forces . . . are reminded that self-restraint, courtesy and consideration of the feelings of others on the part of the troops whose good fortune it is to be victorious, is essential."

At the peace of 1919, Britain received the mandate over German East Africa and the Union over German South-West Africa; and, in 1924, Germans of South-West Africa automatically became Union citizens.

The days of Hitler arrived. The citizens of South-West Africa declared themselves to be Germans as well as South Africans but, compelled during the war to choose between one or the other, decided in the main to be Nazis, and continued, as before the First World War and between the two World Wars, their policy of using South-West Africa "as a base for intrigue . . . for the undermining of our liberties and the seducing of our citizens."

Indeed, five months before the coming of the Second

World War, General Smuts, as Minister of Justice, took over the South-West police force, added to it an armed detachment of Union police, and thus (he came to say) perhaps prevented the Second World War from starting, not in Poland, but in South-West Africa. . . .

It is not, then, for reasons of prestige alone the Union has, since the last generation, wanted not only a mandate over South-West Africa but possession of it. And though Dr. Malan's offer of representation in the Union Parliament to South-West citizens was obviously to the advantage of his party, General Smuts did not oppose it.

To begin with, how could he? He himself had gone to the UN to plead for the incorporation of South-West in the Union. South Africans not only felt that Germany had taken what should have been theirs by "fraud and force," but also two wars had proved President Steyn's words that South-West was a menace to the Union.

It was said at the UN that the Hereros of South-West preferred to the Union the vague protection of Britain, the United States, or the United Nations. South Africans could not see in the African continent any natives better treated than theirs. They could see the natives of neighbouring British dependencies coming, despite all prohibitions, to the Union.

In South-West the lands of the natives had been increased, since the time of the mandate, by ten million hectares; security of tenure was given to the lands they possessed. And if black men had proportionately much less land than white men, where except behind the Iron Curtain (said some ironically) were the lands of the great divided among the small? . . .

Finally, Smuts agreed to the matter of South-West representation in the Union because he could not help himself. Dr. Malan had enough followers to do as he chose. Smuts could only hope that some of the Germans of South-

West Africa might, since Hitler's defeat, have become anti-Nazi enough to vote for the man who had fought the Nazis.

But, as there were South Africans who, studying South-West, had foreseen the coming of the two German wars, so there were some who now, looking at South-West, judged how far Germans in Germany had it in them to become democrats.

The Germans of South-West voted entirely for Dr. Malan. He got all six seats of South-West Africa, and here was written finis to General Smuts's frightfully declining hopes and life.

II

When General Botha became the Union's first Prime Minister, there were people who called General Smuts the brain, and General Botha his mouthpiece. But it was General Smuts himself who said: "In Botha's profound common-sense, I see a deeper statesmanship than in all the astuteness and cleverness of smaller men."

For a long time General Smuts's opponents called him "Slim Jannie"—by which they meant precisely that he himself was astute and clever; but none ever called him a small man. The trouble was that they found him only too big—beyond them, concerned with this or that sort of universal scheme, but not with people.

Which is why General Smuts, the greatest of all South Africans, was a lonely man.

But he was also a romantic man. He could not help his loneliness, and he could not bear it.

His father was a Member of the Cape Parliament and his mother was, for those times, an exceptionally educated woman. Yet Smuts did not learn to read and write until he was twelve.

To begin with, he was a feeble child—not expected to live

long. And then there was the family idea that his elder brother would become a predikant and the important education should therefore go to him. Jan would be a farmer, and whatever he picked up would do. . . . The business of education reverted to him when his elder brother died; within four years he had matriculated, and he then wrote to a professor at Stellenbosch near Cape Town to consult him about his future, saying, in the course of his letter:

"I trust you will favour me by keeping your eye upon me and helping me with your kindness. . . . I shall be a perfect stranger. . . . Of what use will a mind, enlarged and refined in all possible ways, be to me, if my religion be a deserted pilot, and morality a wreck?"

He asked the unknown professor to be his friend.

A boy of sixteen is almost a man. He is almost the man he will ever be.

Smuts was more than double sixteen when, after the Boer War, he wrote a letter to a Miss Hobhouse, a middle-aged Boer sympathizer (and later a German sympathizer):

"They call me cynical and bitter. . . . I prefer to sit still, to water my orange trees, and to study Kant's *Critical Philosophy*, until in the whirligig of time new openings for doing good offer themselves."

There were other things in the letter which induced her to publish it in *The Times*, and which almost ruined him. But more than anything he felt the continual references to himself as the man with a watering-can in one hand and Kant's *Critique* in the other. He did not reproach Miss Hobhouse. . . .

He was three times sixteen when he said to his own people:

"I know I do not possess the confidence of many of the Afrikaans-speaking people as General Botha did, but . . . I am following the policy handed on to me by my leader. . . . We are a small people here and we have no

friends in the world. . . . Do not let us pit our small handful against the world. . . . I feel convinced that both the
League and my work here will prove a success, because if
these things fail, the world fails."

He was four times sixteen when he said to English South
Africans who doubted him:

"If I cannot be trusted after what I have done for a lifetime then who can be trusted in this country? . . . If I
cannot be trusted who can be trusted in the world?"

He became five times sixteen and still he was the man
that wanted a friend; that consoled himself with philosophy; that *had* to believe in the League and South African
unity since, if such things failed, the world failed; that
asked who, if not he, could be trusted in the world. A man
is young in every age. He has hardly learnt to be one age
when another is thrust upon him and he has to learn to
be this. Approaching eighty, finding that everything he had
striven for (except the emergence of the State of Israel) had
evaded him, Smuts asked himself: what could be done now?
He had to begin again.

He sat in Parliament, looking entirely different from
everyone else. All great men reveal themselves, but not all
great men are seen. Who can tap an unseen man on the
shoulder to tell him things? He remains alone.

Was Smuts a silent, sombre man? Not at all. Vitality
lifted the air as soon as he approached. To the end he was
gay, smiling, brilliant, gallant, eager—he offered his spirit to
humanity. But then he remembered that his offer had not
been accepted. The struggle had not availed. Though he
spoke, as ever, of hope, where was it to be found—where?
The light left his eyes as he looked for hope in the world.

When Smuts said that he knew he did not possess the
confidence of his people as General Botha did, it was true,
he did not. There were times—such times as war times—

when his followers could give him a passion amounting to
worship. Now they understood him; now, thank heaven, he
was with them. But when the war ended, their community
ended too: they were again in different worlds. He was high
up there, remote from a hot, struggling, perplexed popu-
lace. He could not reach them; they could not reach him; it
angered them; it was as Bernard Shaw said, in his Preface
to *Saint Joan*: "Their fellows hate mental giants and would
like to destroy them, not only enviously because the juxta-
position of a superior wounds their vanity, but quite humbly and honestly, because it frightens them."

Never did Smuts, never could he, even attempt to delude
his colleagues into believing he greatly admired their ability; he did not flatter them by letting them imagine he leant
heavily on their advice. His mind was swift; it was sharply
made up; it could not bear the hampering association of
smaller minds; he had not the patience or instinct to dis-
guise his mental intolerance; when he led a party, there was
no question who led; when he was in government, he was
the government.

In his later years, in the years of the Second World War,
it fell to him, as Minister of Defence, to go often to North
Africa or England. Then most of the work at home was
done by J. H. Hofmeyr. He did General Smuts's work (he
was Deputy Prime Minister); he did his own work as Minister of Finance and Education; he sometimes held three or
four other portfolios as well. He worked so easily, so naturally, it never seemed there could be too much work for
him. It had indeed been like that from his childhood, when
at twelve he had been placed first in the matriculation, at
fifteen and sixteen first in the B.A. and M.A. lists. He had
then written a political life of his namesake and kinsman,
the J. H. Hofmeyr of Rhodes's time, and, at eighteen, gone
as a Rhodes Scholar to Oxford.

At Oxford he had not only taken a Double First, but acquired an unobtrusively perfect English. Many thought him the best orator, after Mr. Churchill, in the Commonwealth.

He returned to South Africa to become, in his twenties, Principal of the Rand University and then Administrator of the Transvaal. For a time, he was both together. In his thirties, he refused a further term as Administrator, he refused also the High Commissionership in London, and entered Parliament, a Smuts man and—as it turned out—the conscience of the country.

In his early days he was not, because of his utter devotion to Smuts, what men called a leader. By the time he became a leader, the work he had so willingly done had proved, after all, beyond his strength. He died partly through overwork; partly because, like Smuts, he was of those mental giants his fellows like to destroy.

It is possible that nothing in Smuts's whole life so tormented him as the death of Hofmeyr. When he stood at Botha's graveside saying: "For his friend was reserved the hard fate to bury him and to remain with the task that even for him was too much," he was speaking of an older man, a man who had long faced death. When he buried Hofmeyr, it was his spiritual heir he lost; a man a generation younger than himself, in whom he saw the future of South Africa; a man who had had too little out of life where he had had so much, so much—it was enough for a hundred men, and yet it was not enough for him. He remained, unfulfilled.

Sometimes General Smuts called himself a divided man. The team, indeed, his soul drove was the Pegasus of his Desire and the Donkey of his Duty, and both were strong: the swift Pegasus, the labouring Donkey—they made a hard team to drive.

Again, he was a visionary. He could not bear the little in-
termediate steps that joined beginnings to ends; at the same
time there was his temperament—eager, energetic, dynamic
—which would not rest. In a world then, not composed of
Smutses, he too often quested solitarily over the ideal, a
leader out of touch with his followers, who could see neither
him nor the way.

In his absolute confidence in his goal, he could be reckless
of his means of approach. But it was not a cynical reckless-
ness. He simply relied on the creature his flesh housed that
it would not lead him astray.

Although he loved the big games of life—politics and,
despite his anxiety for peace, also war—he was indifferent
to wealth, to possessions, to luxuries. As Prime Minister of
the Union he had to live in the house under the mountains
of Cape Town which Rhodes bequeathed to the future
Premiers of South Africa. But he found a greater ease in the
old military clubhouse he bought for three hundred pounds
and moved to his farm near Pretoria—to that he eagerly
returned whenever these big games gave him pause. Only,
in the end, he could not rest even there; he could not rest.

What General Smuts loved above people were the things
of Africa: the stones, the leaves, the mountains, and the
nights. He was an essential European, a fruit of civilization,
a citizen of the world who yet had in him the Boer and a
primitive passion for Africa. The people, they came and
went, but Africa was eternal.

In the eternity of Africa, he grew impatient of the tem-
porary wants and desires of its people. The Boer War was
hardly over, the children of the Voortrekkers were still
nursing what he himself had described as a Century of
Wrong, when he called upon them to rise from their bed
of pain and walk briskly in the sunlight.

For, with the close of the Boer War, he had accepted it

that this Boer and Briton business had to end, that this handful of whites had to fuse. Countrymen of his might despise him—as they despised General Botha too—for doing the quick and convenient thing; for ceasing so soon to grieve and resent; but South Africa's destiny was clear in his eyes and, as ever, he was prepared to leap the spaces.

Other Boers were not. The very conciliation policy which endeared General Botha and General Smuts to the English estranged them from their own people. The Boer might know in his heart that, sooner or later, all white South Africa must be one nation, but what of decorum? The widow had to mourn a respectable period, the funeral baked meats should not grace the marriage table. He could not bear this haste. . . . The two men who were great in the eyes of the world had the hearts of their own countrymen withheld from them because they hurried so indecently towards peace.

Well, there was General Hertzog. He was moving with appropriate slowness, with bitter backward glances and many turnings and haltings. A man like General Hertzog, careful, strong-hearted, passionately single, devotedly narrow—such a man does not walk too far ahead of his nation, does not wander away out of sight. The steps by which he advanced from an aggressive hostility to Britain towards an acknowledgement that South Africa could not stand alone were so gradual, so unnoticeable, actually so unrealized by himself, that his followers' feelings were not outraged when he brought them at last to where General Botha and General Smuts had stood a generation before—asking that of the Boers which only time had a right to demand, calling for an eager admission where a resentful acceptance was the proper style.

And so it was General Hertzog who at last brought the Boers to make peace—a peace so like the dictation of victory that it was really a triumph for General Hertzog over

Generals Botha and Smuts. South Africa might just as well
have been happy all those years. Yet, again, human nature
being what it is, it was perhaps compelled to be unhappy.

Even then, General Hertzog's peace which was only *like*
the dictation of victory did not in the end prove enough.

Victory itself, the Boer's victory of the Boer War, was
still to come.

General Botha died. They spoke in South Africa of his
deep and universal humanity, yet he died hated by many of
his own countrymen, and General Smuts remained alone
to work for a United South Africa and its security in the
world.

Decades passed, during which his opponents reviled him
—one might say unendurably, but that he endured the re-
vilings. England would have been glad of his assistance in
the years that followed the First World War, but he saw in
the very bitterness against him in South Africa the best reason for staying at home. Every Boer was raised in the world
because Smuts was a Boer, yet the Boers themselves repudi-
ated him.

He put in irons his impatient pride. He sat in Parliament
under the insults of his opponents as silent and unprotest-
ing as though he did not hear them. He spoke, while they
rose in the House and ostentatiously departed, as though he
did not see them. He ignored the contumely of caricature,
press, and platform. The years went on until men, too
young to have fought for the freedom they now possessed,
arose to carry on the ancient enmity. When General Botha
died, the men who sat beside Smuts were not those who
had fought with him, but those who had fought against
him. His chief support came from those very mining houses
concerning which he had written in 1906: "Our fear is that
our party might be so small in the first Parliament as to be
no real check on the mine-owners." He was, however, des-

tined to have on his side three men with great Dutch names. Deneys Reitz—the son of a Free State President, the author of *Commando* and other books; Colin Steyn, the son of the last Free State President; J. H. Hofmeyr.

He had also with him Patrick Duncan, a member of Milner's "Kindergarten"—a group of brilliant young Oxford men Milner brought out after the Boer War, most of whom reached high distinction in the world.

Patrick Duncan duly became the first South African Governor-General.

III

Before the Boer War, there were the following divisions in what is now the Union of South Africa:

Natal, practically all British, until recently a Crown Colony.

The Free State, wholly Dutch, a Boer republic.

The Transvaal, a Boer republic, with its centre, Johannesburg, as emphatically English as if a London more populous than the rest of England together were a French city.

The Cape Colony, divided, in politics, between imperialism and a South African patriotism.

Upon Union there was talk of a Coalition Government. A Coalition Government seemed the right thing for a Union of Brothers.

But there were difficulties: the chief of them, Dr. Jameson who, after the Boer War, had actually become Prime Minister of the Cape. Jameson of the Raid? It was a bit too soon to embrace Jameson of the Raid.

The four new provinces accordingly had elections. Although Botha, the destined Prime Minister of the first Union Parliament, was defeated in his own contest, the Boer parties, except in Natal, dominated the elections; another seat was found for Botha; from that day to this Boers have directed the Union Parliament, and seem likely to go on doing so. Though, to begin with, they said they were not being sufficiently considered, not only has the Prime Minister always been a Boer, but the majority of people in the House, as in the country, have always been Boers and the government of the country has had to think of the Boers *as* Boers. A Union of Brothers has not, in Smuts's sense, come about—on the model as, for instance, of America, where people derived from every land are simply Americans. Another Union of Brothers has, however, come about. Of that, later.

The Parliamentary Opposition—Englishmen—were the Unionists.

When the Boers of 1910—and particularly General Hertzog—complained that they were not being sufficiently considered, they meant chiefly that Generals Botha and Smuts were too devoted to the British. General Hertzog, however, had a grievance of his own when he wrote in his diary of Botha's "weakness and lack of principle which finds such perfect expression in his manner of carrying out his so-called policy of conciliation." His grievance was that, as head of the Free State's representatives, he had a right to a place, and a good one, in the Cabinet, but when he came for his reward there was delay and dallying.

Why was there delay and dallying? Because Natal thought him anti-British.

In the end, Smuts—not Botha—offered him Justice; and "there was no mistaking the reluctance" (wrote Hertzog in his diary) "with which the Prime Minister accepted me as a colleague."

Therefore, until the day of Botha's death, and afterwards, Hertzog hated him; and in his hatred he included Smuts.

However, he took the post offered him in order to fight, as he said, for his people.

He was not entirely against the British people. Every now

and then he said things like: "There is nothing on earth I honour and respect more than the great British Empire, and the great men and the great deeds by which it was established. If the day comes—I hope it will not—that the British Empire has need of men to help her, then I and others of my opinion will be at our posts, and others" (he scornfully challenged Generals Botha and Smuts) "possibly not."

He even seconded a motion for the removal of the word "National" from the party constitution: "The word National is too narrow. It refers too much to the Dutch-speaking section of the South African people. Our wish is to form a party which will embrace all white people in South Africa."

Botha's party accordingly dropped the word National from its title of the South African National Party, and became the South African Party (which a Cape Party had for long been called). But when, in due time, Hertzog irrevocably quarrelled with him and formed his own party, he naturally (narrow or not) used the name National for it. And when, again, Smuts joined the South African Party with General Hertzog's National Party, well, of course, the new party was the United South African National Party. And when after that General Hertzog's leading follower, Dr. Malan, seceded from the Coalition, Dr. Malan formed the Purified National Party. Upon the war, General Hertzog, being defeated, joined Dr. Malan and they were now the Reunited National Party. Today Dr. Malan leads the party and it is called the National Party. General Smuts's party is called the United Party. The expression South African seems out of it. . . .

If General Hertzog was sometimes for the British, he was so often against them that at last a Natal Minister resigned in protest against his "anti-imperial" attitude. General Botha suggested then that General Hertzog should do the same. He refused. General Botha tendered his own resignation and was at once asked by the Governor-General, Lord Gladstone, to form a new Ministry.

He did so without the respective champions of Boer patriotism and British imperialism.

Among General Hertzog's words that had angered the Natal Minister were these:

"South Africa must be governed by pure Afrikaners. . . . The main object is to keep Dutch and British separated. . . . I have always said that I do not know what conciliation means."

But still, upon his exclusion, General Hertzog said to the British: "Your language, your great men, your historic deeds, your noble characters, are also my language, my great men, my historic deeds, my noble characters, because we are both South African."

Throughout his life, according to his passion of the moment, General Hertzog was sometimes for, but more often against, the British. . . .

After the trouble of 1912 he remained, a year longer, a private Member under General Botha. He then formed his own National Party of nine Members. Steyn, the ex-President of the Free State, and F. W. Reitz, another ex-President of the Free State, joined him (though their sons afterwards came to Smuts). In the Cape Dr. Malan, once a schoolmaster, then a predikant, then an editor, joined him. In the Transvaal, Tielman Roos, a barrister, announced that he would rather "stand with his own people on a dungheap than upon the most glittering platform with strangers," and he joined him. . . .

There were the strikes of 1913 and 1914 that agitated British Labour. The First World War came and with it a Boer rebellion. The Indians were reduced in status and hampered as immigrants. The natives were threatened with segregation.

Within a few years the South African Party that had so triumphantly marched into office after Union had offended Britons, Boers, Indians, and natives. And so emphatically was the party of Botha and Smuts no longer what it used to be that the situation in the House was now not South African Party against Unionists, but South African Party against Nationalists: with a dwindling band of Unionists defending property rights, with an increasing band of Labour men assailing those rights.

The South African Party, in short, when it came to look the situation in the face, found that, really, there was nothing that in these days distinguished it from its old enemy. At the next election it joined forces with the Unionists. General Smuts, Prime Minister since the death of Botha, sat together with the men whom, twenty years before, he had fought; he had for his associates the friends of the mining houses whose activities he had once feared and tried to curtail; he was deserted by most of his countrymen.

The National Party took its stand against the new combination.

There was an after-war depression in South Africa. There was the Rand Revolt of 1922 with an end in bloodshed. There was an Immigration Act which operated against the Jews of Eastern Europe. There was a growing racial consciousness among the natives. They had been to France with the troops of the First World War. They had seen things. . . . There was a succession of bad farming years, a devastation of crops by unprecedented swarms of locusts.

Who was the one to blame for all these things, if not the government? By-election after by-election went against the South African Party and in favour of the National or Labour parties. General Smuts's majority sank down and further down. He could not bear the tension. His temperamental impatience sprang again. He would know what all this unpopularity really amounted to. He had come back, after the war, from the great world that sought him to the small world that more and more, it seemed, rejected him —because it was his duty, because the small world was his world.

Well, how far would it reject him? He would know.

One day, following a by-election fought almost in the nature of a test-case and lost, he told the House and thus, for the first time, his supporters, that the government could no longer continue in this uncertainty. He was going to the country.

A year and a half before it was due, a general election was fought in South Africa.

Suddenly all kinds of people became Nationalist.

Moreover, a combination even more striking than that of the South African and Unionist parties was arranged. The Nationalists invited Labour to join them against General Smuts, and they did so.

"Who could have dreamt such a thing?" General Smuts later said. . . . "The Nationalist Party was a party of land-owners, violently opposed to England. Yet the Labourites joined them. They were blind and mad over the Revolution. They cared for nothing except to break me. Nothing mattered—no principle—nothing—as long as they could break me.

"Well, they broke me, but they broke themselves. Yes, they altogether finished themselves. . . ."

But in the meantime their triumph, in the company of the Nationalists, was overwhelming. After a struggle of twelve years General Hertzog led the government.

A Ministry was formed of eight Nationalists and two Labourites. Among the Nationalist Members there was not a single Briton, among the Labour Members, not a single Boer. The Nationalists were, by heredity, Tory. They were landowners. They were countrymen. They were employers.

They were traditionally against Socialism. They stood for exactly the opposite of the Labour ideal.

Only on two points had the new partners any fundamental sympathy. They both wanted a White South Africa—at all costs, and they both hated General Smuts.

Now, on each side of the House, there sat a combination of Briton and Boer.

Not in thirty years did so much rain fall as, in the summer of 1925, drenched South Africa. The campaign against the locusts succeeded, and whether the government did it, or the rains, or their course was run no one questioned.

Then platinum was found—it was found in the most extraordinary places—and money poured into South Africa. Who, until this miraculous year, would have supposed that, whatever assayers might report, practically every farm in the Transvaal was a platinum field.

In 1927, the Nationalists decided that South Africa should have its own flag and the Labour Members—all these Englishmen—supported them. And when General Smuts did not, the meetings he held ended in riots, with bottles flung and windows smashed and halls wrecked and the police helpless and General Smuts crying: "This is politics in our country. This is what we have come to. This is my nation. . . . No, it is the end. . . . The cup is full."

How far he was from knowing the end, and the gall in the filled cup!

The next election too went against General Smuts. He had unthinkingly mentioned his old dream of a time "when the British States in Africa would all become members of a great African Dominion stretching unbroken throughout Africa." One might have thought the word "British" was the wrong word. It was the word African, or rather the two words African Dominion. General Smuts, the Nationalists said, wanted South Africans to unite with Kaffirs. They called him "The apostle of a Kaffir State." "Voters!" they addressed the land: "Save our children from the Black Policy of the South African Party."

The South African Party was so heavily defeated that General Hertzog found he could govern without the Labour Party.

As General Smuts had prophesied, the Labour Party was broken; it was finished. . . .

But he had said that he too was broken. He had said the cup was full, it was the end.

He was not broken. But also the cup was not full.

The rains ceased. The droughts that had stricken General Smuts struck General Hertzog. It was in his kraal there now drooped the seven kine, poor, lean, and ill-favoured; in his fields there now stood the thin, yellow, stunted corn. And though, not only in South Africa, when the Almighty punishes, does one blame the government, in South Africa one exceedingly blames the government.

Together with the rains, the platinum ceased; England went off gold; Australia and New Zealand dropped their money below England's; South Africa, clinging (without regard to the decreased value of money) to its golden pound, could not sell to England against Australia and New Zealand; misery overcame the land of South Africa. . . .

General Smuts, just returned from England, campaigned against the gold standard. For twelve days during the next session, the House talked about nothing else.

General Hertzog enunciated fourteen points against General Smuts; he was again and again called to order, and General Smuts, for the first time in twenty years, objected to an insult from General Hertzog.

The government said: "We will stand by our policy . . . while the House supports us in that policy. . . ."

The drought increased. The farmers could not sell even

the little their land produced; they could not pay the shop-keepers who could not pay the wholesalers, who could not pay the shippers. Little investors could not get their interest from big investors who could not get their interest from their investments. Bankruptcy ran like a catching fire across the land. The Province of the Free State was bankrupt. . . .

A third man saw his chance.

IV

Towards the end of the year 1932, a South African Appeal Court Judge was inspired to return to politics. It was Tiel-man Roos who, twenty years before, had followed Hertzog out of Botha's Conciliation Camp, saying he would rather "stand with his own people on a dung-heap than upon the most glittering platform with strangers."

On General Smuts's return to South Africa in 1919 he had been his most virulent opponent:

"General Smuts goes about the country like a dog trying to bleat like a sheep. . . .

"He will not any more fool the people with his 'slim-ness.' . . .

"We no longer choose to be the infamous tail of Eng-land. No, we must so develop that England becomes the tail of South Africa."

If he spoke like this in public, in private he could forgive anything but rude manners. Although his large following in the Transvaal called him (and so he was generally called) the Lion of the North, he did not look like a lion; he did not even (though it was a Tielman Roos who gave Kruger his only three months of schooling) look like a Boer. He looked like a short, dark, bald, stout, aquiline Jew; with blue eyes unexpectedly sharp in his jovial face; courtly in style, easy with money. He had also something that General Smuts and General Hertzog had not—an approach to the common people. He loved behind-the-scenes work. He loved sitting in hotel rooms with mysterious people—devising, devising. He was extremely popular.

Illness had brought him to what he scorned as the feath-erbed life of the Bench. Now, while he sat there, improving in health but dying of boredom, the country, smitten by its seven years' drought, its adherence to the gold standard that stifled every industry, a ceaseless wrangling, was being done to death. The party to which he had once belonged could not help the drought but it was responsible, he thought, for the industrial depression and the racialism.

The two, indeed, were linked. For though it may seem, superficially, that a gold-producing country should be the last to give up the gold standard, the fact is that gold, of all commodities, most surely rises in price when money grows cheap. For gold is not only a symbol and a system, it is a metal one works and weighs and packs and sells—like wool or maize or oranges. It quite simply pays the gold mines to get more for their gold.

Even before General Smuts came back from England in 1931 to preach the abandonment of the gold standard, the mines were for it. But others, and chiefly the government, were not. Some were not because they hated to see their money cheapened: earners, rentiers, pensioners. Some felt that a reduction in the value of money was a corresponding theft of money. The government's chief objection was that it meant a subservience to England. What! Trail the noble South African pound behind sterling!

General Smuts published his calculation of an off-gold budget (an extreme understatement, as events proved) and it was denounced, and he was denounced, with passionate derision.

Tielman Roos, sitting on the Appeal Court in Bloemfon-tein, in the province bankrupted by the gold standard, had thirteen years before spoken of Smuts going about the country "bleating like a sheep." He had declared that

South Africa would not be "the infamous tail of England."

It was fifteen months—it was even before he had returned from presiding over the Centenary Meeting of the British Association for the Advancement of Science—that Smuts had begun urging South Africa to follow England off gold. He had, ever since then, gone about South Africa preaching this doctrine.

Now Tielman Roos, despite his words of 1919, saw that Smuts, in his campaign, was right; that South Africa had to attach its economy to England's. He saw also that the country was turning from Hertzog to Smuts. He saw his own chance.

Three days before Christmas, he descended from the Bench and called upon the people of South Africa to unite under his banner, that was Smuts's banner, of Off-Gold.

He spoke to packed halls. He rode through vociferous streets. The people of South Africa, weary of their miseries, hailed him as their saviour. He sat about, as in the old days, with cronies, with emissaries, preaching Off-Gold, speaking of his followers in both Parliamentary camps, bowling over General Hertzog, pulling General Smuts's platform from under him.

It was the Parliamentary vacation, and Smuts was not to be found. A newspaper man traced him to a mountaintop in the northern Transvaal, and so he heard the news about Roos's emergence: that Roos was winning over the country on the very policy he himself had been urging for fifteen months.

One thing, indeed, was clear: that with Roos demanding the same course as Smuts, with the secret adherents he claimed on government benches, with the country ruined by the government's clinging to gold, defeat was certain for Hertzog and the country would go off gold.

South Africa's pound stood forty-two per cent higher

than England's pound; upon devaluation it would equal England's pound.

What was the obvious thing to do?

Not only businessmen and speculators, but just ordinary little citizens, sent their money to England—there to swell to the measure of sterling, thence to be returned to South Africa, enhanced by forty-two per cent.

One took simply no risk. Even, if by some strange event, South Africa did not go off gold, nothing was lost. Nobody did any other business. For three days, and until the transmission of money was officially stopped, South African pounds in their millions were sent overseas. The country, in effect was already off gold when the government, having vowed it would perish rather than abandon the gold standard—refused to perish.

South Africa began the year 1933 on a sterling basis. The money that had been sent to England returned to South Africa, luxuriantly increased. Debtors paid their creditors with delightful cheap money. The thrifty investors in public loans, in insurance policies, in mortgages, the people who always paid their debts at once, were proved to be sorry fools. The merchants tried to put up their prices, and, against every law of sense and economics, prices went down. Only gold, gold, gold went up. Quartz gold, and also that gold whose richest lodes, as Samuel Butler said, lay in the eyes and ears of the public.

It had hitherto been worth four guineas an ounce. It presently became six pounds, and then seven pounds, an ounce.

And now it could be seen that the people who had so cleverly sent their money to swell in England had not, after all, been the cleverest people.

The people who really understood were the people who had at once bought gold shares.

For a more fantastic thing even than increasing one's money forty-two per cent on a word to England was happening in South Africa. Gold shares rose, not forty-odd per cent, but a hundred, two hundred, six hundred per cent. The reason was that gold shares appreciated not merely by the difference between the gold pound and sterling, but by the difference between the old profits and the new.

Thus mines that, on four guineas an ounce, had been able to make a profit of only a few shillings or no profit at all, on six or seven pounds an ounce could make a profit (if they went on working their good ground) of two or three pounds an ounce.

Low-grade mines, mines that had been abandoned, reef that had been despised, became suddenly profitable. The richer mines could now develop, not only their best ground, but also their poorest ground. The lives of mines were doubled.

And although the government presently arranged to take from the gold mines an excess-profits duty of six million pounds, and for a time shares fell and protest meetings were held, and it was said the government was ruining the country, profits so went on accumulating that soon shares were higher than ever. The government itself, out of the ordinary mining taxes, and the excess-profit taxes and its share of the mines it leased, made, during the year 1933, fourteen and three-quarter million pounds—an increase of ten and a half million pounds over 1932.

Then there were the monies got from industries connected with the mines; and the income taxes of all the people who had made money out of mining ventures and gold shares (particularly the stockbrokers); and the customs, swollen with prosperity; and the railway takings after years of losses—all these profits and all the other profits that accrue to a country in prosperity.

The accumulated deficit of three years was wiped out. So

many people were so happy, one all but forgot that everything could have been like this fifteen months ago and that
meanwhile tens of millions of pounds might have been
saved.

South Africa revolved round the Johannesburg Stock Exchange. Men whom the world had mistakenly believed to
be millionaires really did become millionaires. Dead bits of
scrips, abandoned in casual drawers, leapt suddenly to life
again. Dozens of gold companies sprang into existence. On
one boom day alone ninety-five different gold shares were
dealt in on the Johannesburg Stock Exchange. It was said
that brokers made up to three thousand pounds a day in the
simple course of buying and selling shares for clients they
had no time to speak to.

People in London bought shares, not only in Johannesburg mines, but in any enterprise in Johannesburg. More
and more people and goods came to Johannesburg; more
white miners by the thousand, more black miners by the
ten thousand. Johannesburg became suddenly a new city
—not beautiful, just urgently new. The banks did not know
what to do with the money that poured in from all directions. . . .

Considering how easy it was to get rich, it was surprising
how many failed to get rich. Those who did not were the
virtuous, conservative folk who abhorred stock-exchange
speculation and made a merit of earning their money in the
sweat of their faces.

It was terrible for the virtuous folk to see the way the buy-
ers of gold shares grew richer and richer. By all the rules,
the speculators should have fallen on shameful penury exe-
crated by their ruined children. But gamblers had turned
out the prudent fellows; prodigals, the prophets. They went
about with the faces of those who have a secret ecstasy (for

nothing is so worth having as what one has not worked for
—whether genius, beauty, birth, or an unearned fortune);
and they sailed for Europe, and bought new houses and
cars, and wildly embellished their wives, and sent their sons
to Oxford or Cambridge, and became suddenly notable for
their wisdom on every subject under the sun.

How could the wives of the virtuous ones bear it? They
taunted their husbands for their cowardice, and pointed out
that here was the one chance of making money—missed;
and had not easy-come-by money the same power, the same
buying-value, the same meaning in every direction as hard-
come-by money? And did it not, they might have added,
taste the sweeter for being unmixed with heartburn, gall,
and sweat?

When shares rose to a point where it was no longer profitable to buy them, the virtuous ones who had so long been
cautious, who had so long refused temptation—who, in
fact, had so long *feared*—at last, trembling, plunged.

And then, chiefly because of the gold whose richest lodes
lay in the eyes and ears of the public, shares naturally
slumped, and the virtuous ones lost their money.

If the Preacher, the son of David, had lived in Johannesburg in those days, he would have put in before "a time to
weep and a time to laugh"—"a time to buy and a time to
sell."

The enhanced gold price which prolonged the hope of
gold production affected not only South Africa but all the
world. As in the 1880's, when the gold of the Witwatersrand was revealed, as in the 1890's, when Deep Level Mining came into existence, so in the 1930's, when depreciated
sterling made it possible to win gold hard to get, did Johannesburg offer to a puzzled world the certainty of continuing
a while longer its old economic system and, with its old

economic system, also its old civilization. In the 1940's, a further continuity was offered with the discovery of the gold in the Free State. Then there was a boom again.

But that was a boom on prospects—on things to happen in years to come. The boom of the 1930's had to do with an immediate result. It could only occur again (though hardly on the same scale) upon a further devaluation of money.

There came a further devaluation of money. There came relief again. It came at a moment when the country needed it as badly as in 1933—on September 18, 1949.

For two years South Africans had expected England to devalue (with South Africa herself to follow, since she knew better now than in 1932); they had remembered the boom of 1933; upon every rumour of devaluation they had bought gold shares; England had not devalued; their gold shares had gone down and steeply down; they had sold their shares; some had been forced to sell their houses; various mines had gone into liquidation; others had prepared to do so.

Finally South Africans had accepted it that England would not devalue; however shares dropped they were not tempted to buy them; all the mines could talk of was the high cost of production and the low price of gold. . . .

Only five days before (so hard pressed she was), South Africa had withdrawn the last of the gold lent to England by the Smuts government. She got for this gold twelve and a half millions in sterling. She would have got for it a week later, when money was again allowed to move through the banks, eighteen millions.

Gold shares appreciated immediately by twenty to a hundred per cent, but many of them were not higher than they had been a year or eighteen months before on the mere rumour of devaluation, and the higher profits of the mines could not offset the depression that came with the higher cost of living.

V

Meanwhile, what of the man who had brought about all the exhilaration of 1933?

Having come down from the Bench, he had called upon General Smuts—since their policies were one, and he the Lion of the North—to join him in a coalition, go with him to the country and, upon their sure success, come in under him as Deputy Prime Minister in a government that would have five Roos Ministers, five Smuts Ministers, and a Labour Minister.

Only a few weeks ago it had seemed certain that the country must have Smuts back to save it. But he had realized, sooner than Roos himself, that, by forcing the government off gold, Roos had left the country with no further need to be saved. General Smuts, his fifteen months' preaching against the gold standard, the fifty million pounds lost during these fifteen months, Roos's own part in the transformation, were alike forgotten in the turmoil of sudden prosperity. People were so busy making money or trying to make it or agonizing over not having made it that, for once in a way, politics were ignored in South Africa. Who cared who led? General Smuts, General Hertzog, Tielman Roos, what difference did it make which of them was Prime Minister? South Africa's forum was not Parliament, but Johannesburg's Stock Exchange.

Roos, who had travelled forth through crowded stations and streets, to speak at packed and cheering halls, travelled back home, unmet at stations; sick and melting in a coupé of a very hot train; dazed by the discovery that, behind the cheering, there had been no money offered to help his new party; no conspicuous people anxious to join it. Now he too realized that his magic was gone. Neither Smuts, the first champion of Off-Gold, nor Roos, the second champion of Off-Gold, had the strength to govern alone.

There were men in Smuts's own party ready to sacrifice him to Roos. They still had the applause for Roos ringing in their ears; they magnanimously forgave Roos the things he had said about Smuts; they wanted Smuts to go in under Roos's leadership.

Others objected. They asked who these followers were that Roos had in Hertzog's party; who these unknown giants that were to become Cabinet Ministers in the Coalition he proposed; why Roos, with his invisible party, to lead, and not Smuts, stronger than he had been for years?

Smuts requested Roos to name his secret adherents and whether, in the changed circumstances, he could guarantee they would still come to him. Roos said he frankly couldn't, he couldn't now be sure they would come to him and he therefore had not the right to say who they were. At the same time, he still demanded to lead. He said only he could swing their two parties together. He refused Smuts's offer of four places in a Coalition Cabinet: Smuts to lead, Roos to be Deputy Prime Minister.

Then Smuts demanded in the House that, since the Hertzog government was now committed to a policy which, according to its own conviction, was fatal to the country, it should resign, and open the way for a national government.

To this Hertzog answered that when his government had sworn not to leave the gold standard it had meant—not voluntarily. . . .

There were men all over South Africa who so feared the rancour of Hertzog's party, should it ever lose power, that they said one dared not let it lose power. Indeed, the country was prospering now. Why trouble?

But Hertzog himself—shaken by the gold crisis, the disasters of the last fifteen months, the thought of those secret Roosites ready, when it suited them, to leave him—was not so easy as all the new moneymakers. . . .

One day Smuts came down from Table Mountain to find Hofmeyr waiting for him with news: Hertzog's people were as tired as Smuts's people of all the rancour and wrangling; they were prepared to go in with Smuts.

On what terms?

Hertzog to lead.

There were Smuts men as ready to sacrifice him to Hertzog as they had been to sacrifice him to Roos.

Smuts looked at them thoughtfully and said that peace was naturally what he wanted. He said it was right the parties should come together. He said he would stay outside.

It appeared Smuts had feelings! His followers were extremely surprised. He was now sixty-three. He had been Kruger's State Attorney. He had fought as a General in the Boer War. He had been a General in the Great War and all the world could offer had lain at his feet. He had refused the world for his soul's sake, which meant South Africa. Yet the men he led were prepared to sacrifice him to Roos, to Hertzog—full of their fears, they were prepared to sacrifice him. And they were startled—they had seen him silent under so many affronts—to find he had feelings. . . .

But, again, there were others who had served him loyally. Should he sacrifice them rather than himself?

Next morning he saw General Hertzog. Next afternoon he stood up in Parliament and, saying he was tired of discussion and dissension, offered to end both by linking himself in coalition with General Hertzog—under General Hertzog. He became General Hertzog's Deputy Prime Minister. He took also the Ministry of Justice and thus, as he said, ended where he had begun when he became Kruger's State Attorney.

The Nationalist and South African parties, on a Coalition platform, went to the country. There was after all, said

Smuts, no difference between himself and General Hertzog except on the native question, and there were members of his own party who saw with Hertzog, and not with him, on the native question.

It was the easiest election for any Coalition candidate. Only two Roos candidates were returned, of whom one presently joined the three or four Labour Members who now offered to declare themselves the official Opposition, and the other the Smuts-Hertzog group.

Roos himself, opposed in his own district by a Nationalist Minister who was supported by his new colleague, General Smuts, was defeated. . . .

He had taken no advantage of the boom he himself had created. Those he had raised to fortune through it showed him no gratitude. He had lost his position and security. He returned, at fifty-five, to the Bar he had many years ago abandoned. The illness that had made him give up politics for the Bench came back. He sat about with people as before—not complaining, still smiling and courtly. He died very soon, poor, concerned about his young family. Smuts unveiled a memorial to him.

In a remote district of the Cape, Smuts assisted another Coalition candidate, Dr. Malan. Dr. Malan was returned.

VI

And now the thought was fusion. What was there to prevent it? The country was booming. The rains had returned. Never before had so many people been so happy as in South Africa in 1934.

Then let there be peace. The English wanted it. The Boers had everything—so it seemed. The old British colonies were theirs as well as their old republics. Had not all this business of the last few months proved it?

There could not be peace. Not yet.

After the Statute of Westminster, Dr. Malan had said:

"Instead of looking upon Great Britain as the conqueror, we look upon her as the mother of our freedom. . . . Republican Independence is dead. . . . The independence which the Nationalist Party has always lived for is now attained, and cannot well be more complete. . . . South Africa today can only secede from greater freedom and safety to lesser freedom and safety."

But what he now said was that South Africa had to be "free in the *international* sense of the word." He wanted a new South Africa Act to replace the Act of Union. It was his price for fusion. He had his followers.

The new South Africa Act was set going. There came before Parliament new Status Bills, and Dr. Malan's Head Committee asked General Hertzog whether he agreed "that the British Crown, in so far as the Union was concerned, is divisible; that we possess the right of neutrality; and that we have the right of separation."

General Hertzog replied: "With regard to the question of sovereign independence and the removal of constitutional anomalies, it gives me pleasure to be able to state that the intention is as presumed by your Head Committee."

Dr. Malan's Head Committee said: "When the present Status Bill is passed by Parliament, South Africa will be freer than Paul Kruger's Transvaal in 1884."

General Smuts received from General Hertzog a written undertaking that the points on which they had disagreed in the past would not be touched by the new Act—they would merely continue to differ on them.

He said to his English followers:

"You English need ask for nothing. Why should you? You are great. Now you have this little Afrikaner people you have fought offering you peace at last, and their hand. . . . If I were an Englishman I would be glad to take that hand. . . . I submit to you. . . . I submit to you with all my heart: nothing is asked of my English-speaking friends, nothing is asked of you which you cannot honestly accept as a basis of co-operation in the future. . . . I should like to know before I go, and I have not a long way to go in the life of this country, that, after the storms of the past, I have succeeded in my small measure in bringing the people of this country together."

General Hertzog said of a secret society whose object was South Africa for the Boers that it could "no longer be suffered that a secret society consisting of only one section of the people—the Afrikaans-speaking people—should sit and scheme day and night, inside the House and outside of it, to rob the other section of their rights. . . ."

More—much more—was to be heard of this secret society, this Union of Brothers that was not General Smuts's Union of Brothers.

But, in the end, in 1934, there was not the fusion one had dreamt of. There were Englishmen who asked what all this meant about South Africa's being a "sovereign independent state"; why the divisibility of the Crown, the right to secede, the right of neutrality?

They formed a new small party which called itself the Dominion Party.

There were Afrikaners who asked, why the naval base for England, why no neutrality, why no secession?

They became, under Dr. Malan, the Purified National Party.

The Smuts and Hertzog men fused.

This is how the Union of South Africa stands under the Status of the Union Act:

South Africa is one of the "autonomous communities of the British Empire," as defined by the Statute of Westminster.

It is (amending here the South Africa Act on which Union was founded) a sovereign independent state.

The Union Parliament is its sovereign legislative power.

The Executive government of the Union is vested in the King, acting on the advice of the Union Ministers, and may be administered by the King in person or by the Governor-General as his representative.

The King ceases to be, as far as South Africa is concerned, "of the United Kingdom of Great Britain and Ireland," or any other part of the Commonwealth: the Parliamentary oath of allegiance is to the King (as one might say) of South Africa. The King's representative has to be a South African. Union nationals are born in South Africa. Under the Status Act a British subject could by right acquire Union nationality after two years' domicile in the Union. There is now a new Citizenship Act according to which he has to wait five years and must then be approved by the Minister of Interior. A foreigner of European descent has to wait six years for naturalization.

The meeting of Commonwealth Prime Ministers in April of 1949, in effect, confirmed South Africa's Status Act so that other Commonwealth states have now more or less the same system. But the decision that India may be a republic and yet remain within the Commonwealth lays down a precedent encouraging to South Africans desirous of a republic. The Citizenship Act has made it impossible for immigrants brought in by General Smuts's government to vote for his party at the 1953 general election unless they were here two years before it became law.

The actual form of government remains as at the time of Union, except that there are twelve, instead of ten, Cabinet Ministers.

There are two Houses of Parliament.

The Senate, which sometimes has an effective moment, consists of eight representatives from each province, and a further eight, nominated by the Governor-General-in-Council, of whom four are nominally selected "mainly on the grounds of their thorough acquaintance with the wants and wishes of the coloured races in South Africa." Jan Hofmeyr once resigned because a Senator was selected who had not, in fact, that thorough acquaintance with their wants and wishes.

The House of Assembly is composed of Members directly elected by the voters. At the time of Union, a voter in the Cape Province had to be male with property worth seventy-five pounds or a salary of fifty pounds a year, and he needed also the ability to put in writing his name, address and occupation. There was no colour distinction. In the other provinces, a voter had merely to be white, male, and twenty-one: for Natal gave natives a franchise under conditions so onerous that a vote was about as accessible to him as a white skin itself; and the two northern provinces, holding from their republican days that there shall be no equality between white and black in Church and State, excluded the native completely.

Women had no vote until, in 1930, General Hertzog introduced a bill to confer the franchise on all women of twenty-one or over. The Synod of the Dutch Reformed Churches formally opposed the bill on the ground that the enfranchisement of women was in direct conflict with the word of God, but it was handsomely passed, and it had the following interesting results:

While white men in the Cape still needed the old property and educational qualifications, white women fell into the universal-suffrage scheme of the rest of the Union.

While, again, coloured men in the Cape had the vote, their women were excluded from it because the Women's

Enfranchisement Act conferred it only on the white women of the Union.

And when, next year, Dr. Malan brought forward a bill which did away with distinctions between Europeans in all the provinces, the white men in the Cape became exempted from the property and educational tests, but the coloured men did not. They still—and only they in the Union— had to have seventy-five pounds or earn fifty pounds a year and be able to write their name, address, and occupation. But yet they treasured their rights, even under this discrimination, because at the same time only they, among non-Europeans in the Union, had a vote at all.

What flowed from this situation was even more striking than the situation itself:

The coloured vote was a South African Party vote and the vote in the north was strongly Nationalist. The flooding, therefore, of the north with white women voters while in the south coloured women did not at the same time get the vote, and coloured men had restrictions white men had not, greatly strengthened General Hertzog's hold on the country, just as once the cry of "Equal rights for every civilized man"—without regard to his colour—was designed by Rhodes to strengthen his own hold on the country. . . .

Then, in 1936, General Hertzog passed a measure (with the required two-thirds majority of both Houses) that took the Bantu voters off the Cape roll and allowed them, instead, three white representatives in the House of Assembly, four elected by themselves in the Senate, and two in the Cape Provincial Council. . . .

And, since the privilege of voting with the whites at all now puts the Cape coloured people in a different category from the other coloured people in the Union, and since the right even of indirect representation puts the Bantu people of the Cape in a different category from the other Bantu people of the Union, it is, in these days, decided that the Cape Coloureds be put in the position of the Cape Bantus, and the Cape Bantus in the position of the rest of the Bantus. . . .

General Hertzog further arranged, in 1936, to give the Cape Bantus their own Representative Council, with local Councils and white advisers; and the business of this Representative Council was to consult together and make report on matters concerning the interests of natives.

In later days General Smuts said the trouble of this Council was that it could do nothing but talk. And this is why, indeed, the Natives' Representative Council, during the black miners' strike in 1947, adjourned, and it has not met since.

General Hertzog was a hard-bitten man, but also an honest one. He said about the new legislation: "The white man can never, with a true heart, go and use his power really to advance the native. He dare not do it. The native, as long as he remains a danger to civilization in South Africa, has no right to expect the white man to assist and support him."

One of his chief followers said: "If we lose our colour feeling and the non-Europeans are developed and civilized, we must become a coloured nation. . . . There is only one policy to follow if you wish . . . to remain a European race in South Africa, and that is to follow a policy of separation between the races. . . . Yes, our attitude is that the Europeans must remain masters in South Africa."

There are said to be several million not wholly white people among the hundred and fifty million Europeans of the United States. There are said to be five or six hundred thousand not wholly white people among the two and a half million whites in South Africa. The blackness in the States seems not to have prevented America from becoming the greatest power of the day. But the South African's problem is different. He is outnumbered, four to one, by the dark

peoples. There are another hundred and fifty millions beyond his borders, and not many whites.

And so he fears.

The people of the Union are not evil. Mr. Churchill, who
has spoken of South Africa's plight at Empire conferences,
is not evil. Abraham Lincoln was not evil, though he said
he "did not understand the Declaration to mean that all
men were created equal in all respects. The Negroes are not
our equal in colour." South Africa faces a question beyond
solution, that is all.

Excluding the three members for the natives, including
the six members from South-West, there are a hundred and
fifty-six members of the House of Assembly. The Transvaal
has sixty-six, the Cape, fifty-five, Natal sixteen, and the Free
State thirteen.

To make a balance between the sparsely peopled country
areas and the thickly peopled city areas, the country voters
are fifteen per cent fewer to a constituency than the average number of voters, and the city voters are fifteen per cent
more. This is held to give the Nationalists a constant advantage in elections.

Except that South Africa has no hereditary ruling body
(and has also abandoned titles), the Legislative Assembly
stands in relation to the Senate as, in England, the Lower
House to the Upper; and, equally, the real vitality of government is concentrated in it. The term of a Parliament
(unless it is previously dissolved) is five years.

In addition to the Governor-General-in-Council and the
two Houses, each province has an Administrator, appointed
for five years by the Governor-General-in-Council, whose
status is about equal to that of a Cabinet Minister. Each
province has, besides, a Council consisting, in the Transvaal
and Cape, of as many members as there are electoral divisions; and in the Free State and Natal, of twenty-five mem-

bers each. Of these Councillors, four form an executive of which the Administrator is Chairman.

The Provincial Councils are subordinate legislatures to the Union Parliament, and have entrusted to them, among other things, considerable taxing powers.

South Africa is, finally represented in England and the other Commonwealth lands by a High Commissioner; it has Trade Commissioners, Consuls, Ministers in various parts of the world, and begins now to appoint Ambassadors.

Though England's representative, who also deals with the High Commission Territories, is the most important of the emissaries, he used to rank, and so did the other Commonwealth representatives, below the higher-titled men of other lands. Within recent years, however, it has been arranged that all shall rank equally, and seniority goes by length of tenure.

South Africa has an Appeal Court of five, sitting in Bloemfontein; a Supreme Court of thirty or so, divided among the provinces; a Magistrate's Court for two hundred odd magisterial districts. A magistrate is a civil servant who tries cases of limited jurisdiction and attends to such other matters as poor relief, pensions, marriages, deserted wives, mental patients, land bank loans. He presides over committees that have to do with liquor and other licenses. In the countryside, he is the community's father. He is constantly moved about, and gets poor pay.

About the time General Hertzog headed South Africa's Coalition government, Hitler and his Nazis began that business in Europe which affected all the world and, with it, South Africa.

Since the time, in the 1880's, when Rhodes was struggling for Bechuanaland, partly to ward off the Germans, there had been the shadow of Germany's hand over South Africa.

The Germans offered to help Kruger get Bechuanaland, and Rhodes remarked that the next thing would be some German quarrel with the Transvaal—some question of brandy, guns, or something—and in the end Germany would stretch from Angra Pequena (Luderitzbucht) in South-West Africa to Delagoa Bay in East Africa; and there South Africa would be completely blocked off at the bottom of the African Continent. When Dr. Jameson, in 1895, spoke of a South African economic and political federation, Kruger said: "When we asked her Majesty's government for bigger clothes, they said, 'Eh, eh, what is this?' and could not see we were growing up." But Germany, he said, would help the Transvaal get an adult's wardrobe.

There was, after the Raid, the Kaiser's telegram of congratulation to Kruger, and his offer to support the Boers against England, which was not fulfilled in the Boer War; and there was, upon the outbreak of the First World War, his telegram to the Governor of South-West Africa, saying: "Guarantee Boers existence Boer Republic if they attack immediately. . . ." "We expected," said the Germans afterwards, "that British India would rise. We expected trouble in Ireland. We expected a triumphant rebellion in South Africa."

There was a plan of collaboration made between the Germans of South-West Africa and rebellious Boers of the Union. On the borders of South-West Africa, Boer and German forces met. There was a Boer rebellion. General Smuts spoke of the full freedom given by Britain to South Africa and honourably maintained; of a pledge to be maintained by the Boers too; and the rebellion was quelled and South-West conquered.

General Hertzog, for his part, had from the beginning said this was not South Africa's war; he did not know if it was a just war; the Germans were a powerful people whom the South Africans should not antagonize.

When the war was over and a British Note to the Allied Powers said: "No peace is possible until reparation has been made for violated right and liberties and the principle of nationalities and the independence of small States recognised," General Hertzog felt the first reparation, the first independence, might well be to the old Boer republics of South Africa; and he and others went to the peace-making in Paris and said to Mr. Lloyd George: "We are here today to ask you that the wrong which was done in 1902 may be undone," and General Hertzog told Mr. Lloyd George then that he had German blood and a third of the people of the Union had German blood. . . .

General Hertzog rose to power. It was now he who represented South Africa at Imperial Conferences in London. He was a naturally courtly man; he enjoyed the conferences; he became so pleasant towards England that followers of his who had not yet met England's charm at home began to call him an imperialist. . . .

And then there was Germany again—the whole German business overflowing again from South-West Africa into the Union of South Africa.

The year 1938 was the hundredth anniversary of the Great Trek—that time when the Boers had left the Cape to separate themselves from England in a land of their own. The festivals of National Socialism were teaching other lands. . . .

An idea! A commemoration, a recapitulation, of trekking, of trekking away, throughout the year of 1938!

At first the British, the satisfied Afrikaners, did not realize what was happening. No less than the dissatisfied Afrikaners were they entranced by the thought of a year of celebration. Least of all had the Dominion Office in London any understanding of what was meant by all this business of beards and bonnets in the style of 1838.

Waggons followed the paths away from the Cape of the 1838 Voortrekkers. At the waggons, Nagmaal (communion) was celebrated. Children were christened, couples were married, at the waggons. The very grease of the waggon wheels was treasured. All the time there were barbecues (Braaivleis) and other jollities.

The newspapers, English no less than Afrikaans, with warmth described and portrayed the great doings. Newspapers in England did so too. As the waggons approached their destination near Pretoria, small-town mayors came out in their chains and robes—English-speaking mayors—and were turned back. It was probably at this stage that the general public for the first time felt not only that this was a year of July the Fourths, but that the Nationalists of Dr. Malan had captured the whole commemoration, root and branch, leaf and flower.

Where the celebrations ended on a height near Pretoria, there slowly began to rise an edifice whose foundation stone not even General Hertzog (now allied with General Smuts) was allowed to lay; and, after much argument, it was laid by three old women, descended from distinguished Voortrekkers. Mrs. Hofmeyr, the mother of Jan Hofmeyr, was also proudly descended on both sides from distinguished Voortrekkers. Mrs. Smuts, the wife of General Smuts, had Voortrekker antecedents of repute and always said she coveted no higher honour than to follow humbly where they had led. Not they.

A Voortrekker Monument had been thought of since 1923, but there had never been enough money for it. Now, after the gold boom, there was enough money for it.

In amusing effect, it was chiefly the mines that paid for the Voortrekker Monument which, in the end, cost three or four times as much as was expected. It looked like the Leipzig Memorial. . . .

And from waggon to waggon, young men carried a torch

that lit a new flame in the hearts of Afrikaners, and in October 1938 a body was formed to perpetuate the ideals of the Great Trek—the freedom the Boers had then sought, their brotherhood, culture, dress, and even games—the Ossewa Brandwag, the Sentinels of the Ox-Waggon.

Behind it seemed to be the ideal of a Herrenvolk. It was even agreed with Dr. Malan that the aims of the Ossewa Brandwag were not political—only cultural. Many well-meaning Boers, in this dream of a national renaissance, joined the Ossewa Brandwag.

One saw the Second World War coming. One saw the two Generals—Hertzog and Smuts—going along the divergent paths they had followed in the First World War. In April 1939 General Smuts, Minister of Justice as well as Deputy Prime Minister, sent three hundred policemen, with machine-guns, to South-West Africa. He told Parliament his idea was to form the South-West with the South African police in their "ordinary duty of maintaining law and order . . . because of warnings that in the near future incidents might take place in South-West Africa in breach of law and order. . . . Members must remember what happened in the case of Austria."

VII

When Russia's pact with Germany was declared, everyone knew it meant war and Members of the Union Parliament, which was in recess, hastened to Cape Town and met on September 3.

That afternoon General Hertzog said to his Cabinet: "I am going to remain neutral. Under no condition will I allow South Africa to enter the war. . . . Gentlemen," he answered the protests of General Smuts and his followers, "I am Prime Minister of this country, and that is what I have decided upon."

The day Britain declared war on Germany, Dr. Malan offered to support General Hertzog in his neutrality. Exactly a quarter of a century after it had met to consider its attitude on the First World War, South Africa's Parliament met again to consider its attitude on the Second World War.

There was now a Cabinet of twelve. General Smuts, with six supporters, was for war. General Hertzog, with five supporters, was against war.

For here was a war, said General Hertzog (as a quarter of a century ago), in which the Union had not the slightest interest. If indeed the German Chancellor meant to dominate the world, said General Hertzog, then he himself would be "the most fiery" advocate for war against him. But where was the proof of it? There was not the slightest proof of it. He was not prepared, said General Hertzog, to see South Africa dragged into a war merely because there was this idea that the German people and the German Chancellor wanted to dominate the world.

He asked the House's approval of the policy he had laid before his Cabinet: "The existing relations between the Union of South Africa and the various belligerent countries will, insofar as the Union is concerned, persist and continue as if no war is being waged."

South Africa was to remain neutral.

General Smuts too spoke as he had done a quarter of a century ago.

"I am in my soul convinced that we are up against vital issues for the present and future of the country. . . . I say that it is not only a question of loyalty and self-respect. . . . It is a question of the greatest importance to South Africa. . . . Not only Great Britain, but our other friends of the British Commonwealth of Nations have declared war and severed relations with Germany, and if we dissociate ourselves markedly, conspicuously and deliberately from their policy and say Germany is our friend—if we do this, we shall get what we deserve. . . . And when the day of trouble comes, and it is bound to come—when we are faced with the demand for the return of South-West Africa at the point of the bayonet, then we shall have to say whether we are going to meet this issue alone, for our friends will be against us."

He moved an amendment to the Prime Minister's motion:

"It is in the interests of the Union that the relations with the German Reich be severed and that the Union refuse to adopt an attitude of neutrality in the conflict."

General Hertzog's motion was defeated, and General Smuts's amendment carried, by eighty votes to sixty-seven, and five absent Members later associated themselves with General Smuts.

General Hertzog resigned. The Governor-General called on General Smuts to form a government. The Union, with the rest of the Commonwealth (except Ireland), was in the war against Hitler.

General Hertzog, in Opposition after fifteen years as Prime Minister, joined Dr. Malan's Purified Nationalists. They called their party the Reunited National Party.

The Germans, and later the Italians and Japanese, conducted their affairs from Portuguese territory, as, across the seas, from Irish territory.

The Union had a permanent force of five thousand; a citizen army of thirteen thousand, with no equipment; two tanks, twelve guns, seventy planes (either trainers or obsolete); two minesweeping trawlers; nine hundred ox-drawn bushcarts, some of which were, in the end, used to remove refuse from prisoner-of-war camps. The creator of the bushcarts, the Union's Minister of Defence, was, like the Union's Commandant-General of the First World War, on the side of the Germans.

Now General Smuts was Minister of Defence as well as Prime Minister and he set about collecting an army and making munitions of war.

The Ossewa Brandwag, the offshoot of the 1938 Voortrekkers, declined (since its function was culture) to deal in politics. But it would serve, it said, where it could serve. And when, a year or so later, the Administrator of the Free State resigned his post to lead them, he demanded of his followers the abstract virtues of "discipline, constancy, patience and fortitude," but he added that, in welcoming all Afrikaners, he included National Socialists.

1940 came, and General Hertzog reiterated that there was "no proof," "not an iota of proof," that Germany wanted world domination. May 1940 came—the taking by the Germans of Norway, Luxembourg, Belgium, and Holland, and General Hertzog said: "Europe has landed itself in a terrible mess. Through the stupidity of General Smuts, we are in it too."

General Smuts spoke of the fight within, no less than without, and said: "I am going to fight Germany, and I don't care where it is, so long as it is against Germany. Some want to fight it behind this river or behind that mountain and hope to heaven the enemy is not there. But we want to fight Germany. She is the enemy of the human race. Germany is a big place to fight in."

He said this because the Union Defence Act required service only in defence of the Union. General Smuts decreed that defence of the Union meant going beyond the borders of the Union. Volunteers were called for service anywhere in Africa.

When France surrendered, General Hertzog and Dr. Malan saw "England and her Empire now fighting alone, without any support on the Continent of Europe, with poor prospects of finding new allies, and with the whole of the western coast of Europe, so near to her, in enemy hands. And General Smuts offers South Africa once again—and perhaps for the last time—on the altar of his imperialism. . . ."

General Smuts said:

"Freedom, honour and self-respect are the foundations on which we mean to build South Africa, and we shall face suffering, danger and death to save them for our people."

Those who believed in a German victory—who dreaded it, yet were not prepared to fall with a people they themselves had fought a generation ago—got ready to dissociate themselves from the falling Commonwealth and declare a Boer republic.

And suddenly General Hertzog did not want this republic. What was there in his tempestuous heart that made him suddenly not want the Boers' grail of a republic? He had passionately spoken for Germany and against England. Where now was his tossed spirit leading him?

It all had to do with this other Union of Brothers that was not General Smuts's Union of Brothers—a body that *called* itself the Band of Brothers, the Broederbond.

The Broederbond had been formed during the First World War, after the Boer Rebellion had failed, to fight to the same end—only not with the same methods: not openly; secretly. Also not with the same sort of people— men who rode horses and used warlike weapons; but with an elite of men who used pens and tongues and brains, who softly moved and softly removed, who entered high places and so worked towards the ultimate aim, a Boer republic. There were never more than three thousand five hundred Broeders.

While General Smuts was putting before the Lords and Members of the British Parliament his plan for a British

Commonwealth of Nations, the greatest possible Union of Brothers, a thing for the whole world, the Broederbond was working towards a directly opposite end: "One Folk, one land, one tongue." Its influence began to be felt in Church, State, commerce, finance, news, education, and particularly education.

It evolved a plan which it called Christian National Education—Christian meaning the three Dutch Reformed Creeds of the Afrikaners, National meaning the Afrikaners' culture.

Under this plan Afrikaans-speaking children would be separated in their schools from English-speaking children; all would be taught according to their separate creeds.

There were indeed already such schools, not only in South Africa, but throughout the world: Catholics had Catholic schools; Anglicans had Anglican schools; private English schools, requiring attendance at chapel, remained exclusively English; all sorts of missions from all sorts of countries had, according to their separate religions, their separate schools. But it seemed somehow not the same when one was compelled to do what one wanted to do.

Only non-European children would not be taught according to their eleven hundred-odd Christian creeds or the Bantu creeds of their parents. They would be taught according to the precepts of trusteeship, non-equality, and segregation. Like the natives of the Belgian Congo (who might not attend a university unless they proposed to study for the Catholic priesthood) they would be taught chiefly to work with their hands; they would not be exposed to foreign ideologies; they would not demand what natives should not demand.

Also the white children would not be exposed to these foreign ideologies—the "deadly danger," in short, of Communism.

Towards this end, they would all, when they reached the

universities, be gathered together under Christian Nationalism; the teachers and teaching would be Christian National.

For years to come, people spoke of the Broederbond without knowing altogether who were the Broederbond. Now this one was denounced as a Broeder. Now that one admitted himself a Broeder. Now here seemed the work of Broeders.

Dr. Malan was a Broeder.

General Hertzog was so far from being a Broeder that, above all things, he hated the Broederbond. Who was ruling the country—he or the Broeders?

As the years passed, it appeared, increasingly, the Broeders.

Despite his conflicting passions, General Hertzog stood fundamentally for the peace he had signed at Vereeniging; for the Union to which he was pledged; for equality between Briton and Boer in South Africa—that equality he himself had brought the Boers by fighting, from the first, for the rights of their language. He said in Parliament that it could "no longer be suffered that a secret society consisting of only one section of the people—the Afrikaans-speaking people—should sit and scheme day and night, inside the House and outside of it, to rob the other section of their rights."

When Botha died, when he wrested power from Smuts, he could have been happy but for this new dominance, this intrusion upon his leadership, of the Broederbond. Once more he was frustrated.

He struggled against the Broederbond and steadily lost the struggle. All that struggled against the Broederbond lost the struggle. A strange thing now resulted. Though both General Hertzog and the Broederbond were for neutrality, their thoughts about Germany were not alike. General Hertzog could not believe the Germans were wicked. The Broederbond could not believe the Germans would fail. They came to advocate terms with Germany.

Suddenly General Hertzog began to warn Afrikaners against a Germany that, upon victory, would utterly disregard South Africa.

There was a Nationalist Congress in November 1940. Hertzog came to it to demand the security, to protect the rights, of the English. He was not in his old age prepared, he said, to join in a policy in which these were not secured. "We still need the co-operation of the English-speaking people. We have already driven off the Jews and the coloured voters. We have made enemies of everybody. Now we are estranging people who are already united with us. This Party is heading for the desert where it will meet its death."

He resigned his leadership, his membership of the Party in the Free State. He said: "We remain Afrikaners. Let us not do anything unworthy of the nation. . . . Time will heal."

With his chief associate, he also resigned from Parliament and founded a new party—the Afrikaner Party.

Now Dr. Malan led the Reunited National Party—the Nationalist Party.

"I am tired," said General Hertzog.

Nearly a year later, brooding on his farm, he was persuaded to declare that he had been wrong about National Socialism: the reason he had said a triumphant Germany would disregard South Africa was that he feared Hitler would not treat with a democratic government. But he had now discovered, he said, that National Socialism accorded closely with the real character of the Afrikaner people, their moral and religious outlook and their inheritance as republicans. He warned the Afrikaners against the malicious, inaccurate, hostile reports about National Socialism. . . .

Who had thus persuaded General Hertzog? Who had told him that the National Socialists were so much like the Afrikaners?

There were people who thought of the Ossewa Brandwag.

For what had happened about the Ossewa Brandwag—the Sentinels of the Ox-Waggon—this body which had arisen out of the Voortrekker celebrations of 1938 and which many Boers, dreaming of a national renaissance, had joined—was that it had ceased to be merely a cultural body. Upon the success of National Socialism, it had conceived a future for South Africa in alliance with Hitler.

It now wore the Swastika and gave the Nazi salute; it held rallies, upon the model of Nüremberg, at Majuba where, sixty years before, the Boers had defeated the British; it spoke about thinking with one's blood, about *"Blut und Boden," "Sturm und Drang,"* "await the hour," "the Day." It chanted: "One God, one Faith, one Folk . . . our land, our Folk, our God." It even sang: *"Deutschland Uber Alles,"* and: *"Wir fahren gegen England."*

It mobilized a secret army and drilled at night; it had barracks, on whose doors were the names of München, Nüremberg, Danzig, Memel, other German towns, former German colonies. It had storm troopers. It attacked Jews and soldiers. It bombed buildings and disrupted communications. It aspired to take over the mines and key industries. It threatened the life of General Smuts.

By the end of 1940, the Ossewa Brandwag claimed 350,-000 adherents. General Smuts said it had swallowed the Parliamentary Opposition.

But it had not swallowed the Parliamentary Opposition, for that would have meant swallowing Dr. Malan and the Broederbond, and Dr. Malan and the Broederbond hated the Ossewa Brandwag—this pagan body of plebs that was National Socialist and not Christian Socialist; that aspired to leadership against the exclusive Broederbond; that threatened to split the Boer nation; that derided democracy and scorned Parliament.

In his own way, Dr. Malan was a democrat and he believed in Parliament.

It was because Dr. Malan so utterly disdained the Ossewa Brandwag that Ossewa Brandwags (people imagined) had gone to General Hertzog with the tale of Nazi-Boer affinity.

A year later General Hertzog was dead.

It was said of him: "Our whole people bow their heads in silent respect and homage. . . . Future generations will perhaps discover that he was the greatest Afrikaner of all time. . . . His body is dead, but his spirit lives. We will seek to find guidance through that spirit."

The newspapers wrote with sorrow of his death. The judges paid him solemn tributes in their courts. The shops and stock exchanges were shut during his interment.

He was buried, at his own sad, resentful wish, quietly, without public ceremony, on his farm.

VIII

South Africa in the War:

The year 1941:

America will spend twenty-five thousand million dollars on the total defence of Democracy. Hitler says: "I thank God the struggle against Democracy has fallen to me while I am fresh and vigorous." The Lend-Lease Bill. Headlines in the papers say: BOY KING DEFIES AXIS. " 'This means,' General Smuts says of Yugoslav Coup, 'that the Battle of the Balkans is lost to Germany.' "

The South African soldiers have long since gone beyond the borders of South Africa. They are in the north. They

have taken Abyssinia. Among them are all the races of
South Africa. Their badge is the springbok.

On his seventy-first birthday, General Smuts becomes a
British Field-Marshal and a Zulu chants:

> *Listen, you upon the mountaintops,*
> *Tell it to those below. . . .*
> *The cloud rose above the Union*
> *To hail its leaden rain upon Somaliland,*
> *Libya, Eritrea, Abyssinia,*
> *And make men wonder.*
> *He marshalled his volunteers. Springboks*
> *Answered to his call. . . . .*
> *The thunder peals over Addis Ababa. . . .*

But General Smuts talks about his soul: "Our soul is invincible." There is trouble for the body when General
Smuts talks about the soul. In fact, the Germans have
joined the Italians against the Greeks and Yugoslavs. Hitler
rides into Athens. The Swastika flies over the Acropolis.
The Germans and Italians enter Egypt. Crete falls. Anyone
can now see that Germany is going to attack Russia, and
she does. The world agrees that Russia will last six weeks
against Germany. Dr. Malan says Britain has lost the war
and South Africa's only salvation is to break with both
Britain and Smuts.

General Smuts with Mrs. Smuts visits his boys in the
north. He tells them: "You will get a more severe test here
than you had in East Africa and Abyssinia. . . . So far as I
am concerned, I will keep South Africa right."

America and Japan enter the war. The victories of Japan.

The year 1942:
In South African harbours lie warships and convoys.
Even the *Repulse* and *Prince of Wales* have rested on their
way to the Far East in Cape Town harbour; and General

Smuts has addressed the men on the *Repulse* and spoken to Admiral Phillips; and now they are all gone, dead, destroyed by the Japanese and lying on the floor of the sea.

Notices say: "Don't talk about ships and shipping." But anyone can see the great things, right there under one's eyes. People visiting the Union from Portuguese East can see them as well as anyone else. They can talk, and hear talk, about ships and shipping. They can talk, when they go back to Delagoa Bay, to the Germans, the Italians, and the Japanese. The Germans, the Italians, and the Japanese can send messages home, and messages from home can tell commanders of ships and U-boats where ships are going, where troops are moving. Many, many ships are sunk round the coast of South Africa.

Directly opposite Mozambique is Madagascar, later to be taken by British and South African forces that Axis submarines may no longer infest Mozambique Channel and dart out to sink Allied ships.

General Smuts says:

"The Indian Ocean is the key to the situation. We are the gateway to the Indian Ocean. We hold the key to victory. You can imagine what a prize the Cape must be in a world at war. I have promised our Allies to keep this country safe."

The German radio says Germany never has wanted, and does not now want, to rule South Africa. Japan says she "could not bear to see a single drop of South African blood shed."

And meanwhile Tobruk has fallen, defended by half South Africa's forces and Britain's best equipment in Africa.

"Avenge Tobruk!" General Smuts exhorts on platform and radio. "Avenge Tobruk! Avenge Tobruk!" Other South Africans bitterly say: "Redeem Tobruk!"

Yet General Smuts's forces do indeed avenge Tobruk.

The Times and the *Manchester Guardian* report that in

the last days of June the safety of Egypt hung on two threads—a few South African Air Force squadrons in Boston day bombers, and a South African infantry division with its twenty-five-pounder guns. For forty-eight hours they held Rommel's army piling up against our El Alamein positions, his shock-troop divisions, two panzer divisions, and seven supporting Italian armoured, motorized, and infantry divisions.

British armoured cars and planes helped to harass the enemy. "But, for a time, the first South African Division, under General Pienaar, sending back all men not required to fire the guns, faced the enemy virtually alone—at Pienaar's own suggestion. Auchinleck said: 'Agreed!' "

Roosevelt announces from the White House:

"United States Army, Navy and Air Forces started landing operations during the hours of darkness this morning at numerous points on the shores of North Africa."

The year 1943:

Many months are to pass before Mr. Churchill can say: "One continent clear," but by the end of January 1943 General Smuts's eyes have already moved from Africa to Europe, and he asks the House to approve of "the employment, on the basis of voluntary recruitment, of South African troops beyond the Continent. . . . It would be impossible for us, at this stage, to sit back and say: 'Africa is clear. Come home, boys!' . . . while the battle for victory is going on further north."

President Roosevelt tells the world that, in 1942 alone, America has produced forty-eight thousand military planes, fifty-six thousand combat vehicles, six hundred and seventy thousand machine-guns, twenty-one thousand anti-tank guns, ten billion rounds of small ammunition, and that the American forces are now seven millions.

South Africa began life at the same time as America. But

it has never, Union and all, been a united country and one cannot live on Fried Flag, one cannot grow great on bread-and-butter politics, there are ways in which independence is merely the saddest of dependencies—dependence on one-self alone.

Therefore South Africa has barely begun its industrial revolution. That it has begun at all is largely due to the two German wars and the genius of Hendrik Johannes van der Bijl, destined to great suffering and an early death.

Now he is able to tell of South Africa's war contribution of tens of thousands of aerial bombs, shells, grenades, land mines; scores of millions of rounds of ammunition; hundreds of thousands of tank spares; armoured cars; millions of boots; clothing, food, transport and so on which South Africa is sending the troops in the north. South Africa is also feeding and aiding the convoys going round South Africa's shores to and from the Middle and Far East. The women of the country devote themselves to the passing soldiers and sailors.

In this year an election is pending in the Union. Because the Nationalists are against Britain they are for Germany; because they are for Germany, they are against Jews. The talk about Jews, all this talk in the world excited by Hitler, puts others too in a turmoil about Jews. Even the supporters of General Smuts wonder whether it is wise for him to say: "If we allow the Jews to be destroyed, then Hitler has, after all, beaten us—morally, he has beaten us."

But he declares to the nation:

"I stand where I stood after the South African War, where I stood after 1910, when South Africa became a united country. I am still for fusion, for union, for the union of all. . . . I have carried on a long fight. The old horse runs for the last time." In 1943, he is seventy-three. It is ten years since he has begun to wonder if now—or now—may not be the last time. It is not yet the last time. . . .

Soldiers, allowed to vote from the war fronts; their cared-for families; the country's war-workers; well-paid workers in the new industries; people stirred by the war; his like-minded followers, stand together behind General Smuts and he defeats his divided opponents by a hundred and five votes to forty-three, and with Independents and the three Natives' Representatives he commands a hundred and ten votes in Parliament.

But the victory is rather over General Hertzog's party than Dr. Malan's. Dr. Malan's party is increased by two. General Hertzog's party, as he prophesied, is thrown into the desert, though not, as he prophesied, to perish altogether. Not a member of the Afrikaner Party is returned to Parliament. The Ossewa Brandwags, having offered themselves vainly to Dr. Malan, have very often, in their rage, voted for General Smuts.

At the same time, various young English-speaking South Africans have decided that there is no reason why South Africa should not, like Eire, become a republic within the Commonwealth. They feel, quite like Kruger, that South Africa is growing up and needs bigger clothes.

The year 1945 . . . the years after:

The war ends. The returned soldiers are given loans and grants of up to fifteen hundred pounds to qualify themselves in their trades and professions, to go into business or on the land. The injured and deprived receive high pensions. The cost of demobilizing and resettling South Africa's soldiers amounts in eighteen months to thirty-five million pounds.

But the new South Africa can carry it all. For South Africa has been discovered in the war. The soldiers that had her hospitality; the privileged who fear England's Socialism and hate her austerity, come, with the means they have in money or energy, to the sunshine, the luxury, the black man's service, the barely touched opportunities of South

Africa. Ships, called Debrett Ships, are laden with aristocrats fleeing as from the tumbrils of Revolutionary France. Planes are laden with them. Other people come with their cars down the unmade roads of Africa to the land of promise at its foot—the Union of South Africa. . . .

General Smuts, thinking of the fate of small countries in the war, of the difference in numbers between the black and white races of South Africa, plans a great white upthrust for South Africa. He competes with Canada and Australia for the disillusioned people of the Old World. He is not calling to the weary—creators though they may have been of the America that is now carrying Europe on her shoulders; that, with her labour and passion, is now sustaining the Democracy all but lost in the war world and still menaced in the postwar world. South Africa is not strong enough, with her two and a third or half million Europeans, to maintain the weary of the world. So it seems.

The people now coming to South Africa are those with something to give—brains, technique, training, and especially money. They buy South African land and houses, they create in South Africa industries. The price of land and houses rises threefold. General Smuts begins to think of South Africa as the great industrial nation of the continent —as the land that will sell, from the Cape to Cairo, the goods that the English, the Germans, the Americans, the Japanese used to sell.

The factories that, a few years after the First World War, were under seven thousand, employing a hundred and fifty thousand people, have risen by 1948 to eleven thousand, employing five hundred thousand people. In 1947 alone, nearly two hundred million pounds has been invested in thirty-six hundred new companies.

There are British, Dutch, French, Swedish, Americans desiring to set up industries to supply all the Africans of Africa.

General Smuts is inhibited by only one fear: too much money, hot money, escape money, is coming to South Africa. It is in the shares, banks, businesses, houses, lands, goods of South Africa. It is so dangerously raising the prices of things South African, it has to be limited; it has even sometimes to be sent away.

Dr. Malan has another sort of fear: Kruger's old fear—only he applies it to what used to be the two British colonies as well as the Transvaal Republic. His fear is that so many Englishmen will come to South Africa that never will the hope be fulfilled of making South Africa a Boer republic.

The Nationalists find in General Smuts's gay welcome to the immigrants something more than lies in the eagerness of Canada and Australia for immigrants, something beyond the question of black preponderance: these new British settlers General Smuts is bringing to South Africa are all potential Smuts voters. And Smuts, a leader in Kruger's republic, a fighter for Kruger's republic, is the last man now to wish for a republic.

It falls to South Africa to see Dr. Malan beat General Smuts; to see General Smuts's immigration plan stop at seventy-two thousand; to see these subjected to new citizenship laws that make it possible for only twenty-five thousand of them—those who arrived before September 1947 —to become citizens within the original two years' probation. The rest have to wait five years.

IX

How quickly time has gone, what miracles it has wrought! General Smuts can hardly believe he is five years older when 1948 arrives. It seems to all incredible—so gay and vital and inspiring he is, flying about the world; so proudly South African; so laden with honours, the countries can hardly think what more honours to give him, they can only exalt the land that has produced this remarkable man. The peers, the plebs, the people with the money, creative or secretive, have merely to see him to desire ardently this land, South Africa.

Jan Hofmeyr is his Deputy Prime Minister. His work lies entirely in South Africa. He is a short thickset man with a gay voice; his skin is not clear and fresh, like General Smuts's, it is yellow, it is grey, over the good bones of his face. Since his childhood, indeed, Jan Hofmeyr has not been strong, and he is not strong now. He has those troubles that go with overwork. He blithely continues, without the strength of ten, to do the work of ten.

There is a warning his party gives him: he is too devoted to the cause of non-Europeans—the Indians, the mixed-breeds, the Bantus. They remind him that 1948 is election year. They refer to the elections lost in 1924 and 1929 on the cry of colour. Hofmeyr does what he can to placate the party: he says—he feels he can say no less—that he is for Christian Trusteeship.

But everyone knows he is a Liberal. To call a man a Liberal in South Africa is like calling him a Communist in America.

And indeed the election of 1948 is fought on the principle that won the elections of 1924 and 1929. Its crisis is the Liberalism of Hofmeyr. The Nationalists stand for Apartheid—Aparthood—the separation of black and white.

The Old Horse is now seventy-eight, but he runs again. Again, as before the 1943 election, he dares to stand by the Jews. Long before England and the rest of the Commonwealth, he recognizes Israel. There are Englishmen who, because of this, vote against him.

Perhaps they would not have done so if they had imagined it would lose Smuts the election: they blame the Jews, indeed, when the election is lost. If Smuts had not recognized Israel, they say, Englishmen would not have voted against him and then he would not have lost the election.

In fact, it is not Israel or Englishmen that lose the election. It is the menace of Christian Trusteeship. The election is narrowly won by the party of Dr. Malan in agreement with the old party of General Hertzog.

As nobody doubted that General Smuts would win the election, so nobody doubts that Hofmeyr, with his Liberal colour-policy, has lost it. Opponents and friends alike declare he has lost it. He thinks himself he may have lost it. But then how far, he wonders, shall a man consider results in doing what he feels is right—even results that may shatter what he feels is right?

He tells his friends he does not care about the contumely heaped on him. He adds: "My lack of sensitiveness is a sign, no doubt, of my mediocrity."

They say there is a sound that will break a glass. The cry against him breaks the vessel which is Hofmeyr.

A month after declaring himself so insensitive Hofmeyr dies, at fifty-four, of his heart.

"But yesterday," says General Smuts, "I paid my tribute to Hennie van der Bijl. . . . Today, when we are burying him, comes the passing of Jannie Hofmeyr, that wonder-child of South Africa. . . . Happy young country that could, within a few years of each other, produce two such brilliant sons. Unhappy country which could, within two days of each other, lose them both. . . . I buried my great friend, Louis Botha, at a moment of South Africa's greatest need, and had, with my poor strength, to continue his work—I who now lose my right hand and the man I had hoped would continue my work."

He has to continue it himself. When he buried Louis Botha, he was forty-nine. In a few months, he will be seventy-nine.

.   .   .

General Smuts says of 1948 that it ends with a drought in the land that is "nothing to the drought of the spirit from which we have been suffering. . . . The war, with its dangers, anxieties and nation-wide appeal to continued effort, braced us and kept us on our guard. . . . It was followed by . . . a slipping down of spirit, a tension, a descent to a lower level in our national atmosphere. . . . Wherever we look over a grim, a bleak world scene we instinctively feel we are not yet out of the danger zone."

It is not the way he felt, six months ago, when the people and their money were rushing to South Africa and he saw South Africa as the great industrial nation of the Continent, selling its goods from the Cape to Cairo.

But yet it is the way Dr. Malan, the conqueror, feels.

For Dr. Malan, too, is old; and he is not well; and he knows there are younger men waiting their chance to go further than he, so that even his opponents pray for his health.

Therefore, like General Smuts, he says:

"In the international world dark clouds are gathering on the horizon. The human race is tired of war, and exhausted; it is praying for peace; but it seems as if an evil spirit is irresistibly dragging civilization to its doom."

General Smuts once (when he was quite young) taught Dr. Malan at Sunday School. He had been a Minister of the Church.

It would be strange if he did not feel, as they stand today, in their seventies, facing one another, a little of what General Smuts feels, a small sense of kinship.

It is now his turn to go, like Botha and Smuts and Hertzog, to Prime Ministers' Conferences in London—to dine with the King and stay with Britain's Prime Minister.

The Dominion Prime Ministers are in London to discuss the question of India's remaining, as a republic, within the

Commonwealth. One no longer says British Commonwealth, as Smuts did, when he spoke before the two Houses
of Parliament in 1917. One says Commonwealth—a Commonwealth of Nations—as Rosebery said in Adelaide in
1884.

South Africa and India are the deepest of enemies; the
Indian question in South Africa grows ever more embarrassing; but now Dr. Malan and Pandit Nehru have a pact,
they are supporting one another on the matter of being republics, and yet within the Commonwealth. And Dr. Malan says:

"We regard ourselves as being" (within the Commonwealth) "so free that no restrictions can be placed on our
free development . . . even should we decide, as a nation,
to become a republic. . . ."

He adds that the National Party is not an Isolationist
Party. It is not so stupid as to think that any country can
stand apart from all other countries and have nothing to
do with other countries of the world. As it supported the
League of Nations, so, setting aside the Big Five nations and
their veto which Russia continually uses to endanger the
world, does it support the United Nations.

Yet since it seems that, in spite of the United Nations
and the devastation of the last two world wars, another war
is not excluded; and since, for this reason, there has been
established the defensive alliance of the Atlantic Pact,
now, therefore, South Africa, for its part, is desirous of an
African Pact that shall include the European countries having possessions in Africa.

Of all countries, says Dr. Malan, South Africa, faced by
the menace of a continent of armed Africans, an Asiatic alliance, and an overflow of Asiatics on the African continent,
has most to fear from Communism.

In a war against Communism, he says, the weakest part

in the defence system of the Western Powers is the Middle East. For this reason, the Atlantic Pact needs South Africa and South Africa needs the Atlantic Pact. South Africa, says Dr. Malan, is ready to play her full part in a war against Communism.

Both sides of South Africa's Parliament cheer him. His leading opponent in the Senate says his speech will go far towards uniting South Africa.

A Nationalist Senator brings the subject to earth again. He says that, whatever the Opposition chooses to think of the Prime Minister's remarks about the Commonwealth, his party stands for a republic.

The year is 1950. It is the year—May 24 is the day—of General Smuts's eightieth birthday. At the end of the month he is due to fly to England, as Chancellor of Cambridge University, to confer degrees.

What shall South Africa do about General Smuts's eightieth birthday?

Since his defeat in 1948 General Smuts has had no house to live in during the Parliamentary sessions in Cape Town. His home is the same old corrugated iron house in Pretoria he has had since Union. In Cape Town he lives in a hotel, and he is not the sort of man that can live in a hotel. He is the sort of man that needs an outside to his house. His followers of the Cape therefore arrange to give him, for his eightieth birthday, a house on a slope of Table Mountain. He speaks of his gratitude, but he says to one: "A house? But I am a transient, a ghost."

Other towns decide to give him gifts. He is to be made—no, not the first, but the third—freeman of Johannesburg City—he, who has the freedom of so many cities, the degrees of so many universities, so many orders, so many honours, that he cannot at all say the number of them.

His birthday itself is to be celebrated in three of the Union's provinces—in Johannesburg and Pretoria; in Cape Town; in Durban.

But has not the Union four provinces? Why no celebration in the fourth province?

In the fourth province, the Free State, General Smuts has only one Parliamentary follower, the son of ex-President Steyn. And, as General Smuts's eightieth birthday is not going to be honoured by the nation, but only by his party, therefore no celebration in the Free State.

Since the end of 1949, General Smuts has had a pressure on the sciatic nerve which has given him, he says, the greatest pain he has ever known. He cannot sleep, he cannot sit. The festivities of his birthday are to begin in Johannesburg on the day before, the 23rd. On that day Johannesburg has its first winter frost.

He drives through the streets without a hat or coat and stands up to speak to the multitude. He speaks outside and inside the City Hall. He arrives, limping, at the banquet in the City Hall and sits staring, in pain, before him, and turns for a moment to whisper: "They have not given me a minute's rest. They are killing me."

On the balcony of the City Hall there is a dais, shaped like a birthday cake, with eighty giant electric candles. Still without hat or coat he goes, after the banquet, to speak to the people outside.

Four days later the newspapers are full of Smuts's illness. He has, one upon another, pneumonia and a coronary thrombosis; he has a mysterious temperature that turns out, in the end, to be the malaria he has continually had since the German-East campaign of 1915; he has influenza; he has his sciatica; he falls over a radiator and badly burns himself; he has blackouts and, confused, says he must see Churchill—again and again, over nearly four months, he is thought to be dying and he does not die.

And then there is Dr. Malan's complete victory in South-West Africa; the final knowledge that he will never lead the country again; the accumulated knowledge that all he has worked for his life through (a Jewish state apart) has failed. There is no brotherhood in South Africa; there is no brotherhood in the world. . . .

An activity comes on him which seizes people before they die. On the night of September 11 he suddenly dies.

Dr. Malan hears the news at a Nationalist Party Congress. He covers his face with his hands and weeps.

Later he speaks of "the shocking event." He says words that would have eased Smuts's agonized heart to know. He says Smuts's place cannot be filled. He tells of his intellect, will, energy, endurance—his life as a student, thinker, warrior, party-leader; statesman; leader in the Boer War; leader in the two great wars; his work in unifying South Africa, in the League of Nations and the United Nations. He calls him a great historic figure. South Africa's wealth, he says, lives not only in gold and diamonds but in men like Smuts "who, by their personal qualities and deeds, are able to leave, deep and indelible behind them, their footprints in the sands of time and of their own country's history. . . ."

It may be that, of all people in the world, Smuts's bitterest opponent most bitterly feels his death.

Part

T W O

CHAPTER SIX

The Afrikaners (Dutchmen, Boers)

I

IT may be said the fate of South Africa was written the day the first man in the world stood erect in the land that, two hundred years ago, became the country of the Bechuanas.

But, in the days of our history, the fate of South Africa has fallen upon us from Europe. It came with the first adventurers from Portugal and Holland. It came with the Huguenots of France; with the French Revolution; with the battle between Napoleon and the world and England guarding the Cape against Napoleon—nominally, on behalf of the House of Orange and the hated Dutch East India Company, but, profoundly, on the world's side in the wars of Napoleon.

So, in 1795, began the enmity of Boer against Briton which led to the Boer's continuance of their trekking that had begun in the days of the Dutch East India Company; which led to the Great Trek of the eighteen-thirties—the Trek of the Voortrekkers; which led to England's pursuing authority over the trekkers—even into the new lands across the Mountains of Snow and Dragons, the rivers Orange and Vaal—the lands of Natal, the Orange Free State, and Transvaal. . . .

Diamonds and gold were found, the fortune-hunters

came, Rhodes came. To the borders of the new lucky lands the desirous Germans came, that were never henceforth to allow the two earlier nations to unite in peace.

To make a home in the new free lands were Jews, escaped from the pogroms of Russia; a few British and German Jews came with the other hunters after diamonds and gold.

Indians, engaged as indentured labourers by the sugar planters of Natal, brought their families, brought their followers.

There were the Cape People, a new nation: the fruit of white men and the Malay and Hottentot women of the Cape.

There were the overriding black men, driving and driven.

Youth, as everyone admits, is rebellious. It is not as original as it thinks itself, nor as inspired: for it slavishly follows the current fashion, and that which ends as principle begins, very often, as pose.

And so, in Europe today, inherited privilege is poorly defended, and questing young men become Socialists or, it may be, Communists.

But in South Africa today it is difficult for a man to be a Socialist or Communist. In South Africa he is faced at once with a situation which neither precedent nor imagination can overcome. He is brought up against the problem of the Kaffir—the native, the Bantu, the African, as the black man has variously been called in South Africa.

Indeed, the Socialist or Labour man—the sort of man who would be supporting the Socialist or Labour government in England, is in an impossible position in South Africa. For it is his plight that he must specifically act against the interests of the very people who, no less now than in Trollope's time, are the real workers of the land. The Revolution of

1922 had chiefly to do with the Labour man's horror of the black man as an equal or associate.

The natives do nearly all the unskilled work in the land. Legislation excludes them from competing with the skilled whites.

So, in the mines, they, and not the white miners, work on the stoeps. On the farms they, and not the farmers, do the planting and reaping and breeding. They pass the bricklayer his bricks and the plumber his pipes. They dig the trenches, they mix the concrete, they lay the roads.

They collect the refuse, and deliver the milk, the meat, the groceries, the papers, the parcels from the shops. If they do not come in a van, they ride on bicycles with slips of paper they cannot read, looking for addresses they cannot find. Long before daylight, they are at the housework. Every time a South African steps on a ship to go overseas, it is a shock renewed to see a white man cleaning basins, scrubbing floors. It gives him a sense of shame to find, in England or on the Continent, a white woman washing a doorstep. A white South African has to be poor indeed not to keep his Kaffir. An Indian selling fruit or flowers has his Kaffir. The first thing a European gets in South Africa is a Kaffir. There is probably not an avowed Communist in the country who hasn't his Kaffir, even if he does call him an African or, in embarrassment, "the slave."

Nor does he pay him more than the customary wage. It is, indeed, the capitalist who pays the native a fair wage, since he is generally richer (though not always) than the Communist.

So when, in South Africa, the Socialist or Labour man speaks of a chance for all alike, he does not mean—he cannot mean—the black man of the land.

For if he did, where would he himself be?

Therefore he is bewildered and, being a divided man in

his own conscience, he cannot hold together a political party. All he can do is support trade unions and adhere to this or that more or less liberal Parliamentary grouping.

It is, then, not towards Socialism the young South African tends. Even the backveld Boer who has long since replaced the Cornishman on the mines—even he, especially he—is not a supporter of Labour or Socialism. Today the official Labour Party supports Smuts. But the Labour Party that, in 1924, joined Hertzog had not a Boer name among its Parliamentary Members, as General Hertzog's Nationalist followers had not an English name: except, that is, a British name accepted by the Boers, like Smith, Murray, Conroy, Ross. Today there is a Boer Mine-Workers' Union that specifically supports the Nationalist Party. In short, the South African of Boer descent, with the spirit of youthful revolt in him, votes Nationalist.

The description of what used to be the Boer or Dutchman is now the Afrikaner. Actually, if one speaks to men who fought the Boer War (which is, in these days, decently called the South African War) they say wistfully that of all names they have borne or could think of, they love best the homely name, meaning farmer, under which they fought for their freedom. It may be modern to say Afrikaner, but they love it, it smoothes their romantic old hearts, to call themselves Boers.

There are other Afrikaners who speak of all white South Africans being Afrikaners together. But it seems doubtful whether English-speaking South Africans will call themselves Afrikaners; and, if they translate the word into Africans, then this of course makes them black men. So all they can do is to use the term English-speaking South Africans.

When Smuts, addressing the two Houses of the British Parliament, said: "I think the very expression 'Empire' misleading, because it makes people think as if we were one entity, one unity"; when he then preferred to "Empire" the term "British Commonwealth of Nations," he added: "I think the man who would discover the real appropriate name for the system of entities would be doing a service, not only to this country, but to constitutional theory."

The real appropriate name is now being used—simply Rosebery's "Commonwealth of Nations," which opens the way to all nations. Smuts's own countrymen, however, remain without a national name. They have no name which embraces them all. Here is another reason why they are not unified.

The official name of the country is the Union of South Africa. Whether white people like them or not (though useful all find them) there are black men in South Africa. But they cannot be called South Africans, for this would make white men of them. The Indians, whether of Pakistan or Hindustan, remain Indians (except to those who, wishing to insult them, call them Coolies). The Jews, whose blood-brothers are Israelis, are generally classed with English-speaking South Africans, even though many use Afrikaans as their home language. The mixed bloods are called Bastaards, except in the Cape where they are called the Cape coloured people, or simply the Cape People. The Afrikaners call the Cape People, officially, Kleurlinge (Coloureds); but they sometimes call them Hottentots, which they pronounce Hodnots. This the Cape People find highly offensive, though they do have Hottentot blood in them. On the other hand, the Hottentots the first Dutchmen found in the Cape were known to them as the Cape People: so that, originally, the names Hottentot and Cape People were interchangeable.

In these pages the Bantus are called, according to the time, circumstances, and official mode, Kaffirs or Natives or Africans. The members of the nation described by General

Hertzog as "the older population" are, similarly, called Boers or Afrikaners. The mixed breeds are, according to the general style of the country, called Coloureds or, sometimes, half-castes. The other peoples have names that adequately define them.

One has to note how the political and patriotic fashion has changed.

The Boer, before the Boer War, was not particularly proud of his nationality; and, though he did not love the Englishman, he stood in awe of him.

Nor was the Boer encouraged to self-respect by his English neighbour. And the same thing happened to the Boer as, until the resurgence of Israel, happened to the Jew. He was made to feel unhappily conscious of his ancestry. And, equally, he could escape his discomfort in only two ways: either by shunning his despiser, or by shunning that in himself which was despised. The Boer did not begin to brood, in those days, over the possibility of despising his despiser. At most, he dreamt of revenge.

Then came the Boer War. And though, in the Cape, there remained people adhering to the English side of things, whose Dutch names meant no more to them than the Dutch names of the American Knickerbockers, in the Transvaal and Free State, boys of fifteen were swept into battle and a sense of race.

In later years, some of these boys were the men who, with their white-bearded elder brothers, rode out from their farms and villages to meet General Smuts when he came back to them from the affairs of the great world. Then he mounted a horse, and they turned homeward and he rode with them.

But some, again, could not forgive him for forgiving the Boer War and going into the great world and becoming a leader in it and not only their particular leader; and they

preferred to join the young people who had not fought in
the Boer War but upon whom had descended the consciousness that one white race alone had ever shed Boer
blood and that, for Empire's sake, the British race. And the
greater, therefore, Britain's Empire became, the more their
passion grew against England. They clung to Germany, so
they said, not for Germany's sake, but "to break the over-
weening pride of British Imperialism which had crushed
their national independence by guile and by force."

The Englishman, meanwhile, became aware that the
Boer had ceased to regard him with awe. Most naturally he
regretted it and desired once more to be thought a fine fellow. As the Boer stepped back, he stepped forward.

A few years after the Boer War came England's consent
to General Smuts's request for Responsible Government for
the old republics. Union followed. England, having done
something noble, glowed in the warmth that accompanies
magnanimity. It contemplated the Boers with the sentimen-
tal air we bend upon our beneficiaries. Generals Botha and
Smuts became heroes in England. In South Africa, young
Englishmen in the schools and colleges began to make a
point of using an occasional Boer idiom—apart from the
fact that (through General Hertzog's doing) it was now
officially and commercially desirable to be bilingual. In England people gave South Africa as an example of England's
genius for making friends of her enemies. And, concerning
this amity in South Africa, General Smuts said, thirty-five
years after Union, that "the story of South Africa this
whole period is one of the highlights of history."

The Boer, however, his pride awakened by his upward
spring, was both cautious and somewhat arrogant. The
First World War found him divided between an inclina-
tion to respond to the new spirit of English brotherliness
and a suspicion of it. He expressed his uncertainty by fight-

ing with England in Africa and France, and by striking again for independence in the Union. Now the young Boer no longer admired, as twenty years ago, the Englishman. He met him, without awe, as an equal.

When General Hertzog formed his National Party, young Free State, without qualification, supported him. It was presently joined by the victims of the Rebellion, by the reaction, the depression, that followed the war. General Smuts was swept out with other institutions of the past. Young Boers on the Rand, young workingmen, became not Labour but Nationalist. In their universities there was a spirit of Afrikanerdom (as one now called it) abroad; and often it was a spirit of exclusive Afrikanerdom.

Undergraduates began to speak with enthusiasm of the flexibility, the sonority, the literary adequacy of that Afrikaans language which, by natural growth and conscious development, had now completely overridden the High Dutch of Church and State.

The new language had a simpler grammar than the old; but in other ways it was not so simple. It developed increasingly a sort of public-school style, a vocabulary, an accent, that overwhelmed people brought up in the old Boer tongue. They often could not understand (old Boers confessed) the smart new Afrikaans language. They lightened, they brightened, when they heard the old folk songs in the old Boer language, when they told one another their Bill Rogers type of joke, for which one absolutely needed a homely language.

At the University of Pretoria, Afrikaans became presently the sole medium; the students refused to affiliate with the students of English-speaking universities; they demanded the exclusion of English professors and, at their meetings, they flew the old republican flags of the Transvaal and Free State, but not the flag of Britain or even the flag of the Union. By 1950, there were four Afrikaans-speaking universities which excluded non-Europeans. There were four English-speaking universities that admitted non-Europeans —one in separate buildings, though also with the sort of food for Indians that their religion required. The separation grew.

On tables, on bookshelves, in Afrikaners' homes, rested the new Afrikaans Bible; novels and verses in Afrikaans that received an almost holy appreciation.

On walls hung the paintings of Afrikaners that followed contemporary trends. . . .

In three hundred years in Africa, the Boers have not achieved any work of the highest art. Yet there certainly is a Boer renaissance, and out of this ferment may spring such work. The writings—chiefly the lyrics—of several Afrikaner poets, the books also of two Afrikaner naturalists, have quality. The novels, in a land remarkable for its English-writing novelists, have not. The novels, nevertheless, together with the other writings in the new language, are the classics of their day. Through them, children, students, the nation, learn the new language. They have to. How else?

But, indeed, they glory in their own art. It is possible to find a university graduate claiming that the Afrikaans poets are the greatest the world has known—the whole world, the whole time; to read in a school examination paper a request for a comparison between various embarrassed Afrikaner artists and Michelangelo, da Vinci, and Rembrandt.

Far now is the Afrikaner from the Boer who was shy of the nationality he yet defended with his blood. Now he flaunts his Afrikanerdom as if it were not merely a shield, but a gay keen weapon, and his aggressive prancing disturbs the English-speaking South African who cannot, in his declining position, allow for the ardour of the new spirit and thinks sadly of that quiet courtliness he failed to appreciate in time.

·   ·   ·

The Second World War came, and the new Boer saw only a struggle between England and Germany—England the perennial foe, Germany the perennial friend—in word, if not in deed. To him, therefore, it did not mean what it meant to the rest of the democratic world that England, for a year, solitarily defended that world. He refused to believe in a Nazi cruelty unthinkable among Boers themselves. Against all fact, argument, and reason, he compared the Nazi concentration camps with the concentration camps of the Boer War.

II

What sort of a person is the South African who has some French and German blood, but is mainly of Dutch descent? Does he resemble the Hollander who came with van Riebeeck in 1652?

It may be said at once that, just as the Hollander has been moulded by the physical characteristics of his country, so has the Afrikaner.

In Holland there are nine and a half million people living in an area which might comfortably spread itself on rather less than five per cent of one of the Union provinces. In Holland there are nearly seven hundred people to the square mile. In Holland the highest mountain is little more than a thousand feet above sea level, and a quarter of the land is below sea level. In Holland one may go from one end of the country to the other on water, and water is the powerful insidious enemy that has to be held at bay for very life's sake.

The Union is nearly four hundred and seventy-four thousand square miles big, and it accommodates five white people to the square mile. Huge mountain ranges traverse it. Its physical problems are the conquest of space and drought. Where the Hollander, jostling against hundreds of other Hollanders on his little square mile, works and works and works for life, and tries to push the sea away, the South African Dutchman, discovering four other white beings settled within a mile of him, thinks how crowded the country is getting, and worries about his water rights.

He has as much space and air and sunshine as a man can use; he has at hand a dark people made, it seems to him, by God to save him the hardest physical effort, and he stretches his limbs, and moves at his leisure, and waits for the seasons to wind themselves off the reel of time.

The light and warmth have made him big in bone and muscle. The unrestrained spaces have developed in him a passion for freedom—at least for himself. The companionship of nature has awakened in him a vague poetry which moves him towards the desolate earth, indeed, desolation. And, if the Hollander has developed an obstinate strength through his constant struggle against water and a crowding humanity, the Boer has developed an obstinate strength through his constant struggle against drought and his knowledge of loneliness.

The virtues, however, which his circumstances have engendered in him are counterbalanced by defects. To his isolation he owes not only his love of liberty, but also a certain narrowness of outlook; not only his hospitality, but also an evasive suspiciousness. If to be placed beyond the reaches of comparison gives a man a dignified serenity, it deprives him, very often, of an intellectual grace. Observing around him neither superiors nor inferiors, the Boer has the outlook of an aristocrat, but on the other hand he has, too, a limited idea of his own position in the world.

One might continue at length to show how the conditions of his life have moulded the character of the Boer, and yet one could never be accurate, for conditions and their influence are not always the same, and, like the people of other nationalities, Boers vary.

There are, for instance, those who are called backvelders.

They have been described as if they were a peculiar growth, but, in fact, a backvelder is simply a person living out of range of urban civilization. There are backvelders all over Europe. There are backvelders in England and America. One may meet, in casual travel through countries highly developed, people much meaner in intelligence and outlook than an ordinary Cape Coloured person; and South Africans who, during the First World War, shared German prison-life with Russians (Czarist Russians, let it be emphasized) thought them more crushed than the South African natives, even though the Russians have a genius that has penetrated their utmost degradation.

That the backvelder may, in certain circumstances, be a person deficient in morals or manners is, of course, true enough. If he lives on the veld, out of reach of trains, out of touch with education and educated opinion; if he knows nothing, hears nothing, is told nothing, obviously he will be undercivilized—like any other of the world's backvelders. A man who has only nature to instruct him has a poor guide to those qualities which arouse our trained admiration. None of those virtues we extol—not *esprit de corps*, nor self-sacrifice, nor honesty, nor chivalry, nor generosity, nor sympathy, nor gratitude, nor self-restraint—are instincts. Instincts are those gross characteristics—those irrational compulsions—we spend our lives in trying to overcome. . . .

In one respect, however, the South African backvelder is different from any other kind of backvelder. He is never the lowest in the land. So far is he from the subservience of the European backvelder that, on the contrary, he is always someone's "baas." Whatever he may be, the white man—any kind of white man—merely because he is white, is baas, is boss, master, to the black man. One's black servant will speak of the baas who is begging at the door, of the baas who stole the broom. He will assuage the beggar, he will apprehend the thief, and address each, in doing so, as "Baas."

To three quarters of the humanity in South Africa, then, every backvelder is an aristocrat. But just this aristocracy is his ruin.

There is in South Africa a class of person called a "poor white." There is a corresponding class in America, and its origin is the same.

A poor white is someone of European extraction who cannot support himself according to a European standard of civilization, who cannot keep clear the line of demarcation between black and white.

A Carnegie Commission, sponsored by the Dutch Reformed Church, found in 1932 that twenty-two per cent of the white population of the Union might be classed as poor white; and another thirty-four per cent as economically below normal: unable, that is, without government assistance to clothe, feed, house their families or educate their children.

By the time of the Second World War, it was thought that twenty-five per cent of the white population of the Union was poor white—unemployed or unemployable. Yet not necessarily degenerate. Men doing field work among them while the Commission sat found that the intelligence of the poor white children on the backveld was actually above the average: perhaps because they had to be self-dependent.

The Second World War, that drew many backvelders for the fun and money of it and paid their people at home more in a month than they normally got in a year, did much to civilize them. Then there were the war industries that employed them. Then, after the war, there was work for everybody.

Now, as elsewhere, there is no longer work for everybody and so poor whites will be created again.

This is, very often the genesis of the poor white:

In the old days a man could have practically all the land he wanted for little more than the asking. There was enough of it and it belonged to nobody in particular. In the days of the Dutch East India Company the rental for six thousand acres was five pounds a year.

So, as he went trekking along, the Boer settled himself on six thousand or twelve thousand or twenty-four thousand acres of land; and this was his farm. He built on it a house of unburnt brick with a roof of thatch; he fenced in a yard; he built a kraal for the cattle that grazed on the land; he dug a well; he planted as much as he could manage. Then, when he got tired of the Dutch East India Company or their English successors and wanted new grazing-land, he moved further and further from the Cape and its governors; and where he settled was his land; and then, because he had settled there, it was his nation's land.

Well, that trekker became a patriarch. He had a large family, and most of his children remained with him at the homestead. When he died the land was parcelled out among them, for there is no system of primogeniture in South African law. According to the common law of the country, there is community of property between husband and wife. In practice, a mutual will is made which leaves the survivor in possession and enjoyment of the property. On the death of the survivor it is equally divided among the children. . . .

On these subdivided portions the children, in turn, begat large families. And, again, death and inheritance broke up the estate.

By this time the man who had not fitted himself to be a town-dweller, or who had not learnt the science of agriculture, could not make a living on his strip of ground. And still, owing to the presence and cheapness of the Kaffir, he had never acquired the habit of labour. Now he could no longer afford to be an employer, nor was he trained to be a worker. Occasionally he compromised by settling on someone else's land and acting as a kind of superintendent in return for the privilege of using the farm also for his own purposes. He was then called a *bywoner*—literally, a co-dweller.

But still one could find a white man from the land, living in a room, a yard, among natives and Asiatics, without money, without a trade, unable to command a white man's wages, unable to live on a black man's wage. And, living so, the distinction between coloured and white could not be maintained. The descendant of the aristocratic landowner was, in short, become a poor white.

Living in the same yard, there might be an Englishman, come to South Africa before the dole and the Second World War, without money or training or capacity, because in South Africa, he had heard, there was no need to work: one simply picked up the gold and diamonds. He too was now a poor white. And the children bred by poor whites, from women of all colours, in their turn (if they turned out to be white at all) were poor whites. And these poor whites would be seekers after relief, charity, or casual opportunity, but yet sheltered under the banner of the white man's pride.

III

Among the backvelders, then, are those who have been overwhelmed by the spaces of Africa and enervated by the use of the black man.

But there are others who have conquered themselves and the land and who are in the position European landlords once had. As in other parts of the world, too, they have a strong hold on any government. Always the farmer has to be placated. One might, of course, regard him as a sort of civil servant, whose pay takes the form of reliefs and subsidies. But in South Africa there is quite peculiarly the matter of his vote. No politician would today dare tell the story (as Smuts did forty years ago) of the old man who discovered a really serious drawback to farming in the Transvaal: "The ground is too low. You have to bend your back to work," or answer the question if he understood what was needed in farming: "Yes. Sweat."

In the Second World War, while the government was taking fourteen of the twenty million pounds real profit earned by the mines, it was paying the farmers seven and a half millions in subsidies—the difference between South Africa's and the world's price for their products.

Of this money a third was given to the wealthy sugar-farmers of Natal who, in their persistent greed, had brought upon the country its Indian question, yet held autocratic power in Natal; and the rest to the country's wheat, grain, and dairy farmers whom, for all that, General Smuts's party could not win. "No control," said a commission in 1940, "was exercised to avoid inefficiency. . . . Unhealthy farming practices" were accentuated. The help given to sugar and maize farmers persuaded them to produce more, and the more they produced, the more it cost the government in subsidies.

At the same time, the South African farmers do, remotely, follow modern ways; they have, increasingly, the right machinery; they have cars even when they escape taxes; their children take agricultural courses and bring home new ideas.

There are, mentally and temperamentally, two kinds of Afrikaners.

One kind reveres learning, is solid and thorough rather than agile and swift; his patient exhaustive brain fits him peculiarly for the law (in this case, the Roman-Dutch Law, inherited from Holland where, since Napoleon's time, it is no longer practised) and the legal system and tradition in South Africa are as highly developed as any in the world. He occupies many academic posts. He has ability as a doctor or engineer. It seemed at one time strange that the descendants of the merchant adventurers of Holland should have so little capacity for commerce. It appears, however, to have been only a traditional adherence to the land that once tied him to the disintegrating life of the stoep. Now the Boer has money and he understands the affairs of money; he begins to trade and manipulate.

Strangely, it is not the Boer—whose name means farmer—that is the best farmer in South Africa. It is, first, the Jew, and then the Englishman. When the Boer calls himself farmer, he should rather say landowner. That at least he used to be, more than a worker of the soil.

The Afrikaner becomes, almost too readily, a teacher or civil servant. He is, by disposition and habit, a politician: the English have largely lost their influence in South Africa because they have not that absorbed passion for politics which inflames, it seems, every Afrikaner's heart. The Dutch Reformed pulpits are the rostrums of men trained in local colleges and seminaries. Where the clergy of other Churches are generally imported from overseas, so that they can never quite adapt themselves to the unique conditions of the country, the Afrikaans predikants, born of the soil, have extreme power over their flocks—social and political bound up with spiritual.

That is one kind of Afrikaner.

The other kind is brighter, sharper, passionate for the arts, no less a politician, a swifter rebel, an easy cosmopolitan.

Both kinds are, in looks, barely to be distinguished from

the South African of British descent. The backveld Boer—even the poor white (such is the potency of the land)—is no less big and handsome than the privileged Boer. That the Boer is so big and heavy probably explains why his game is rugby football. It is seldom cricket or tennis or golf. When the British M.C.C. came in 1948 to play South Africa in cricket there was only one Boer name—of olden days—in the South African team. When the New Zealanders came to play South Africa football in 1949, there were in the principal test matches thirteen Afrikaners and two Jews. English South Africans have recently won first places in world tennis and golf events: no Afrikaner even entered the matches.

Socially, the Afrikaner is not at all inhibited. Until lately any white man was his equal. Through the nineteenth century, no casual white traveller on the veld needed to hesitate before a Boer homestead. He was welcome to enter and join the family. The members of the family would, one after the other, trail past him, slipping into his grasp a characteristically limp hand; and he might eat with them, and sleep with them, and find with them accommodation also for his beast, his conveyance, and his Kaffir. And there would be no self-consciousness in his reception; no agitated striving to impress; no embarrassment over any inadequacy.

The spirit of the veld came with the countryman to the town. He met the important person without diffidence and the inconsequent person without pride. His manner, especially towards the old, was comforting and courteous. So Paul Kruger was Oom Paul, the uncle of his nation. So Mrs. Smuts became Ouma Smuts, the nation's grandmother.

The best-bred Boers have still that old simplicity. General Smuts extended, to any guest he had the time to see in his corrugated iron house, the hospitality he himself so naturally received from the world's princes and premiers; he extended the hospitality that any guest received—no more —to the princes and premiers that visited him. At the Prime Minister's official home in Pretoria, two rooms, reserved for a valet and maid, were what General and Mrs. Smuts chose to take for themselves. J. H. Hofmeyr, with his overwhelming brain, addressed his mother, with Boer deference, in the third person. And, again, if this brain awed lesser men into something like anger, the simplicity that went with it made him Hoffie to boys in holiday camps.

Not long ago there died in Hofmeyr's constituency an old Boer, a wealthy butcher, who every Christmas celebrated his Christianity by inviting all, black and white, to come and feast with him. And, among the hundreds who came to his unparalleled entertainment, was Jan Hofmeyr in a matching humanity. . . .

A fuller civilization has now begun to wear down the courtliness of the ordinary Boer. The departure of the patriarchal mode has dimmed his reverence for his elders. Too much contact with his fellows has brought a limit to that hospitality which, when calls on it were not so frequent, could be exercised without restraint.

Ideas of form and status have entered his head. He is no longer so ready to extend his slack hand and courtly welcome to any stranger, saying confidently and confidingly, as if he were offering the honours of the world to a traveller from another planet: "Ek is van Aardt"—"I am van Aardt" (of the earth, that might mean) or whatever else he happens to be called. He has learned, through a fuller civilization, that a man must be introduced and have credentials.

He has not, through a fuller civilization, learnt to change his attitude towards his dark-skinned neighbour. Today, almost as an instinct of nature, the white South African is hostile to the black. Children of English parentage born in the Free State or Transvaal—for that matter, in Rhodesia, Nigeria, or any other African territory—are not less Negrophobe than children of Afrikaans parentage. In the Cape there is a tradition of a humane, and at least politically equal, treatment of the black or coloured person. In Natal the attitude is quite like that of the southern United States; and more in Natal than anywhere else do the white people speak the language of the black—that is, in Natal, the Zulus.

The sentiment that, in general, the South African has about colour—whether consciously or unconsciously—is that which once spurred the exodus of the Voortrekkers: God made the black man different from the white man, and it was against nature to deny that difference. The modern man may not, like his ancestor, find his justification in the Bible: "Cursed be Canaan, a servant of servants shall he be to his brethren," but he cannot help feeling that the native hardly belongs to the same order of creation as the white man. If he goes here beyond the Bible, which does use the word "brethren" of the children of Ham, his colour prejudice has still something almost religious about it.

He positively believes it his duty to humanity and civilization to uphold the difference between the children of Ham and Shem. Apartheid—Apart-hood—is the cry of General Smuts's opponents. But General Smuts, no less than Dr. Malan, was intent on maintaining this "outpost of white civilization." Nor would Apartheid prove so profitable an election call for Dr. Malan, if the Boer did not, from his heart, want it.

He wants most deeply to have, and not to have, the Kaffir. This courtliness the Boer shares with the Virginian is bred of the ease and lordship that comes of having slaves.

The Prussian used to address his servant in the third person, as if he were speaking to him (so inferior he was, one could not acknowledge his physical presence) through some ghostly intermediary.

The white man of the southern United States was amiable, so one hears, to his slaves; the Little Father of All the Russias, if he happened to be a good Little Father, was patriarchally kind to his serfs; the feudal lord of England was dutiful and charitable to his valets and varlets. The Boer, too, is genial to his Kaffirs.

Yet the root of all these relationships is the same: if one does not, in the Prussian way, ignore the very presence of an inferior, one still maintains the position of owner and chattel. And with the Boer the chattel is less human than with the Russian or the Briton for the same reason as in the southern States: there is the extreme difference created by colour. There exists, besides, a past of fighting and fear —fear in the past, fear for the future—that has no counterpart anywhere else.

The Boer began by having real slaves and servants that were in the position of slaves. When the Hottentots and Bushmen died of their liberty, there were, for servants, the half-castes—the Cape People—bred through them. After the Boer, fighting the Kaffirs for his life, beat them he had his Kaffir servants; and the attitude of the Kaffirs was that the conqueror commands.

It is with less excuse the newcomer to South Africa often sheds, in Africa, the ideal of fair treatment which holds in the country he came from. Quite soon he catches the prevailing infection of racial arrogance; and, at the same time, his attitude is not qualified by either experience or understanding. Thus it happens that, in practice, the Boer often treats the native better than the Englishman. And, apart even from this matter of experience and understanding, the Boer, being less class-conscious, will (without prejudice) chat with his native servant, take a personal interest in him, as an Englishman, despite Socialism, still class-conscious, cannot bring himself to do.

Even when the Englishman is strong enough in spirit to maintain his national tradition of justice, the difference remains that which once existed between the northern and southern United States. The Northerners fought for the rights of the Negroes, but the Southerners had an affectionate intimacy with their Negroes not customary among their more highly principled countrymen.

Which should the black man prefer: the justice of the state or the condescension of the individual? Undoubtedly the justice of the state—the right, and not the favour.

CHAPTER SEVEN

The English

THE ENGLISH South African is not quite the same sort of person as his brother in England. And, indeed, one may distinguish the Englishman in three ways: according to whether he is at home, abroad, or born on the soil of a dominion.

The Englishman at home is a most attractive being. There has never been a Boer Prime Minister he has not charmed into a benignity quite unwelcome to his brooding brothers in South Africa. The Prime Ministers go to conferences in London; they are secretly smitten with the beautiful island, its ancient treasures, its hospitality, its style; and, back home in South Africa, it takes real hard work to get them again into the proper mood of traditional hostility.

The Englishman, indeed, is kinder to the stranger (accredited) than to his fellow Englishman. The reason for this is that the Englishman is clever and he fears boredom. The social life of England is largely based on this fear. A stranger will soon go away; one will not for long be afflicted with him and so one can afford to be kind to him. But the man next door—now he is dangerous: he can so easily prove a bore, unendurable, inescapable—one has to be very careful with the man next door.

When it comes to neighbours, the Englishman prefers

the Old Testament to the New. Not "Love your neighbour" is his heart's theme, but "Let thy foot be seldom in thy neighbour's house, lest he weary of thee and hate thee."

Or the other way about.

The Englishman abroad is reputedly a bore to other people: it is said he regards them in their own lands as uncivilized foreigners. But it is not this Englishman who is being considered here. It is the Englishman, come on his own behalf, or his country's, to live in a distant land. This is the man who is supposed to be the genius of the British Empire: he knows instinctively how to handle inferior peoples, how to make them love and respect him, both together.

But the truth is that he can only handle them as long as they feel themselves inferior. The moment they do not, they cannot tolerate the conduct that is based on the belief in their inferiority; and off drops another bit of Empire.

There was a time when the Englishman who came to South Africa completely changed his character so that his nationality stuck out of him like the quills of a porcupine. He lost the smooth and genial charm of the Englishman at home, and disported himself with an assertiveness that not only emphasized the difference between himself and the man he called a Colonial, but that was haughtily meant to emphasize this difference. He was as deliberately an Uitlander—an Outlander—in the Union as, long ago, in Kruger's Transvaal; and the real South African, even of English descent, resented it. At root he had a sincere admiration for the Englishman. He might not acknowledge it, but, regarding the matter judicially, and comparing the English with this nation and with that, and seeing perfection nowhere, he could not but help coming to the reasoned conclusion that, after all, no other race was finer. . . .

Nevertheless, he had a quite human objection to being considered anything but the Englishman's equal; nor did he like to be thought of as a Colonial—a little brother—a term now generally applied to the coloured races.

To himself he was not a little brother: he was a citizen of the British Empire of South African nationality. He did not care—although he tried to correct it—to be told he had a Colonial accent. He did not admit—although they were in fact his model—that English customs were superior to his own. He did not like to hear England called "home" as if South Africa was exile. He would not, in short, be patronized. And instinctively, and defensively, he clung to his fellow South African, whatever his ancestry.

The South African of English descent was, indeed, feeling himself quite at home with the South African of Boer descent—when he found himself checked by a bewildering discovery—the Afrikaner was putting on airs towards him!

What, dramatically, had happened (a taste of what was beginning to happen throughout the world) was that the Afrikaner had come to appreciate the significance of his numbers in the Union: the fact that there were more Afrikaners in South Africa than all other white races combined —half as many again as English; and that, since England was letting South Africa go its own way, and a vote was a vote—why, the Afrikaner had the power, political and national, he had the country!

So has England, spreading her industrial revolution and her democracy, undone herself. There is no comfort; there is no moral.

The realization that, after a hundred and fifty years of struggling, power had so simply come to him was more than the Afrikaner could contain with equanimity. His exhilaration was immense. He threw out his chest. He threw up his head. He offered to show the world.

In pursuance of this ambition, he sent his ambassadors to

foreign countries and asserted himself against his English-speaking neighbour.

At first the Englishman could hardly believe it. Then he had to believe it. England had won her war, yet the conquered was the conqueror. He himself made the money, but the other fellow made the laws, and then he made the money too. The Afrikaner could tell the Englishman to do this and do that, and he had to obey.

Chagrin overwhelmed him, anger, grief and, worse than anything, a sense of helplessness. All he could do was black-ball people from his clubs, and, in the end, that came home to him too. At least two blackballings have made—and are making—history in South Africa.

The very coalition of General Hertzog and his own champion, General Smuts, he looked upon as a submergence of himself. Even when General Smuts assured the South African English that the new Constitution under the Statute of Westminster did not require of them more than was right, the Englishman remained distrustful, afraid, unhappy and, but for a small, out-of-date sort of movement, supine.

Now days are here when the might of the Afrikaner's numbers leaves him helpless and true union can only come about either by the Afrikaner's good will or the unifying misery of an economic collapse. He is not yet convinced of this good will; he does not want an economic collapse.

So what is he to do?

Dr. Malan invites the whole *volk* to come together on Dingaan's Day at the opening of the Voortrekkers Monument and celebrate as one the Great Trek and the Boers' conquest of the Kaffirs. General Smuts, still dreaming of the Union of Brothers he preached only seven years after the Boer War, tells his following that they should go: "The most illustrious and biggest event in the history of our country was the Great Trek. It was symbolic of the courage

of the South African people and the idea of a greater South
Africa. . . . My call to you is to take a whole-hearted part
in the celebrations. The whole of the people have paid for
the monument and the whole of the people should go to
the celebrations. . . . We must not let it become a sec-
tional affair. . . . I shall be there, and I shall have my say."

How noble General Smuts is, the Englishman thinks,
how courageous. But shall he himself hastily grow a beard;
buy corduroys and veld-shoes and a tie decorated with ox-
waggons (since the Voortrekkers travelled in ox-waggons)?
Shall he buy for his women the dresses of the eighteen-thirties, with the proper bonnets and mittens? Shall he ride in
the Voortrekkers' commandos, bearded, with Dr. Malan's
followers? Shall he eat with them at their barbecues—their
Braaivleis? Shall he, in short, pretend that he is a descendant of those people who, assured, as they said, that the
English were as little eager to keep them as they to remain,
had left the fruitful land of their birth to enter a wild and
dangerous territory—only to get away from them? What
part had he, really, in this "most illustrious and biggest
event" in South Africa's history declared by General Smuts?

He had indeed tried once to delude himself that he had
a part. This was in 1938, when the Voortrekker Centenary
started the new South Africa. There was fun and festival
going on around the Voortrekker waggons, and mayors in
their chains and people that were not Boers had come out
to welcome the waggons and join in the fair . . . only, of
course, to be sent back.

He knows that General Smuts will be there and have his
say to help him and for the good of all. If General Smuts
says he is to go there, he will go there. He will be different
from the real celebrants, with their beards, corduroys, veld-
shoes, ox-waggon ties, waggons, horses. He will not be coming, like Dr. Malan's followers, from every berg, dorp, and
stroom in the Union, and so he will be greatly outnum·

bered. But still, however strange his position, he will be there. . . .

He goes, and nothing happens. Nor would anything happen if a Protestant entered St. Peter's.

Now what shall be the English South African's celebration? He does not deny the sufferings and successes of the Great Trek. But he denies that the Great Trek opened South Africa. All modern lands are the creation of industry. And industrial South Africa, he feels, is the creation of the industry of Britons.

He might add, though he does not, that is equally the creation of Jews, the industry of Jews.

So to what shall the English South African erect a monument? On what English monument would state treasuries dare to spend £400,000? What passion has the English South African that would drive him to demand monuments in praise of himself?

Rhodes—good, bad, and great, all together—would have known the answers. Other Englishmen do not. Since Rhodes's death they have had to depend on Boers (crying a union of Brothers, Unity Is Strength)—on Botha, Smuts, and Hofmeyr—for their leaders.

And now they, too, are dead.

CHAPTER   EIGHT

The Jews

FOURTEEN or fifteen years ago a Dutch Reformed Synod, meeting at Bloemfontein, decided by sixty-four to sixty-one votes that the Jews were not, after all, God's Chosen People and thus to be specially favoured; the Transvaal Synod, considering the question of Jewish persecution (then much to the fore, owing to the teaching of Hitler) left the treatment of Jews to Christian consciences; the Natal Synod failed to penetrate God's will.

To them all the Chief Rabbi of the Transvaal commended the words of Tolstoi:

"He whom neither slaughter nor torture for thousands of years could destroy, he who was the first to produce the oracle of God and has been for so long the Guardian of Prophecy, is everlasting as eternity itself."

However, eternity, as Spinoza says, is now. Hitler presently destroyed almost all the Jews of Europe. The Jews, living for too long on words—on the Word—were not comforted.

There had been a time, sixty or seventy years ago, when a Dutch Reformed Synod would not have debated how one ought to treat Jews; when, if the Bible said the Jews were the Chosen People, then that was enough for the Boer. He believed the Bible.

And so it fell to the bent fugitives of ghettoes to have an experience unique in Jewish history: to receive a welcome as by brothers of brothers.

The Boers, indeed, saw a peculiar kinship between themselves and the Jews. The Jews too had once been Voortrekkers. They had fled from Egypt to found themselves a national home. They had crossed the Red Sea and sojourned in the wilderness and drunk of the bitter waters of Marah.

So had the Boers fled from the oppressor, and crossed the Vaal and sojourned in the wilderness and drunk of bitter waters. All along the route of the Voortrekkers are Biblical names. Bethel and Bethlehem and Bethesda; Elim and Hebron. They even had a Nylstroom, a River Nile, which it is said they took to be the hidden source of the Nile itself, reached in their long-continued wanderings—a very link with the Jews of Egypt. . . .

The Jews, having found a place where it was not yet known how civilized people ought to treat them, wrote to their friends and relations and told them (as did others, of America) that here was another Promised Land; that here a man might go where he liked, do what he liked, say what he liked. And, following a few early Jewish adventurers, English, German, and Hollander, there began now to come, emerging bent and bewildered from the ghettoes of Russia and Poland, fleeing from pogroms, a trail of Jews. They went across the veld with a bundle of goods on their backs, and they halted at Boer farmhouses; and they sold the Boers their goods; and they brought them news of the towns and tales of the old world they had left; and exchanged jokes with them and slept the night.

A few months later they reappeared. But this time they had a Cape cart and horses. Then they bought and sold ostrich feathers and ox-hides. Or they became cattle-dealers. Or they settled down somewhere; opened a little shop; im-

ported a bewildered wife and several children and decided
that one of the boys would be a doctor. If they were bache-
lors, they sent for a girl from their home towns, but sometimes they married the big solemn daughters of their Boer
hosts and these became their faithful wives and did their
best to bring their children up in the right Jewish way. . . .

But diamonds and gold had, by this time, been found,
and a different sort of Jew came to South Africa—not only
the Russian and Polish Jew, cautiously lifting a humbled
back, but a recurrent form of the earliest Jewish emigrants
to South Africa: the self-confident English or German Jew
with a head for big money. He worked with diamonds and
gold and concessions. He came to live in Johannesburg.
Other Jews came to live in Johannesburg. There presently
seemed to be quite a number of Jews about the place.

The creators, through diamonds and gold, of modern
South Africa are, but for Rhodes, Jews.

Yet only the leaders of the mining world are today Jews;
and, though they make great money deals with other Jews
overseas, they do not, as a rule, employ Jews on the mines.
Nor are the businesses in Johannesburg that supply the
mines in Jewish hands; nor the great engineering or electri-
cal companies; nor the great wholesale or retail stores.

But they have nearly all the smaller wholesale stores, and
the Woolworth type of shops which in South Africa are
called bazaars. They are not among the great builders, but
they are the jewelers.

They are, increasingly, the country's manufacturers.

They have become the best farmers of maize, potatoes,
tobacco, oranges, apples, and bananas. They are not among
the great wine-growers or cattle-breeders.

They control the theatre world. Law and medicine are
largely in their hands.

They have no influence in politics. Though many Jews

have been Members of Parliament, only one has become a Cabinet Minister. No Jew has been an Administrator or diplomatic representative. Many Jews are mayors.

Over a third of the Union's hundred and seven thousand Jews live in Johannesburg; and in Johannesburg they are one in nine of the white population; and in Cape Town, one in fifteen; and in Durban, one in forty-six; and in Pretoria, one in fifty-four.

The reasons for this disproportion are probably that Jews coming from Europe entered the Union at Cape Town; stayed if they could make a living; if not, went on to Johannesburg where the opportunities were greater.

In Durban, they could not compete against the Indian traders and were not socially acceptable to the British. In Pretoria, a town of officials, they either did not seek or were not offered government appointments.

1926 was the last census year that classified Europeans in the Union according to their descent. Today one can only guess at their numbers by their religion. At that time the Jews were four per cent of the white population. Later they became four and three-quarters per cent of it. They are now under four and a half and likely to decrease; first, because they are not readily admitted into the country; second, because the Nazis have frightened Jews out of having many children; third, because a number are going to Israel.

For voting purposes, the Jews are classed with the English. This is because they follow General Smuts, who has been their undeviating friend for half a century.

It is curious how few concessions are made to the Jewish vote, considering the power it gives the three per cent of Jews in America. This may be because it is taken for granted that they will vote for General Smuts.

There are Nationalists who resent it. What, they ask, of the time when their forefathers welcomed the Jews as no other people had ever done? Did this mean nothing to them?

It meant much. But General Smuts represented that tradition. He was the man who spoke for the Jews, who spoke against quotas, who fought Hitler. Even then, he almost lost them because the English, with him too, supported England when she forbade Jews their homeland while the Nazis were destroying their kin.

Yet, even before the coming of Hitler, the position of the Jew in South Africa was not what it had been when, in the old days, he came to lonely farmhouses offering, in a broken tongue, to sell the goods on his back. He was less a stranger when his loneliness and poverty matched the Boer loneliness and poverty than when he prospered and grew numerous.

For if, as has been said, it is easy to bear the troubles of others (indeed, exhilarating, since, by comparison one's own troubles seem lighter) there is, again, nothing that makes so godlike a demand on human nature as for the benefactor to watch benignly the swelling of his beneficiary into a rival or, worse, a patron.

Even the Jews, who so ardently strove for Hitler's refugees, resented it when, within a few years, they were very prosperous. No more than any other South Africans could they tell themselves judicially: "These people were fugitives. They came to a land that did not want them; whose language they did not speak; without money, without friends. And immediately they have risen so high. What valuable citizens they will be!"

However, this was not the attitude. It is, indeed, one of the Jew's problems that he does not stay down. The will to survive, to succeed, to grow, is in his blood; and his very survival, success, growth, make him not more but less welcome.

There is another thing which makes the Jew unwelcome,

and it stood out particularly when Hitler specially illumi-
nated the strange man, the Jew, who had nowhere to be
except in an alien world. For, naturally, one's instinct immediately rose up against a man who had nowhere to be
except in an alien world and might possibly—and the more
others rejected him—wish to come to one's own world.

This, indeed, is what happened in South Africa when
the United States made its Quota Act which involved Jews,
and it was feared that the Jews who could no longer go to
America might, instead, come to the Union. South Africa,
accordingly, that so desperately needed whites to offset its
blacks, also made a Quota Act.

It was in 1930 that General Hertzog's government, while
General Smuts was out of the country, brought in a Quota
Act which was supported, not only by his own party, but
also largely by General Smuts's party; and against which, at
the third reading, General Smuts fought an almost lone
hand.

This Quota Act spoke of Eastern Europeans, but since
few other Eastern Europeans came to South Africa, it
meant Jews; and it cut down to fifty a year the immigrants
from such countries as Latvia, Lithuania, Poland and Hun-
gary—from any country, in short, east of a line running down
Europe.

This was a concession, later abandoned, to the Jews' feelings: no race was mentioned—only a section of the world
that, included, for instance, also Greeks; but it had one extraordinary result: When, in 1933, the Germans attacked
the Jews, they were able, being west of the Bar, to escape
to South Africa, and they did so.

After a few thousands had come (whose numbers were
exaggerated into hundreds of thousands) an Aliens' Act was
passed in 1936 which laid down that an Immigration Board
had to judge whether a person was of good character "likely
to become readily assimilable with the European inhabit-

ants within a reasonable time of entering the country . . .
not likely to be harmful to the welfare of the Union . . .
not likely to pursue an occupation which in the Board's
opinion is already overcrowded."

The last possible fugitives to escape the ban reached Cape
Town towards the end of October 1936. As they got off the
ship, five hundred of them, students of an Afrikaans University demonstrated against them; and even the English,
seeing so many coming together, felt as if the country were
being invaded.

But this was, in effect, the end of Jews coming to South
Africa; for it was only needed to say of a man that he was
not assimilable or followed an overcrowded profession, to
keep him out.

During the war years, when even England, so near Germany and desperate for food, took in sixty thousand Jewish refugees, the safe prosperous Union took in fifty a year
and Rhodesia took in six a year. Nor could General Smuts
do anything to prevent it: his followers too wished their
exclusion.

They probably damaged themselves by doing so (if the
Nationalists benefited) for the Jews were potential Smuts
voters. And when, later, the English in South Africa blamed
the Jews in South Africa for the work of a Polish-Yemenite-
Arab gang in Palestine, and voted against Smuts for recog-
nizing Israel, which made it the fault of the Jews that the
election was lost, then the Jews asked themselves in bewilderment who, really, were their friends in South Africa.

Ninety-nine per cent of the Jews of South Africa were
Zionists. For some unexplained reason, they were the most
ardent Zionists in the world, the greatest individual donors
to Zionist funds, the largest in numbers to go fighting for a
Jewish Palestine.

Now, having too the easiest life, physically speaking, of
all Jews, a great many of the younger ones went to settle—

to do what in South Africa was called Kaffirs' work—in Israel. They grouped themselves together, still wistfully South African; and, because their language was English, the other Israeli solemnly called them the "Anglo-Saxons."

And, in fact, being "Anglo-Saxons," coming from South Africa, had done something for them. They had grown, in South Africa, big, strong, and vigorous. They had shared the legal democracy of Europeans in South Africa (and if various individuals did not like Jews, it was their human right); they had inherited some great traditions; they were, no less than the Voortrekkers, leaving the fruitful land of their birth to enter a wild and dangerous territory: with only the wish to live quietly and justly; molesting none unless molested; at peace with all; under God and their own laws. These were the words of the Voortrekkers; and because South Africa had been the Jews' birthland, they were thought the best of Israel's settlers.

CHAPTER NINE

The Indians

I

THERE is a people in South Africa whose condition is the opposite of that of the Jews.

The Indians had a homeland of their own when they came to South Africa. They have it today, and, in its new independence, it shows a proud face to the world. It remains, nevertheless, full of miseries; and the thought of all Africa is that too many Indians of India will abandon their homeland to join in the new scramble for Africa; and it is the chagrin of all South African governments that nothing will induce the South African Indians to return to India. No pains, no bribes—nothing.

There are Indian plants in Rhodesia that may have been planted there by Indians about the time King Solomon, every three years, sent his ships (and those commissioned from Hiram of Tyre) to fetch African gold and silver, ivory, apes, and peacocks. The gold they brought back was in such quantities that Solomon's very targets and shields and drinking-vessels were of gold, and his ivory throne was inlaid with gold, and gold was so easily had it was nothing accounted of in the days of Solomon.

It may be that, even in those days, there were Indian planters and traders to provide for the needs of prospectors

and diggers and hunters in Africa. There are some who say
that Indians, and not Arabs or Phœnicians or Africans,
built those stone walls and temples whose ruins remain one
of the mysteries of Rhodesia; and who knows but that ancient Indians walked about the land a Portuguese navigator
two thousand years later sighted on a Christmas Day and
called Natal?

For the purposes of this book, however, the Indian story
in Africa begins in the year 1860, when the English sugar-
planters of Natal complained that the Zulus would not
work and begged the government to let them import labour
from India. And the fear Africa has of the Indians today begins with the arrival in Natal of the Indian gentleman of
birth and culture, Mohandas Karamchand Gandhi.

The idea of the sugar-planters was to indenture Indian
labourers and pay them ten shillings a month, rising yearly
until, in the fifth and last year of their indentures, they
would be getting fourteen shillings a month. One might
plant sugar profitably like that. And one might encourage
the Indians to settle in South Africa and keep up the supply of labour by giving them land and citizen privileges instead of return passages to India; or one might arrange that
they should stay on for at least five years after the expiry of
their indentures.

The citizen privileges were presumably those conferred
upon Natal when the British annexed it in 1843:

"There shall not be in the eyes of the law any distinction
of colour, origin, language or creed."

The Indians came to Natal. They spread themselves over
the land, not as trespassers, not merely as licensed foreigners, but as invited compatriots, indeed, as guests paid to enter the country and stay there. . . .

Until, in the eighteen-eighties, there was a thing the

Transvaal and Orange Free State, no less than Natal, could not fail to remark—the growing number of Indians.

The Boer republics took measures.

The Transvaal, in 1885, reversed an agreement made with England only the year before, according to which all people, other than natives, had full right to live, trade, and own property anywhere in the Transvaal. It now forbade Indians these rights except in certain areas, and later, immigration was stopped altogether. Today the Transvaal has thirty-seven thousand Indians.

The Free State, in 1891, not only forbade Indians to trade or farm in the Transvaal, but, without compensation, deported them. During the Boer War, a certain number came in, as servants with the British forces. Of these and their descendants, fourteen remain.

There was, before Union, no colour bar in the Cape, but it was not easy for the Indians to come from Natal to the Cape. The Indians and near-Indians in the Cape are today seventeen thousand.

Natal itself grew alarmed in the eighteen-nineties. The provision about Indian labourers remaining in Natal for five years after the expiry of their contract was deleted—against the will of the sugar-planters who, in 1911, when indentured Indian labour was finally abolished, made last great efforts to get in as many Indians as possible. In the eighteen-nineties, two shiploads of Indians were forcibly prevented from landing. The Prime Minister, Mr. (afterwards Sir Harry) Escombe, introduced bills, which subsequently became the Licensing and Immigration Laws of 1897, pointing out that "Unless an arrestation was put upon the introduction of immigrants from India, the whole social polity would be disturbed . . ." and that, "having regard to the character of the people who were coming into the country" (mostly deck passengers, who paid only two pounds or so for their passages) "it was easy for the whole of the population of this country to be, as it were, submerged by the new arrivals, entailing a competition which was simply impossible as far as Europeans were concerned . . . on account of the different habits of life."

Two years later there was the Boer War; and, though Gandhi thought abstract justice was on the side of the Boers, justice for the Indians was one of the things the British were fighting for, and so he said: "Every single subject of a State must not hope to enforce his private opinions," and the Indians accordingly stood with the British.

After the war, Gandhi (with a neat little moustache, a high collar, and a striped tie) came to Milner to receive the Indians' reward—those rights the British had fought for.

To him Milner answered:

"I hold that when a coloured man possesses a certain high grade of civilization, he ought to obtain what I might call white privileges, irrespective of colour. For the present, however, there is no prospect whatever of their prevailing —certainly as far as the Asiatics are concerned. . . . The Asiatics are strangers forcing themselves upon a community reluctant to receive them."

The Indians found, in short, when the war was over and the British took control, that the little finger of Lord Milner was thicker than the loin of President Kruger. Kruger had required them to pay a registration fee on entering the Transvaal, and had (officially) refused to permit them to own land. Lord Milner not only suggested that they should reregister—should go so far as to give their thumbprints that residents might be distinguished from would-be immigrants —but sought to prohibit immigration altogether.

He had the support of the South Africans (except the sugar-planters of Natal). It was all very well, they said, for the Indians to claim the privileges of citizens of the British Empire, all very well for the British Empire to feel a duty towards India, but were the actual Indians coming to England, or were they coming to South Africa?

Were the South Africans to pay for Great Britain's nobility? Were they, already burdened with an overwhelming colour problem, to be made the dumping-ground for the overflow of a polygamous people, hundreds of millions strong, coming out chiefly as labourers, waiters, hawkers, and small tradesmen, forcing their European competitors out by underselling and underliving them? Could they help it that India was a land where people got born and died with such depressing ease, and that existence there so bitterly depended on whether the Lord sent a monsoon that year or not? Could they permit the cheap, embarrassing Indians to force out the rare and precious Europeans?

Between the Indians and South Africans stood the Imperial government, anxious to do its duty towards the Indians, but still more anxious to conciliate the latest colony—very, very anxious not to interfere. After refusing on its own behalf to sanction any anti-Asiatic legislation, it left the matter in the hands of the Parliament newly set up by England in the Transvaal.

The new government, represented by General Smuts, its Colonial Secretary, went briskly to work. The compulsory registration of Asiatics, their identification through certificates bearing fingerprints, their almost total exclusion from the Transvaal, were put in force.

Gandhi approached Smuts on behalf of his fellow Asiatics, making demands and suggestions, making diminishing demands and diminishing suggestions. Let there be any administrative restrictions they pleased, he finally said, let them admit in a year six Indians—no more than six, and only of the highest standing—six men to lead and stimulate the outlawed community in South Africa, but let there, nominally, at least, not stand any longer against all Asiatics this grievous Act branding them as one with criminals. . . . In opposing, in 1925, the Colour Bar Bill brought in by General Hertzog's government, General Smuts repeated Gandhi's words to him: "Do not dishonour us. We recognise that there must be distinctions, but do not cast a stigma upon us in the laws of your country. . . ."

But the repeal of the Act was refused. And it was now that, conciliation having proved useless, Gandhi had resource to the weapon which he then named Passive Resistance—the exercise of soul-force, but which he, a generation later, in India, called Non-co-operation. It was in South Africa India began to pull out of the British Empire.

II

When, in 1888, at the age of nineteen, Gandhi came confidently to London, the son, the grandson, the nephew of high ministers at the court of an Indian prince, to read for the English Bar, he had passed through spiritual and religious conflicts, but he had not yet awakened to the sense of a racial conflict. He was prepared to like England. He did like England. He set himself (the withered, ascetic, loin-clothed being of later days) to learn what he took to be the accomplishments of an English gentleman: dancing, elocution, French, and fiddling. But he was troubled in his intercourse with other English gentlemen by vows he had taken to abjure wine, flesh, and women—by thoughts of the wife and family that, at nineteen, he had at home. And, in the end, he gave up his dancing, elocution, French, and fiddling, and went to live solitarily in a room on vegetables and a pound a week. . . .

Then he came to South Africa. He came as a barrister to fight a case, as an Indian gentleman of caste and culture who owned a frock coat and top hat, an evening suit, and refused to wear a ready-made tie.

On his second day in Durban Gandhi went to see the

law courts, wearing his turban of an Indian barrister. The magistrate told him to remove the turban or leave the court. He left the court.

Having to be in Pretoria for his case, he took, as a barrister should, a first-class railway ticket. But a fellow traveller objected to travelling with an Indian. Gandhi was asked to sit in the van; refused to go; was thrown out, with his luggage, by a policeman; spent the night in a dark waiting-room, considering whether he should at once return to India. . . . The history of the British Empire might have been different had he done it.

Through the Transvaal one needed to travel by coach; and the conductor suggested that, in order to avoid unpleasantness with the other passengers, Gandhi and he should change seats. Later, however, he wanted his seat back again—he wanted to smoke—and told Gandhi to sit on the footboard. "Sit on this, Sammy," he said giving him a piece of sacking, and calling him by the term South Africans have derived from "sami"—the ending of many Indian names. When Gandhi would not move, he struck him in the face.

In Johannesburg, he was denied admission at a hotel.

Still determined to travel as a barrister should, he called on the Johannesburg stationmaster in his frock coat and top hat that he might be given a first-class ticket to Pretoria.

In Pretoria he was arrested for being out after nine without a pass. . . .

Gandhi entered upon a twenty-one-year struggle for the Indians in South Africa.

He ceased to be a barrister and became an attorney in Johannesburg. He began to practise Satyagraha—soul-force.

He commended it to his fellow Indians. They were not to register or give their fingerprints. They appealed to England. The Speaker of England's Parliament found that fingerprints were used in India: ex-soldiers and ex-officials had to give their fingerprints before getting their pensions.

The South African Indians said only one fingerprint was given in India and even Milner had only required their right thumbprint. They said they didn't mind giving right thumbprints, for in India right thumbprints were taken of Muslims going to Mecca, who often returned with plague. But left thumbprints were taken of habitual criminals. They would not give their left thumbprints, still less all ten fingerprints.

Smuts said that thumbprints had been found insufficient. Fingerprints, he said, were the only safeguard against the forged certificates an Indian could buy in Johannesburg, Durban, or Bombay. He insisted on ten fingerprints.

Out of ten thousand Indians subject to registration, only five hundred gave their fingerprints. The rest offered to go to jail; many did so, and Gandhi with them.

The jails of the Transvaal had not been built to house thousands of Indian passive resisters. Their religion forbade them to eat the food usual in jails. It was hot. A number of them became ill. There were protests from England. Smuts let them out, replying to criticisms of his weakness: "I do not mind climbing down. I am accused of being too prone to climbing down. . . . I secured my object."

The arrangement between Smuts and Gandhi under which Indians were let out was that if they registered *voluntarily* they would be forgiven for not having done so compulsorily; and those who had the right would be allowed to remain in the Transvaal. It does not seem much of a gain for Gandhi. But it appears that Smuts visited him in jail; they had a philosophical discussion; Gandhi drew from it the idea that the immigration laws would be repealed. Smuts said, naturally not.

So passive resistance was resumed. The Indians tore up their registration certificates with the voluntary fingerprints and moved backwards and forwards across the Transvaal-Natal border. They were arrested, imprisoned, released, crossed the border again.

There was Union. The laws that had been applied to the Transvaal were applied to the country. A new Act excluded "any person or class of person deemed by the Minister (of the Interior) on economic grounds or on account of standards or habits of life to be unsuited to the requirements of the Union or any particular province thereof." Smuts "deemed" all Asiatics, for these reasons, unsuited to the Union.

It was the year 1913. For the last time Gandhi led his followers in a Passive Resistance Movement. Over two thousand Indians crossed again from Natal into the Transvaal, and allowed themselves to be arrested. Gandhi himself was sent to the Bloemfontein jail where "the prospect of uninterrupted study for a year" filled him, he said, "with joy." Other Indians were sent to jails. Those who could not be housed in jails had to work in the mines.

Gandhi won. That is to say, the word Asiatic was not henceforth mentioned in connection with the Immigration Act of 1913. No longer was a stigma cast on Asiatics, as such, in the laws of the Union.

And those laws now, in effect, apply to all would-be immigrants to the Union. Only last year the power to reject any immigrant was placed in the hands of the Minister of the Interior.

Now Gandhi felt himself entitled to go home. He arrived in England two days after the beginning of the First World War, and from England he went to India, to practise there the lesson he had learnt in South Africa.

During the war Smuts said to the Indians who had served with him: "I have had no more loyal, devoted and brave troops under me than those from the Indian Empire, and I think the young South Africans who went with me, who fought side by side with those heroes from Asia, today have more kindly feelings than they had before towards the Indian population of South Africa."

Three years after the war, however, he had to explain South Africa's attitude to the Imperial War Cabinet, and he said:

"We started as a small white colony in a black continent. In the Union the vast majority of our citizens are black, probably the majority of them are in a semi-barbarous state still. . . . The Indian question with us is an entirely subordinate question. . . . But you cannot deal with the Indians apart from the whole position in South Africa; you cannot give political rights to the Indians which you deny the rest of the coloured citizens in South Africa. If you touch the Indian position you must go the whole length."

Some delegates were shocked by this, but Mr. Winston Churchill said it would be affectation and humbug to pretend there would be no great changes in the law of the land if hundreds of thousands of Indians—or perhaps millions— were to enter England and seriously compete with the working and clerical classes. He said he understood South Africa's embarrassment.

In denying Indians the rights Gandhi claimed, Milner had said: "There is more chance in the case of the coloured people of South African birth; and no doubt their claim is a stronger one, inasmuch as they are natives of the country, and have no choice but to live here. . . ."

It was what General Hertzog came to say in even stronger terms. The white man, he said, was not responsible for the Indian's existence. But he was responsible for the Eurafrican's existence. It was therefore the Eurafrican he had to carry with him, rather than the Indian.

The Indian was determined that it should be otherwise. From the time of Kruger, he had been forbidden entry to the Transvaal, yet he managed to come in. Here was one way. An Indian already living there might bring in his child under sixteen. Little Indians from India were accordingly brought in as the children of Indians legitimately in the country and, receiving certificates to remain, later (since they themselves were innocent) had these certificates ratified.

There were laws preventing Indians from owning fixed property, except in certain areas. So they had their properties registered in the names of white people, or they formed themselves into limited liability companies which, being merely abstractions of law, could not be subject to racial restrictions. Provisions then had to be made to exclude from holding land such companies as were controlled by Asiatics, and also, later, white trusteeship over Indian-owned land.

Yet, somehow, the Indians increased, and also their wealth.

General Smuts's government fell. General Hertzog took over. Stricter measures still were being prepared against the Indians when England intervened.

So now, upon an "appreciable number" of Indians returning to India—travelling free, with bonuses—the Union made concessions:

Married Indians might bring in their wives and children. Equal pay would be given for equal work. The government engaged itself to raise the Indians' standard of life and receive an Indian Agent to guard their interests. The standard of life had to do with health, labour, industry, education, social welfare. The Clause about it was called the Uplift Clause. The Agreement—the Cape Town Agreement—was called by the Indians their Magna Carta.

The Indian Agent duly became a High Commissioner. Seventeen thousand Indians returned to India.

The people of Natal asked what use that was to anyone. Seventeen thousand. How long would it take the Indians to produce another seventeen thousand? And nearly all in Natal.

Of the Union's three hundred thousand Indians, two hundred and fifty thousand were in Natal, and the other provinces would not take over any of them. In Durban alone there were (compared with the Europeans' hundred and twenty-eight thousand) a hundred and twenty thousand Indians, and it was reckoned that, fifty years hence, Durban would have twice as many Indians as whites.

One might amuse oneself with the expression "fifty years hence." One might speculate on Natal, the Union, India, the world, fifty years hence.

Though the Union to this day struggles—by offers of free passages and gifts of money—to persuade the Indians to go home to India (the Union says "home"; the Indians do not; Pandit Nehru supports them) the Indians are not, in fact, undesirable citizens. If even the Jews cannot compete against them, it is because the Indians work so hard. Though they commit commercial crimes, they seldom commit crimes of violence. According to the latest records, the *serious* crimes of natives are twenty-seven thousand a year (women, two thousand); of whites, two thousand two hundred a year (women, two hundred); of Indians four hundred a year (women, twenty-five). Proportionately, the coloureds by far commit the more crimes.

Yet their hard work, their light record of crime, are not

the things the people of Natal particularly notice about Indians. They notice their penetration into white areas. They cannot fail to notice their terrible fecundity.

Through the streets of Durban they walk, the little sad-eyed Indian mothers, with their little sad-eyed children. Though ninety per cent of Indian children go to school, the girls go only for a year or two, since from twelve they must be kept at home to be saved (their parents feel) from desirous men—to marry at fifteen or sixteen and become little sad-eyed mothers themselves.

It is the breeding of the Indians the Europeans fear. But they have more to fear.

III

The Indians came to deny that the Uplift Clause in the Cape Town Agreement was being fulfilled. Hofmeyr threatened to resign when an Act, called the Pegging Act, said of this Agreement and of Indian penetration into the Old Borough of Durban: "Thus far and no further.". . . "Every time," he said, "a surrender is made to racial and colour prejudice . . . we are sapping our moral foundation of leadership." He withdrew his threat when General Smuts, promising not to maintain the Pegging Act longer than three years, offered to bring the matter before a Judicial Commission.

Upon this Commission two Indians were to sit, but they declined the invitation. A new Act decreed where Indians might freely live and where they might not. The Indians refused to sit on a Board that was to carry out this "Ghetto Act." An Act was passed giving them the sort of parliamentary representation the natives had—with three Europeans to stand for them in the Assembly and two in the Senate. They refused to avail themselves of it and demanded equality with the whites. If they had accepted it, General Smuts would have had a majority of one in the Senate at the next election, and all but equality in the Assembly. Dr. Malan repealed the Act.

They looked, indeed, to the new India. . . . For, in the Second World War, the Indians of India had seen their opportunity; and there was Gandhi now practising the Passive Resistance he had applied to South Africa that always led to violence; preaching the brotherhood of men that made his brethren kill him.

Now Gandhi advised the English to preserve their souls by inviting Hitler and Mussolini "to take what they want of the countries you call your possessions . . . your beautiful island with your many beautiful buildings"; yet, at the same time, he advised the Indians to drive the English from India's beautiful country and beautiful homes. "Quit India" became the Indians' cry to the English.

When Gandhi, in February 1943, undertook one of his great fasts which General Smuts said "undermined reason," his son wrote in the paper he edited in Natal: "Gandhi is fighting a battle to free India from the foreign yoke. . . . It is as legitimate as the British fighting to be free from the Nazi yoke."

Towards the end of 1944, the new Delhi Central Legislature debated the disabilities of Indians in South Africa; and decreed equal disabilities for South Africans in India, economic sanctions, and the recall of their High Commissioner in South Africa.

A leading member said:

"I wish India were in a position to declare war on South Africa here and now. If she were, I should lose no time in taking an army to South Africa. . . .

"We must declare throughout the Commonwealth and the civilised world that we are determined not to submit to this racial arrogance. . . .

"Some day India will come into her own and be in a po-

sition to take more effective action against those who persist
in assailing her national honour and self-respect. . . . Our
patience" (he said in the words of Hitler) "is now completely exhausted."

Another member said: "Even in the war Indians have
shed their blood for South Africans. I wish very much that
the Indian regiments which knocked the macaroni out of
Mussolini could be sent to drive some sense into the South
Africans."

Two years later India arraigned South Africa before a
United Nations composed chiefly of non-Europeans, and
General Smuts went himself to state South Africa's case.

His words were received in disdainful silence. Mrs. Pandit, Nehru's sister, cried:

"Over many years my Government . . . has appealed,
complained, protested and sought compromises and agree-
ments and has finally been forced to bring the matter before the bar of world opinion."

The audience rose to its feet and applauded her.

Next year she demanded a division of the Union into
three full Dominions, one for the whites, one for the Indians, and one for the natives—each people being given an
area proportionate to its population.

This demand too was applauded.

General Smuts had said in 1946: "Indians should be the
last persons to throw stones at others and make charges of
class distinction and discrimination."

One of the Indian delegates to the UN had been a High
Commissioner in South Africa. He said, quite truly, that
many of the UN's members would not be allowed into a
European tearoom in South Africa. But it is also a fact that,
from the time the first Indian Agent came in 1926 to the

time the last Indian High Commissioner left in 1946, no
Indian representative, Muslim or Hindoo, at any private
(obviously not public) party ever had as a guest a fellow
Indian.

Nor had this to do with white social feeling. The Europeans invited were of the sort that had no prejudices against
Indians. It had to do with the social feeling of the Indian
representatives. They admitted their great loneliness in
South Africa and that there were no Indians with whom
they could, on any but official terms, associate. . . .

General Smuts added:

"The Indian delegation knows well enough that, if the
present restrictions against Indian immigration into the
Union were lifted, scores of thousands—nay, hundreds of
thousands—of Indians would be only too glad to escape
from their own country and settle in the Union, notwith-
standing the discrimination alleged."

Yet Mrs. Pandit returned to the attack and, in 1948, it
fell to a Nationalist to represent South Africa at the UN,
and what he said was:

"The bombings of Hyderabad are still echoing in the ears
of the world. There is still fresh in the minds of civilised
people the ruthless slaughter of tens of thousands of fellow
Asiatics—Muslims of Kashmir and the Punjab. . . . It ill
becomes any delegate of the Indian Government to make
charges of ruthless discrimination when in India there is
practised the most vicious and cruel form of discrimination
the world has ever known."

He might have added that it was the religious believers
in this social discrimination that killed Gandhi.

The replies of the South African delegates were the obvious thoughts of South Africans. They felt also that, with
the Union government begging them—bribing them—to go
"home" the Indians had not the right (however natural

their desire) to want to live in one country under the protection of another.

It was what they had felt when, in Kruger's day, the Uitlanders had appealed all the time to England.

But they had other feelings too. To speak indignantly was a great pleasure, a great relief, but words did not change the values of figures. There were two hundred Indians in India for every white man in South Africa. Their very numbers made them long to leave their hungry, crowded land for Africa, made them look with close, attentive eyes at things happening in South Africa.

What, though, of the Africans in Africa: forty of these for every white man? If the Indians came to knock the macaroni out of South Africans, what would the Africans do?

Would they stand, colour by colour, against white?

Whom did the black man prefer: the Indian or the European?

The latest South African delegate at UNO had barely finished contrasting the beam in India's eye with the mote in South Africa's eye when the matter of African, Indian, and European was tested in South Africa.

IV

On the evening of January 14, 1949, a Zulu boy had a dispute with an Indian boy, serving in a shop. The Zulu boy struck the Indian boy. The Indian shopkeeper punished the Zulu boy by striking him too, and the Zulu boy fell against a glass window, which broke, so that he was cut about the head by glass and blood flowed.

He was not much injured; but natives, waiting outside at a bus terminus, saw the flowing blood.

Could one imagine that out of this event alone a racial

fury would arise, a real pogrom? The shopkeeper was later fined a pound, or seven days, for common assault.

The beginnings are far back.

First we have the South African wanting life, liberty, and the pursuit of happiness, not, like the American, for all, but for himself alone. So, for a while, each soldier remains a general.

But now the United States, discovered at the same time as South Africa, has sixty times South Africa's white population, it is the world's director and benefactor while South Africa remains full of fears of numbers—numbers. Numbers of black. Numbers of yellow.

The South African has also, from the beginning, decreed that black, and not white, shall do the hard physical work. Therefore the industrial worker in South Africa produces, on an average, sixty pounds of goods a year, and the industrial worker in America produces four hundred pounds of goods a year.

No wonder, perhaps, the sugar-planters of Natal decided that black men were not efficient and got workers from India.

But there is another point too. Since the dark people are so many and the white so few, the good work—the trained work—is the prerogative of the whites, and the dark-skinned have to stay unskilled and incompetent.

Accordingly, it falls to the small body of whites to provide the benefits for natives and Indians.

And they cannot do it. Until the evanescent war-prosperity gave work to any man, half the white South Africans needed help themselves.

Now, close-packed round the pleasant city of Durban on the Indian Ocean, live Indians and Zulus in houses that are not houses, in foul and noisy slums, and whatever money the white people spend on houses for them can never be enough. The fecund Indians, the crowding natives, will always outrun the money spent, the houses built.

The natives in the slums round Durban have stronger bodies but the Indians have better brains. When natives and Indians go to do unskilled work, the Indians become foremen and the natives continue in the heavy, less-paid work—under them. They mutter resentfully as they suffer the Indians' direction.

The natives have long memories for grievances. It is as hard to win their forgiveness as their gratitude. The reason is that they lack civilization. They have a sense of their own rights, but not of the rights of others.

Thus they will remember for years a trifling wrong or deprivation. They will kill for a stolen grain-sack, for a mulcted sixpence. If they buy something from an Indian and they find that they could have got it cheaper elsewhere, they will feel they have been robbed, cheated, exploited; their hearts will swell with rage; they will brood continually over their wrongs.

But they have also their own standards of the fitness of things. It is right that they should serve the white men, since the white men fought and beat them. It is not right that nations they overcame should be regarded by the white men as their equals. "We beat those dogs." It is far from right that the Indians should prosper that fought no one and beat no one and arrived in the land of the Zulus as slaves.

The native sees the Indian carrying his basket of fruit sixteen hours a day. Presently he sees him pushing his fruit in a cart. Then a donkey pulls his cart. If that Indian does not get so far as a motor van, his son does. Or his son may become a director of a bus-company, a merchant, a property owner.

On the other hand, there are wealthy Indians (mostly Muslims) born of wealthy Indians.

The Zulu sees this.

Again he sees the Indian looking at a Zulu girl.

The Zulu girl is luscious, with a large laugh, and the Indian girl is meagre and puling. The young Indian, with his thick, black, oiled hair, his rich shiny hair that seems to have all the strength of his body, uses his money to draw the Zulu girl. The Zulu is not consoled by the hatred his Indian slum neighbour too has for the wealthy Indian. . . .

Another sort of Indian begins in these days to speak of the glory of his country over the seas. The black people had better look out for us. The white people had better look out. One day the Indian people from over the seas will come to Durban, and then you will see who is boss in this land.

However, there is still another sort of Indian and also another sort of African: the intellectuals. They speak with one voice of the discrimination against people of colour.

And there is the thoughtful, compromising sort of Indian who says:

"We know we are hated, that the European prefers the African to us, that he thinks the African honest, faithful, courteous, colourful, uncompetitive—the sort of inferior he always likes.

"We know he finds the Indian mysterious and cunning, full of Oriental stratagems, not at all, like the African, easy and lovable—that, since India's rise to independence, he sees in all Indians a potential danger.

"But yet" (protests the Indian) "the Indian has lived in the land, and his father and his father's father, for nearly a hundred years. He has lived in it longer than many Europeans. He owns nothing he has not worked for. He feels at home only in this land. South Africa, he feels, is his homeland. He has links with India, but India is not his land. Is it not cruel to talk of sending him away to this strange land over the seas, so foreign to him merely because his ancestors, generations ago, used to live there?"

The South African says:

"You cannot have it both ways. You cannot live in South Africa, and call for the protection of India."

The Indian says:

"But if I need protection in South Africa?"

In homes, in streets, in Parliament, in newspapers, at work, at the UN, there is talk about South Africans and Indians. The African hears the talk. He knows how the South African longs to see the Indian leave the land; that he is so anxious to be rid of the Indian he will even pay him to go away.

Here, at last, is a real sympathy between black and white: the deepest: a common hate.

How one could please oneself, the African thinks, how one could please the white man, if one drove the Indian into the sea!

The African looks towards his lord. Does the white lord's head seem to nod?

As the Zulu boy falls against the Indian's window and the blood flows from his broken head, something breaks too in his people's heads and the hate pours forth.

There are Indians who say the thing did not happen suddenly, like that. They say how could it be that, in localities miles away, the Zulus went mad at the very moment the boy's head was cut in the Indian's shop? They think it extraordinary the way the Zulus went from Indian shop to Indian shop, from Indian house to Indian house, and never attacked a European's shop or house, and also not the shop or house of a Chinese. It was all too methodical, they say, to be utterly spontaneous.

The Zulus burnt, stole, killed, raped. Derelict and de-

graded whites—men and women—cried them on. They
shouted and rushed about the streets in an ecstasy of vicious
enjoyment. They looked like fiends. . . .

The Zulus felt they were doing very well among the Indians when, to their astonishment, they saw hundreds of
armed white policemen coming in to save the Indians.

As the riots continued, more police were sent from Pretoria.

Citizen forces, foot and mounted, were mobilized. There
were naval forces. There came firemen. Casualty and clearing stations were set up. Fifteen hundred Indians and natives lay on hospital beds and hospital floors. Forty thousand Indians and five thousand natives were taken to shelter
and succour. The National Ministers of Justice and Defence arrived. There was an alarum in Parliament. A judicial Commission of Enquiry was set up. . . .

The Zulus could not understand it. Did not the white
people want the Indians out of Durban? Were they not doing what the white people wanted?

No, they could not understand it.

The pogrom lasted for a night and a day and another
night and day, and it also broke out weakly in Maritzburg
the capital, and other places.

And, in the end, most of the hundred and fifty people
killed were Zulus. Most of the thousand treated in hospitals
were Zulus. Nearly all the five hundred charged in court
with public violence, theft, possession of lethal weapons,
were Zulus. The Africans remained muttering.

On the other hand, the fifty shops destroyed, the six hundred and fifty damaged, were Indian. The two hundred and
fifty houses destroyed, the thirteen hundred damaged, were
Indian. The goods burnt or stolen were Indian.

The Indian property destroyed or damaged was not in-
sured against riot or civil commotion.

The Indian shopkeepers said they would not open their

shops again until they felt safe. Stories spread among Indians throughout the country of Indians roasted alive in houses and buses.

The white people in Durban felt it that, during the next few days, there were no waiters, no hawkers, no laundry-men.

Two thousand Zulus applied for shops and hawker licenses. A Zulu applied for a bus license. A boycott of Indian shops was begun which continued. Between a hundred and two hundred Indians applied to go to India though Pandit Nehru reiterated his instruction to them to remain in their homeland, South Africa.

In Madras the President of the Indian National Congress pondered whether "the Durban tragedy was one of those mad outbursts of unaccountable fury which can only be likened to occasional cataclysms of nature," or whether there was more than appeared on the surface "to account for so vile and vindictive a manifestation of mass passion."

He added imaginatively:

"The harmony and concerted action so long in operation between the native population and the Indian settlers over there must have been the strength of the democratic movement."

However, one can see now that, if the Indians came to knock the macaroni out of the South Africans, the Africans would stand with the South Africans.

On the other hand, there are those two hundred Indians in India for every South African.

CHAPTER TEN

The Half-castes (Coloureds, Kleurlinge, Mixed Breeds, Cape People, Bastaards)

IF there was, as the important Indian said in Madras, any "harmony and concerted action between the native population and the Indian settlers," it could only have been in the Cape. There the "native population"—meaning, not the Africans, but the mixed breeds, had something in common with the Indians. They had, from the old slave days, Indian blood in them, other Eastern blood in them. Because of this, and their similar colouring, they were also mixed with modern Indians—"the Indian settlers." They had the same constitutional position. When General Hertzog took the Africans of the Cape off the common roll, he left the yellow-skinned people—the mixed breeds and Indians—on the common roll. When Dr. Malan takes the yellow people off the common roll and gives them what the Africans are to lose—white representation in Parliament— the mixed breeds and Indians will again be classed together.

And though Milner said these mixed breeds had more claim to "white privileges" than Indians; and General Hertzog said the whites had more responsibility for them than for Indians, it is not today, it will not be later, the Indians that will acquiesce in discrimination between themselves and Europeans. Before the last High Commissioner left

South Africa in 1946, he was demanding a vote equal with whites for Indians. And now that India is a republic in the British Commonwealth (helped to this position by South Africa, setting the pace for South Africa); now that India speaks as a member of the UN and has aspirations, the Indians have certainly greater hopes in South Africa than the Coloureds—indeed, any hopes of the Coloureds rest on the Indians.

Though in the United States the white person with some black in him is called indiscriminately coloured or Negro; and the Negro—the pure Negro—is also described as coloured, in South Africa no dark-skinned man is called a Negro; no Bantu is called a Coloured. One says in South Africa "a" Coloured: the adjective is used as a noun. Coloured is, indeed, the official description of the man with mixed blood. The description in Afrikaans is Kleurling: the word which means coloured.

If the coloured man lives in the Cape, he is called a Cape Coloured. If he is of those who left the Cape a hundred or more years ago to settle along the Vaal River, he is called a Bastaard. When the Afrikaners call the Cape People (as one also says, instead of Cape Coloured people) Hottentots, which they pronounce Hodnots, the Cape People much resent it—as the Bantus resent being called Kaffirs and the Indians coolies.

But the terms, unless they are meant to wound, have not an evil background. Until a generation ago, even the missionaries described the Bantus as Kaffirs; they described themselves as Kaffirs. The Indians actually came out as coolies, though many are today wealthy and some are educated and they are not, except in Natal, employed as labourers. The Hottenots were described by the earliest Dutch settlers as the Cape Men and their blood is in many of the Cape People.

Today, however, it can be said that when the words Kaffirs, coolies, Hottentots are used for modern Bantus, Indians, Cape People, they are spoken ignorantly, carelessly, or
with intention to wound. It is only when one speaks histori-
cally or, in a certain sense, descriptively, that one does (and
sometimes must) use the word Kaffir.

When General Hertzog said that the white man was responsible for the coloured man, the reason was obvious—
the white man begot the coloured man.

In the old days—taking one aspect with another—there
were colonists who, like Biblical patriarchs or monarchs,
had their official and their unofficial households, their white
wives and their Hottentot handmaids. But they used their
serving-women as Abraham used Hagar rather than as Solomon used the Shulamite. No Hottentot girl ever preened
herself before her white lord, declaiming: "I am black, but
comely." When the Abrahams were done with their Hagars,
they sent them with their Ishmaels into the wilderness.

And God said: "Also of the son of the bondwoman will
I make a nation, because he is thy seed."

The sons of the bondwomen of the old Cape settlers; also
of men who stopped at the Cape—a little while, a little
longer or, in the end, altogether—are a nation today: not
an accident, a group, a clan, a class, but a nation, a people.

By the end of the eighteenth century, the whites of the
Cape were twenty-five thousand, the slaves thirty thousand,
the Hottentots, Bushmen, and mixed breeds twenty thousand. One says mixed breeds. For it was not only the Hottentots and Bushmen that, mixed with the whites, gave
their name to what became the Cape People. Into the fusion went the slaves—women from the East, beautiful
women—who have left to many descendants their Malay
eyes and features.

Today Cape People form almost half the population of Cape Town. Not counting the half-million that are said to be lost among the whites, they are almost half as many as the white inhabitants of the Union.

Of their forebears, only the whites still exist.

The Bushmen fled from the civilization they could not meet to the clefts of the valleys, the holes of the earth, and of the rocks. Long after they were gone, slain every one by hunger, perished by the spear, white artists and scientists still sought and copied and considered with awe the Bushman paintings in the caves from which they had been shot out, smoked out, driven out, and utterly destroyed. When the art of South Africa is sent overseas, it is the Bushman or Bushman-type paintings that are chiefly acclaimed. . . .

The Hottentots, freed from a servitude that amounted to slavery, fought with white against black and black against white; stole when they could; drank very much; submitted their souls as readily as their bodies to the white people's domination; lost themselves in the whites, Kaffirs, mixed breeds, died of their helpless freedom.

The slaves went into the Cape People.

The Cape People continued to take the blood of casual soldiers, sailors, and other white men. As they grew paler, they edged towards the whites. If they looked white enough, they slipped in among the whites, and it cannot be seen that the white people have lost anything by it. Some of the best people have Cape blood in them. One may also spend a lifetime in South Africa and not meet more than two or three children that have reverted to a coloured ancestor and are darker than their parents. The idea of a black child suddenly appearing in a white family (as in one of Conan Doyle's stories) is mere romance. It is sometimes possible to see dark blood in a person classed as white by the dark neck and forehead, the tinged eyeballs—some say, the very thin legs. Where there is less Malay and more African blood the features are the chief indication. This can often be seen more clearly in photographs than in the flesh, where fair colouring may distract the eye.

In the great influenza epidemic that followed the First World War, many wondered why fewer of the weak Cape People died than of the strong black or white people. The reason was that, even in death, the Cape People, if they could, joined the white people. They were recorded, they were buried, as white people.

Nor do their darker relations obtrude themselves on the coloured people who, as the expression is, "try for white." They sympathetically and honourably lose them to the whites.

There is now a law forbidding intermarriage between black and white. This applies to mixed breeds. It may happen that before the marriage officer a doubt arises; the marriage certificates of parents are called for; if the parents, or one of them, are described as "mixed," the marriage cannot take place; the anguish is fearful.

The Cape People have a definite physical type, a characteristic accent, even a characteristic laugh. There are those who have inherited the looks of their Malay ancestors: they have the colour and strong black hair of Indians: the features of the East too. Their bodies, however, because of the white blood, are bigger. If they are light enough to freckle, there has probably been a recent incursion of white blood.

The Cape People's home language is generally Afrikaans, but on social occasions they prefer, on the whole, to speak English. Their habits and manners are those of Europeans. They dress and live, as far as their means allow them, as Europeans. They are, many of them, highly capable with their hands; they become good carpenters, mechanics, servants. . . .

But it has not yet happened in the history of South Af-

rica that a really coloured man, a man so dark that he could
not, even by a general conspiracy of evasion, pass as a white
—it has not yet happened that such a one has distinguished
himself in any branch of achievement whatsoever. No Cape
coloured man has risen to high rank in commerce, art, science, the professions. Hardly any coloured man, indeed, has
even gone so far as the son of some aboriginal chief, the
owner of land and cattle, who now and then struggles
through a university to a profession.

The young African, it is true, does not gloriously succeed either. His difficult circumstances apart, he lacks the
quality to compete against his white colleagues; and, worse,
he often takes advantage of his less-educated brethren. But
yet, in making the attempt to rise, he does something beyond the coloured man's ambitions. And he is marching on.

It is perhaps for the very reason that the coloured man is
so near the white man that the will to succeed is not in him.
There is the constant comparison, the constant distinction,
the instituted order of things. It has been held through
the generations that he should stand below the white man.
For him to aspire to compete against the white man, to
have dreams of drawing, in any respect, level with the white
man, would seem almost like a violation of nature. Although the coloured man protests often that his heart is as
white as the white man's, that he does not consider himself
the inferior of anybody, his feeling is otherwise. It is this
very heart he speaks of, the spirit within him, that is not
white. However he may have proved himself in war to be
not deficient in physical courage, it is as if the darkness of
his skin descends also upon his soul when it confronts the
white man.

And how should it be otherwise? Consider his ancestry.
In his veins runs, on one side, the blood of slaves; on the
other side, the blood of the careless, the selfish, the stupid,

the vicious—if also, sometimes, of the well-born or very simple. Consider his life—unwanted, as he is, by the world, born into humiliation. Whence, poor, betrayed being, shall pride and hope come to him? It can come, far more easily, to the son of a kraal, where there are memories of strength and power and a growing knowledge of a whole continent full of his kind. . . .

It naturally happens that a pretty Cape girl may honourably attract a white man—it has, almost from the beginning, happened that men in poor circumstances have found it easier to marry girls less demanding than white girls, and that the dark blood is then progressively bleached out in their descendants until it makes no practical difference.

But upon this the final twist of tragedy is achieved in the shame the child has in the colour of his mother, so that he hides, shuns her, and denies her. Yet then, too, the leap is taken from the coloured into the white ranks.

In no circumstances, however, can the coloured man, as a coloured man, hope to pass as the white man's equal. And if he cannot hope, he does not hope.

And so he lives among others of his kind; and, unless awareness from Russia has come upon him, he approaches the white man only as an inferior.

He nevertheless remains a civilized man. He is more civilized than the European peasant (for he is a townsman himself, and seldom a peasant), more civilized than the poor white.

He likes a concert, a cinema, a dance. He goes to school. He belongs to a Coloured Boys' Brigade, a Church, a Society, a Lodge. On the Second of January, he holds in Cape Town his elaborate Coon's Carnival, the only regular carnival in South Africa. His persiflage is that of the lower metropolitan classes. The flirtation of young Cape People,

the conversation of old Cape People, is probably the same
as flirtations and conversations in the East End of London.
He also, like his Hottentot and white, rather than his Eastern, forebears, enjoys his drink.

And yet, the less civilized white peasant of Europe is to
this extent the coloured man's superior: the blood in him
is stronger for advancement. The descendant of serfs may
become a Tchekov. The peasants of Eastern Europe, the
plebs, have seized power from those they once served.

The blood of the Cape man is not like that. It is as if the
offspring of the originally mixed unions had, through generations, and through circumspection of life and interbreed-
ing, achieved a definite, inferior, and static race: a race not
given to rebellion (its mothers were submissive); a race with
something old and civilized about it (its fathers were Europeans); a race made up of weak materials and without the
capacity for great spiritual or intellectual growth.

There are some who suggest that mixed breeds, unless re-
plenished in a generation or two with the blood of one of
the original stocks, tend to die out. The Griquas are given
as an example of a people who, during this century, have
begun to disappear.

The Griquas, however, are not so much disappearing as
becoming absorbed. And the Cape People, intermarrying
all the time, bear out Darwin's denial in *The Descent of
Man*, that mulattoes and half-castes are infertile and are,
physically, at any rate, well-established.

The Griquas here mentioned came originally from the
same stock as the Cape People—one branch adhering to
civilization, the other wandering away, in advance of the
Voortrekkers, through the desert to the Vaal.

Of all the mixed breeds that originated in the Cape, the
Cape People alone retain their identity. Those that went

north are merged with other fugitives—the Bantu fugitives from Chaka, Mantatisi, Moselikatze; the remnants of the hundred years of Kaffir fighting.

But there are still everywhere in South Africa the half-castes—literally the half-castes—of the day's casual and idle begettings.

These are less like the Cape People than the Griquas were. They have no Malay in them. They have not much Hottentot—often no Hottentot. They are the first fruit of the association of white men with the native women of the country.

In native territories where there live a few unattached white men; on gold and diamond diggings; in locations on the outskirts of towns and villages, black women sit suckling yellow babies. Sometimes the babies have the black peppercorned heads of their mothers; but sometimes they have fuzzy brown or rusty-coloured hair, and grey or yellowish eyes. And they grow up with their little black brethren in the location or kraals, slightly despised by them, but living the same lives and marrying and ending among them.

The fathers have no interest in their half-breed children: they neither acknowledge them, nor provide for them. . . .

From which one may see that parental love is not an instinct—not an unreasoning impulse—but a social development. Where the social embarrassment would be intolerable, parents abandon their children. . . .

In older days, when there was no white society to hinder him, a white man took casual girls from the kraals or he took a black woman to live with him in his house in order to satisfy his physical and domestic inclinations; incidentally produced five or six half-breeds; and, unless he was tied down by his circumstances, without any compunction went back to civilization, or wandered off to another part of the country. If he went back to civilization, he married a white woman. If he wandered off, he took a new black woman and with her, too, had a family.

Not very often, he became, as South Africans call it, a White Kaffir; merged himself with the natives; stayed forever with the wives he bought and his African children.

Two men of this kind are outstanding: Buys, the first white settler in the Transvaal; and Dunn, of Natal. They founded clans of half-breeds.

At this day, the descendants of Buys—all named Buys— live on land of their own in the northern Transvaal which is called Marah, after the land of the Bitter Waters to which Moses' followers came; and what their place is in South Africa they cannot understand.

The people of the Union are more generous than the people of the United States towards the coloured that dare pass for white.

In Virginia, for instance, a man with not more than a sixteenth of Indian blood is classed for marriage purposes as a Caucasian. But if a man with the slightest percentage of Negro blood marries a white woman, they may not, legally, live in the State of Virginia.

In South Africa, there are, according to different purposes, different definitions of colour. And though, for the rest, a man is as white as he looks, a new law forbidding mixed marriages is being strictly enforced. Under it, if a marriage officer thinks a bride or bridegroom suspiciously dark, he may require immediate proof of whiteness.

On the other hand, he is not at all likely to go back two or three hundred years to seek out black blood. The nuisance apart, he would not dare to. Who knows what facts inconvenient for quite other people might emerge?

In practice, if a man looks like a white man he may buy liquor in the Union, or vote there, or try for white in marrying there. If he hardly looks a white man, he manages to get away sometimes with talk of Portuguese blood—he may be able to prove Portuguese blood. And though Portuguese blood from Mozambique is almost certainly mixed blood, is the Union going to offend its neighbour by saying a Portuguese, whatever colour he may be, is not white—its good neighbour whence come so many mine-boys?

It is, indeed, seldom that the rule of the eye is qualified by harsh enquiry. The man with the secret drop of black in him is not tormented as in America.

In short, then, it may be said that where the American classes as black any person who conceivably may be black, South Africa classes as white any person who conceivably may be white.

This is partly a matter of humanity, partly a matter of discretion, partly a matter of the bribe that is offered to society. Discounting the romantic shuddering—the conventional hypocrisy—over hidden black blood, the position is that if a person not impossibly dark can pay his way in the coinage of success, he may enter anywhere; he is not rejected socially or even matrimonially; past and future are alike taken on trust.

On the other hand, if socially the South African is kinder than the American to the man of mixed blood, politically—nationally—he is less kind.

The reason is simple. The Negroes—the coloured—of America are a tenth of the population. In time, for all America's precautions, the whites will absorb them and then the Americans will become a slightly yellower race, more akin to their South American neighbours and also to their friends among the United Nations.

The Africans of South Africa (not to mention the other non-Europeans) are nearly four times the number of whites. The Africans of Africa are forty times the number of whites. In Africa, accordingly, if there is a fusion of colour, little will remain of whiteness, very little indeed of the European race and that civilization which, with all its faults, is yet the highest the human race has known.

If the white man, now in Africa, goes out of the continent or into the black man, it will not be the first time such a thing has happened in the oldest of continents: the Americans themselves who scorn the South African's desperate efforts to stay white would not like it if they had before them the continual thought of disappearing before, or into, the Negroes. They might equally deny them chances of overcoming their dark inheritance, they might with greater cause than Abraham Lincoln deny that all men are in all ways equal: "The Negro is not our equal in colour."

Among the first to deny that the black men are their equal in colour are the coloured men. They, more than any, have need to assert their whiteness, and they bitterly do it.

CHAPTER ELEVEN

The Africans (Bantus, Natives, Kaffirs)

W HEN the black man came sweeping down from the north three centuries ago, all southern Africa seemed to be his province. He was bold and virile and prolific. He showed his Asiatic blood by his colour, that was lighter than the Negro's, his differently shaped head, his nose that was often curved, his almond eyes, the oval contour of his cheekline.

In some of his customs too he carried the East with him. And there are many who believe that, as Selous the hunter thought: "The blood of the ancient builders of Zimbabwe still runs, in a very diluted form, in the veins of the Bantu races, and more especially among the remnants of the tribes still living in Mashonaland and the Barotse of the Upper Zambesi."

But what is the origin of the Bantu races? No one knows. Who were the builders of Zimbabwe? No one knows. Actually a Zimbabwe means no more than the stronghold of a chief, though it has now become attached to some imposing ruins in Rhodesia.

There these ruins stand in the country Rhodes took from the Mashona and Matabele, half a thousand witnesses to the story of Africa. But the language they speak is foreign to our ears, and we can only guess at what they try to tell us.

We can think of lost cities. We can see in the ruins the remains of palaces, temples, fortresses. We can reconstruct into an edifice of romance the conical towers, the stairs and floors, the giant monoliths, the parallel passages—rows upon rows—seventy, eighty, a hundred rows of unmortared granite blocks mounting upwards face to face. On a koppie surveying the world there rest the remains of what today is called the Acropolis—there are its walls and passages and recesses and caves and temples and strange symbols and birds of stone that Epstein might have carved. . . .

A tall brown aquiline people called the Bakwena used to work so well in stone, one might almost believe they, rather than the Mashona or Barotse, built those ruins. They could build strong high walls without lime or mortar. Their houses had architraves and cornices and fluted pilasters to hold the roofs. Their walls and floors were polished with a mixture of dung and metal until they shone like agate. The soldiers of Mantatisi, of Moselikatze, of Chaka pursuing Moselikatze, destroyed them, so that never again have they been what they used to be.

But others, again, say that no African, no Bantu built that dead city. They say that men must have come from far lands to build it. They say that religious rites that were never born in Africa were once practised in the temples between the Zambesi and the Limpopo. There are those Phœnicians, chartered by Solomon, who once landed on the coast of Mozambique and came to dig for gold in this land of Rhodesia and built houses there, and worshipped Baal and Astarte, and sacrificed black bulls as some African tribes still do today. There are the Indians who planted Indian trees and flowers and fruits which are found in Rhodesia and nowhere else in Africa. Some even think that the Queen of Sheba came from the regions of the River Sabi in Rhodesia, and not from Ethiopia or Arabia. But this seems unlikely. She could hardly have gone to Jerusalem "with a very great train, with camels that bore spices" (though certainly with the gold and precious stones) in the little coastwise vessels that Hiram of Tyre sent to Sofala in the quest for Solomon's gold.

Milton, however (he may have seen an African map by John Speed, dated 1626), is among those who identify Sofala with the Ophir from which Hiram's navy fetched the gold, for he writes of:

> *Mombaza, and Quiloa, and Melind,*
> *And Sofala thought Ophir, to the Realm*
> *Of Congo, and Angola farther south. . . .*

which would make Rhodesia the land of Ophir. Sofala is indeed the nearest port to the Zimbabwe ruins; and, before the sand conquered it, it was the chief town of a great Arabian state, a harbour abie to hold a hundred vessels.

Hither, to this Arabian state, when the Cross confronted the Crescent, the men of Mahomet fled. And they too came inland to trade with the black men of the country in slaves and gold and ivory. Later, Persian Muslims came. Continually, down the east coast of Africa, men of the East came—as they are coming today.

So this is why there are Bantus on whose faces the East has left its mark, though the religion of the East they refused to accept and thus earned their name of Kaffirs—infidels—men rejecting Mahomet.

Across John Speed's map, about the twenty-second parallel that Rhodes could never cease to think of, lies the land of Monomotapa, that was the land of the Makalanga before they killed the Portuguese Jesuits who were trying to convert them and were then overcome by the Portuguese.

In Monomotapa the Bantu tribes gathered and later came south. The Portuguese, the English, the Dutch did not find them in the country when they landed at the Cape. It was only towards the end of the seventeenth century, a generation or so after van Riebeeck occupied the Cape, that they were met on the east coast by sailors shipwrecked at Delagoa Bay. It was only in the eighteenth century, as the whites moved east and the blacks moved west, each wiping away the little aboriginals of the land—the Hottentots and Bushmen—that the great colour clash, whose climax may not be far off, began.

Today the children of the race of Chaka, the King of the Zulus who "ate up" whole tracts of Africa, who "wiped his spear" in the blood of more than a million people; of Dingaan, his brother, who murdered the trusting Voortrekkers; of Moselikatze, who, flying from Chaka and following Mantatisi, swept bare the land across the Vaal, and challenged the Dutch, and now sits upright on the same Matoppo Hills where Rhodes lies; of Moshesh, the wise and wily Basuto who knew when to make war and when to make peace—today they are all, all the black people who were friends or enemies to each other and challenged the march of civilization—they are all the charges, the servants, the dependants, the victims, the problems, the danger, of the white men.

II

It has already been remarked here that the Africans, Bantus, natives, Kaffirs, aboriginals, black men—whatever one may choose to call them—are no more one nation than are the inhabitants of Europe. Without further consideration of the Bushmen who have passed away, and the Hottentots who hardly exist now as a pure race, one may divide the natives of South Africa into two groups: the Zulu-Xosa and the Basuto-Bechuana. Since Ba and Be in the second group simply mean people, the smarter Bechuana or Basuto now call themselves Tswana or Sotho. A more technical division of the South African natives would be Nguni, Shangana-Thonga, Sotho, Venda, Lemba.

The last two are small nations that do not much resemble the other Bantus, and they both live in the Zoutpansberg in the northern Transvaal (the Salt-pan Mountains) which the Voortrekkers reached in the late eighteen thirties. The Venda have a language and strange old customs which greatly interest scientists. The Lemba have features that are hardly Negroid, a language from far north, and Semitic traditions.

The Nguni—roughly the Zulu-Xosa, composed of many tribes—are the people who went east and southeast from Monomotapa, taking with them Hamitic and Semitic blood and laws. The AmaZulu, People of the Heavens, went east; and among them was the small Zulu tribe which called itself after the name of the whole group and from which Chaka, the great tyrant, sprang.

The land of the Zulu is today Natal.

The AmaXosa went southeast. Among them, too, was a tribe, the Xosa, that called itself after the name of the whole tribe, though the Tembu had a higher royal status. Ranking with the Xosa and Tembu were the Pondo. Among the inferior tribes of the Xosa were the fugitives from Chaka that came to the Xosa, crying "Fenguzi-la"—"We are in want," so that they were henceforth called, in contumely, the Fengu; and also the Baca who, alone among the natives, will carry night-soil. They did it in Johannesburg's more primitive days; they do it still deep down in the mines.

The land of the Xosa is today the eastern Cape.

The Sotho—the Bechuana-Basuto peoples—are also composed of many tribes. They, too, passed through Monomotapa and have Hamitic and Semitic customs. The Basuto settled in land that later became the Orange Free State, but a part of them are in the mountains of Basutoland, under British protection. The Bechuana settled in land that later became the Transvaal, and they have, besides, their own territory Bechuanaland—under British protection.

The Shangana-Thonga live in the northern and north-eastern Transvaal, and among them are still other refugees from Chaka.

The Zulus have, in effect, no Hottentot or Bushman blood. The Xosas have Hottentot blood and the Hottentot click in their speech. The Bechuana-Basuto have much Hottentot and Bushman blood. For this reason, they are smaller and yellower than the Zulu-Xosa peoples and have not their looks. In their wars against the followers of Moselikatze, they could tell when enemies were about by their wider footprints. One can also distinguish between European and African footprints. Despite the Arab blood in the South African natives, their feet are flat: no high arches leaves gaps in the prints.

The South African natives are always typified by the Zulus. But the Zulus are not the biggest, handsomest, and most intelligent of the South African natives. The Shangaans (Shangana) are. They think so themselves. They are very conceited about their looks and brains. At the same time, they regret their darkness; and when they speak of a woman's beauty they generally mean she has a light skin, and for a light-skinned girl, they will pay more lobola.

Lobola may best be defined as the opposite of a dowry, and it is less out-of-date than a dowry. There cannot be so many fathers as there used to be able to pay young men to marry their daughters. But, in the kraals, the fathers still expect young men to pay them for those treasures, their daughters; and even the young men who go to work in towns save their money to buy cattle for a girl at home. A young man has to be very advanced before he will rebel against the paying of lobola, a young girl very advanced (or abandoned) before she will take a young man who has not paid her father lobola. Those are not girls for whom a young man will pay lobola, that go about the towns wearing smart clothes and spectacles. Even if there is nothing wrong with their eyes, they wear spectacles: one may almost take spectacles to be a sign of depravity—at least, as the fashion is today.

It is generally held to be an unfortunate thing that young Africans come to work in the towns without their women. The girls that follow them are more unfortunate: unfortunate, according to the old description, in themselves; unfortunate for the community. It has been said by an authority, who is now an official in Rhodesia, that in half the houses provided by Johannesburg's municipality for natives, men live with concubines; and that in half of these, again, illicit liquor is brewed, and also crime.

The tribal life of the African is bound up with two customs: Initiation and Lobola. Initiation means that a young man goes to what are called the Mountain Schools—the secret schools in the mountains—and that there, with others of his age, he is painted white, confined in huts, circumcized, taught tribal ways and the mysteries of sex, comes out a man and is given a woman. Girls too are initiated, but not so generally now as boys.

Where chiefs have many wives, the first wife is not the principal wife—she is only that one who has removed from him the white paint of his initiation. Nor is her eldest son his heir. He is only the first to come. An important chief's Great Wife is chosen from a Royal House by his counsellors and lobolaed by the tribe. A child of this Great Wife is the heir. The chief has also, granted his sufficient status, a Right-hand and a Left-hand wife.

The lobola is paid in cattle and money.

A woman's children belong to the male head of her family and the lobola is their ransom. But the husband is not cheated by a childless wife. Her younger sister ("the seed bearer") gives him the children for whom the lobola was paid.

There are people, and particularly and naturally young and advancing natives—who are against the custom of lobola. The white people say it makes merchandise of women —slaves to be sold at a bidding. The young natives say that, on the contrary, it makes slaves of the men. Though a father will sometimes give his girl to an old man because he feels she is not beautiful enough to win a Jacob's laborious devotion, he will yet love her too well to offer her as a slave. . . . The Biblical Jacob, when one comes to think of it, had also to pay lobola for his wives.

The young man, however, must deny himself for years to get the cattle and money the father requires for his girl —the present price is about twelve cattle and twenty pounds. He has sometimes, if he and his girl become too impatient to wait for a recognized marriage, to yield to her father their unransomed children. A couple may become middle-aged before their union is hallowed by lobola. An ambitious young man often cannot enlarge his life because he is enthralled to his father-in-law.

On the other hand, lobola is a great boon to the women in the kraals. Where, in other parts of the world, a woman-child is regretted, so that even the most civilized parents wish for sons rather than daughters, and certain ancient nations kill their female babies, among the South African natives there is quite the opposite view. The Bantu must be among the few peoples in the world who hope for girl, instead of boy, babies.

The reason at root may be material, but, because a woman has a potential value in cattle and money, she is welcomed into the world; she is guarded with care; she is treated with honour; she grows up with the assurance of one who knows her own worth; she respects her body and her virtue so that a man may desire to labour for her; she takes pride in her value and despises a woman who cannot command a substantial lobola.

Again, what is paid for is treasured. A man will be moved to guard greatly something which he has been able to get only by eating his mealie-meal in the sweat of his face.

The custom is also of social and economic use to the white man. Lobola makes the native work and it prevents polygamy. If a man has to pay a dozen cattle, and money besides, for a wife, he does not casually decide to have more than one wife or even an extra woman.

So that today, since there is still this old marriage-handicap of lobola, since natives no longer fight one another and men are accordingly not scarce, not ten per cent of native marriages are polygamous. And since cattle are not, in these times, so quickly come by and a native often cannot marry so soon as he otherwise might do; and since, with civilization, his demands and those of his wife-to-be are risen, the African, like his European contemporary, finds himself marrying at a later age than his father did, and also his family is smaller.

In these days, the town natives, unlike the Indians, control their output of children. But, in the old kraal days, the number of children a Bantu woman, on an average, produced was five; and it was the same whether she shared a husband or not, though it may not have been the same if she shared a husband with too many others.

The missionary Moffat wondered that Moselikatze, with his thousand wives and concubines, had so few children. It is strange, too, how little is told of the children of King Solomon's thousand wives and concubines.

The explanation about Moselikatze may be that he was a thinking man who, any day, preferred a conversation with Robert Moffat to the amiabilities of his thousand women.

But Solomon (also reputed to have been a thinking man) seems to have concerned himself not only with philosophy, literature, interior decoration, architecture, peace, religion, and statecraft—he composed the very Song of Love Songs; he won the Queen of Sheba; unlike Moselikatze, who could not be persuaded, even by Moffat, to take on a new god, he allowed his heart to be turned by his heathen wives after strange gods. Solomon must really have cared about women.

But yet the Bible gives all sorts of figures concerning Solomon: his thousand wives and concubines; his thousand and five songs; his three thousand proverbs; the twenty thousand measures of wheat and, again, of oil, he gave Hiram; his levy of thirty thousand soldiers with the seventy thousand labourers and the eighty thousand stone-cutters; the exact proportions of the buildings on which he spent most of his time—it only says nothing of the five thousand children that (by Bantu standards) his wives and concubines should have produced, or even (allowing just one child to two women) of a mere five hundred.

III

The life of the native begins in the kraal.

In the kraals, in those small villages of huts that, like cattlefolds too, are called kraals, whole tribes spring to the command of their chief as soldiers at the word of an officer. He has sway over them more absolute than a European can imagine.

But in the locations outside the towns, and in the towns themselves, there are no chiefs, no tribal regulations. The life of the old-fashioned kraal native is still largely, though not, as at one time, entirely, based on two great principles: obedience to his chief and his tribal laws; a socialism of the most comprehensive character.

The tradition of the first principle keeps him, while he adheres to it, law-abiding. Having, for instance, fought the white man, and admitted the white man as his superior, he follows his chief in giving him his respect and obedience. Within a few years of the time when Dingaan and his Zulus had tried, with their black bodies, to bar the white advance into Natal, one single white man, that same Theophilus Shepstone, who later annexed the Transvaal, was ruling between one hundred thousand and two hundred thousand Zulus in Natal. And so, for thirty years, he ruled them, and in peace.

"Know ye, all Chiefs, Petty Chieftains, Heads of Kraals, and Common People," he proclaimed in the high manner of the Zulus themselves, "a man's life has no price; no cattle can pay for it. He who intentionally kills another, whether for witchcraft or otherwise, shall die himself; and whether he be a Chief, a Petty Chieftain, or Head of a Kraal, who kills another, he shall follow his murdered brother; his children shall be fatherless, and his wives widows, and his cattle and all his property shall be forfeited.

"Let this be proclaimed in every kraal and on every hill, so that none may say 'I knew not!'"

With the native's adherence to his chief is bound up his socialism—that is, the socialism of the unemancipated kraal native; and this socialism has something which the new socialism of Europe has not. For where, with the African, it is natural because it is primitive, with the European it is self-conscious because it is a deliberate changing from a tradition which he believes has failed him: it is in his head and heart and not in his blood.

In the kraal the chief holds the land in trust for the community. In the kraal—and it extends to the town—a man is never utterly friendless. In the kraal no one wishes to possess more than another, to work better, to excel materially at his associate's expense, or to his chagrin. In the kraal of olden times . . .

But even in the kraal of modern times a fellow tribesman is addressed and described and introduced as brother—so that if a European wants to know the actual relationship between two natives, he must patiently enquire whether they had the same father and mother, or perhaps only the same father; whether their fathers were brothers or their mothers sisters; or whether they merely belong to neighbouring families. . . . A man will need money for his brother—his real or so-called brother. "My brother has lost his money." "Well, he is working. He will pay you back." "But it is my brother. How can he pay me back? I must give him the money. It is my *brother*."

If a naked child of three, with his round serious black eyes, and his protruding little belly, gravely performs a native dance at a white person's request and is rewarded, he will, as a matter of course, hand over his reward to some elder child, or, if it is divisible, share it. Any kraal native, young or old, will, in the leanest times, regard the food that is given him as a trust for the common good. . . .

Then, suddenly, he will kill another for a sixpence, for a sack.

When a man dies, not only his possessions but also his liabilities descend on his children.

On the other hand, as the individual has a duty towards the tribe, so has the tribe towards the individual. It is responsible and the government expects the chief to embody that responsibility—for the well-being, the security, and even the misdeeds of its members. As a result the kraal's *esprit de corps* is shown in the directly opposite way from the European tradition. It works out in something like the Russian way.

In the kraal a man tells. (But so, of course, does the European of one who is not in his social stratum). If a kraal-dweller has transgressed the law, his fellow will report him to his chief, for otherwise the whole kraal shares in his dereliction. The cause of the community, which is also his own cause, is hence his agreeable duty.

In the town a man does not tell. No native servant will watch the interests of his employer to the extent of reporting against a fellow servant. He will see a series of misdeeds going on for years, and say nothing. If a native is asked what his evidence will be in the case of a friend charged with a crime, he is quite likely to respond: "What does Sir" (or "Master") "think would be best?" It will not enter his head to tell the mere truth. The court has to go on the probabilities.

It is a question of which tradition seems to work out better. If a Walt Whitman were looking long and long, not into a pen or shed, but into a reed-built, hive-shaped, smoke-filled, windowless native hut, he would no doubt remark how, among Bantus in the same kraal, there is no sweating or whining or repenting or praying—no respectability or mania for owning things; and he would think them higher than other human beings.

But yet, in the process of not sweating or whining or repenting or praying or coveting respectability and possessions, every primitive native in every land destroys his land; destroys his life on the land; can no longer live on the land; and, now that he cannot wander away to empty lands, may be thankful for the civilization that has grown up to sweat and whine and pray and covet and possess the means to save him.

Today, no more than forty per cent of South Africa's natives still live in their own communities. The other sixty per cent live among Europeans on the land or in the towns.

This is how the natives of South Africa have come to their present position:

In 1779, not long after black and white first met in the

eastern Cape, there began those Kaffir Wars that lasted a hundred years; that the white people took on as their own wars, but whose origin was the insult offered by the Tembu Paramount Chief to the Xosa Paramount Chief in suggesting a lobola of only a hundred cattle for his daughter. In those days the Boers named the Great Fish River in the eastern Cape the inviolable boundary between black and white.

During this hundred years, Chaka, the Napoleon of the Zulus, in a great passion for blood and glory, destroyed his own people and many others.

Then, on the Basuto side of the Drakensbergen, the Queen Mantatisi, scorned in love by a fugitive from Chaka, drove forth in rage against the world until what Chaka had done to the Zulus was done by her to the Bechuanas and Basutos. She left their countries so bare that even her own naked, blackened, black-plumed, satanic warriors ended as cannibals.

In the wake of Mantatisi, came Moselikatze, devastating further the Basutos and Bechuanas.

The Boers came, the Voortrekkers. They fought their way through Basutos, Bechuanas, Moselikatze's Matabele, and Moselikatze abandoned to them the part of Bechuanaland that is now in the Union and went further north. There, defeating the Mashonas and other tribes, he established Matabeleland and Mashonaland which Rhodes took from his son Lobengula in the eighteen-nineties.

In the end, all the black people were overcome by the guns and horses of the white people.

After the white people had defeated the black people that had destroyed their own strength, after they were in control and the black people had to give up fighting, the black people recovered so quickly that, in 1894, Rhodes told the Cape Parliament: "The natives are increasing at an enormous rate. The old diminutions of war and pestilence do not occur. . . . The natives devote their minds to a remarkable extent to the multiplication of children. . . ." He asked what was now to be done about them.

He answered.

He was responsible, he said, speaking as Rhodes of Rhodesia, Rhodes, Prime Minister of the Cape, Rhodes, the Chairman of De Beers and his Goldfields companies, for two million human beings.

He put before Parliament what he proudly called his "Bill for Africa." Not South Africa—Africa. "You are sitting in judgment," he told the Members, "on Africa."

The Bill was passed almost unanimously.

In 1947 General Smuts said:

"Today, if you discuss the native question . . . you cannot look at it merely from the South African point of view. If you touch this question, you touch Africa."

Africa is that continent which has a hundred and sixty million blacks and four million whites; and has overcome all previous civilizations below the Nile; and is faced, as in times past, by Asiatic invasion; and is now confronted in its darkness by this group of two and a half million whites, crying, from its thinnest, lowest end:

"Black shall not pass."

IV

There were certain words, certain thoughts, Rhodes applied to the black races. For instance, human. "They have human minds." "Help them use their human minds." He spoke the word "human" as though to combat the suggestion that they were not human. "I do not believe they are different from ourselves," he said boldly, challenging Darwin's thought that, even in God's eyes, they were not as white people.

But yet he called them children, declaring them thus a

people, retarded. Rhodes's Bill for Africa was a measure to separate these retarded people from the advanced white people. . . .

Speaking in Parliament, he went on to say:

"The natives in the past," he said, "had an interesting employment for their minds in going to war and in consulting in their councils as to war. By our wise Government, we have taken away all that employment from them. We have given them no share in the Government—and I think rightly too—and no interest in the local development of the land, which cannot continue to provide enough for all of them. . . . We do not teach them the dignity of labour, and they simply loaf about in sloth and laziness. . . . These are my premises."

This was his solution:

To give the natives, under European direction, their own land, which no whites, except officials, approved traders, and so on, might enter. To train them to govern, manage, tax, and educate themselves; to take liquor from them; teach them to work; train them to build their own roads and bridges and grow their own food and forests.

There would be individual holdings (Rhodes had no faith in the natives' communism, under the dictatorship of their chiefs). There would be primogeniture (he believed this system to be a source of England's strength). Property owners, as was the Cape law, would have a vote. The younger sons would labour three months in the year (a ten-shilling tax on "loafing" if they did not) on Europeans' farms and mines. The reserves were more than natives' reserves. They were South Africa's reservoirs of labour.

So was the Glen Grey Act a success?

Rhodes considered Glen Grey "the best portion of South Africa." The *Encyclopædia Britannica* of 1911 described it as "well-watered and fertile." A government commission of 1932 called it desert.

For this the commission blamed both black and white.

The Europeans, said the commission, had changed the environment of the native, but had not taught him how to adjust himself to the new environment. The native still planted as his forefathers planted; he practised the animal husbandry of his forefathers; he believed religiously in a plenitude of cattle and then could not understand why "man begets, but land does not beget"—why, in short, land eroded by cattle eating its growth to the roots and worn out by continual planting of the same crops should become a desert. . . .

And yet in Glen Grey, thought the commission, lay a great idea. These very reserves, so depleted, might, with help and teaching, be rescued and restored; the native could still be taught to govern himself; the reserves alone offered a basis for the solution of the Native problem—a practical method of natural segregation. Where Glen Grey had failed, Europeans had their difficult material, their limited experience, and not their evil intentions to blame. The policy of segregation, said the commission, should continue. . . .

Seven years later, a leader of liberal opinion in South Africa, the President of the Institute of Race Relations, put it like this: The Liberal, he said, had, for the good of the native, to consider three policies: Total Assimilation, Total Separation, a native life among Europeans running parallel to theirs. "When liberals support or demand some measure for improving the Reserves they are in principle working for Total Separation. When they approve the admission of Native, or other non-European students into Universities which are predominantly white, they take a step on the road towards Total Assimilation. When they encourage the Native to organise for, and among, themselves some service or institution similar to these available for whites, they are practising the policy of Parallelism." As things were in the world, he thought that "total separation should be the liberal's choice."

Today Dr. Malan's supporters, who condemn liberals as the enemies of the white race, say exactly the same: but for different reasons.

Practical men—businessmen and economists—do not know how it can be done: where is the land to come from? Where the money for the industries and developments in the native reserves? Where will their own enterprises get labour if the natives devote themselves too ardently to their own affairs?

The farmers do not want "black spots" among their own lands. They say: "The natives should restore the land they have destroyed" before new land is got for them.

Chiefly, the sort of young natives that call themselves Africans hate the thought of the reserves. It is the white romantic, not the new young African, who sees a noble picture as the native, in his bright blanket, strides along eroded red paths on rock-crested mountains, with his wife behind him, on her head a load, and on her back a child.

What the educated young native sees is the misery of the crowded reserves where the land is so badly farmed and the yield so poor that a cow will give "not even a can of milk"; and the family has to be broken up by its men becoming migrant labourers.

Often, too, these men don't want to come home again. For in the towns, so they say, one learns trades; gets better wages, work, food, education, medical help; a chance to play European games, see films, read news, meet men of other tribes, find out modern thoughts and ways.

Finally, there are the old men at home who so dislike
European interference that they will not let boreholes be
sunk in their lands, or use the government ditches, or send
their children to the pre-school feeding centres. Often their
children starve.

Yet the dream of separation does not fade, and always it
is based on Rhodes's Bill for Africa.

Three years after Union, General Botha, its first Prime
Minister, decided to add twenty million acres to the native
reserves, which were then, with their other holdings, thirteen per cent of the Union's land.

Considering the natives' numbers, this figure does not
look well; but, again, only fifteen per cent of the Union's
land is arable, and the natives, like other people, prefer to
live in towns.

Botha's plan naturally made the price of land go up; the
German war of 1914 began and South Africa was in it and
had a rebellion besides; a depression followed the war; fifty
per cent of the white population was below the bread line.
After General Botha died and was succeeded by Generals
Smuts and Hertzog, there was no more talk of twenty million acres; the best one could now do was thirteen million
acres, but there was also another interesting idea: one would
spend a half million pounds on getting land and sinking
boreholes in it.

What land?

Every Union Prime Minister has bitterly demanded the
three British territories, all dependent on the Union: Swaziland, Basutoland, Bechuanaland. Each seems to have had
secretly in his heart the thought to solve the Union's Native Problem with these—with one of these. Which one?
Which has much space and needs boreholes?

Obviously not Swaziland, a small country whose Queen
mother is the most prolific rainmaker in southern Africa.

Not Basutoland, so eroded that almost every able-bodied man has to go and work in the Union.

Well, naturally, Bechuanaland: a quarter of a million square miles big; a desert, reputed to have under its sands much water; the very land for boreholes.

Only the territories will not come into the Union: they like, under Britain's mild protection, to rule themselves. Particularly will Bechuanaland not come into the Union. Bechuanaland has already a man to each square mile. It is enough. The Bechuanas want no millions of Union natives thrust upon them.

The educated young Africans who hate the reserves deride the thought that one can "change from a subsistence to a money economy; change the whole relationship between people and land; introduce tax-paying and wage-earning as necessities; introduce Western material culture," and then expect the old social structure of Africans to remain as before. "The Africans," they say, "will not willingly go back to the ancient and fast-dying fields of primitive life. Whether we like it or not, we shall have to cope with what the rest of the world coped with—namely the adjustment of our life conditions to the demands of Western culture."

They say that the Europeans too once "lived like savages and constantly fought one another, and all the nations of the world have been through that stage of development."

They recall that Western culture itself came from the valleys of the Euphrates, the Tigris and the Nile and that Peter the Great went west for the civilization he brought to Russia, and "What," they ask, "is the position of Russia today? Is Russia not one of the two World Powers today?"

They know about the French Revolution.

Are not Africans, they say, getting the treatment which

caused the French Revolution? And they too, they vow, would die for an African revolution. . . .

Sometimes they wonder what, after a successful revolution, they would do with the whites of South Africa. Send them back to that devastated old Europe?

The gentler souls think one could not do that. There is room enough in Africa for all. "As other peoples have done, and as other peoples of this land have already done for three hundred years, black and white can develop together. Together we have made this land what it is today. We have made it our joint fatherland. . . ."

There are, however, cynics among these African intellectuals.

Are the white people, they ask, afraid for their white women? "White women," they say, "are repulsive to us."

If only, they say again, the black peoples had in the beginning united to ward off the Europeans from South Africa, "we should not today have a white problem. . . ."

The quotations cited above are from private papers of young African intellectuals, twenty to twenty-five years old, educated in the Transvaal.

Most Europeans feel about such Africans as these that they are "intellectuals entirely sequestered from the thoughts of their people, quite incapable of independent thought, who merely repeat the precepts of their mentors." And it does seem likely that the native intellectual feels himself far away from the people in his kraal. He can no longer think like them, he can no longer feel like them. He has been trained to think and feel like a European. He is not merely—and crudely—a native. He is a particular kind of native: an African with a European standard.

An older African leader says:

"On railways . . . his" (the black man's) "waiting-rooms are made to accommodate the lowest blanketed

heathen; and the more decent native has either to use them
and annex vermin or do without shelter in biting wintry
weather."

V

What, failing the reserves, can South Africa offer the black
man and yet stay white?

Always there is the white man's fear that to give the
black man too much may mean his own submergence.

Therefore the native may become a teacher or preacher
to other natives; he may become a doctor who runs a risk
if he sees a white patient, but who is so desperately needed
for his own people that the government will give him a
bursary to attend a medical school; he may become a law-
yer, and then he treats his fellow Bantu ruthlessly, and often dishonestly; he may become a craftsman, a trader, a
piece-worker in industries or mines.

But he cannot, as in other parts of Africa, get a position
that will give him authority over whites. In the public services he is employed only as a menial or a low-grade clerk,
except in the Native Affairs Department where he may become an agricultural demonstrator, an interpreter or a
clerk. In the police or defence services he cannot get a
commission.

He can—he somehow does—run a business, a bus, or a
taxi.

France's colonials are divided into three groups: the few
thousand "*citoyens*," highly tried for their French civilization; the lesser "*Notables Evolués*," the millions of "*sujets*"
(many of whom do not want the obligations of a superior
status) who fall under native law.

That they may be citizens, even on rigorous terms, is as
much as friends of the South African natives ask for them.
It is what members of the native Parliament, the Bunga—a

rather helpless affair, directed by white officials—mean when they say: "We think that peace will only come about in this country when all the positions are open to us and we can fill them. . . . If the native is sufficiently educated, he is fitted for work any other man can do. . . . Why has the native departed from his former primitive state and acquired education and trustworthiness if he is not allowed to go forward?"

This is just and reasonable, but can this going forward include the vote, direction of the country?

Many friends of the natives say it should include the vote: they say no more is asked than the French give: that is, full equality—citizenship—according to a man's civilization. This, they say, would mean that only a few natives, and not dangerously many, would get the vote.

But do they not also think every native ought to be educated? And, should not every educated native then get the vote? And would this not be dangerously many for the white people that are a fourth of their number and, above all, want to maintain their white civilization?

What South Africans say is:

"Frenchmen have France to live in. We have only South Africa. We cannot afford to do what Frenchmen can do."

Yet even the French colonies had forced labour until 1946. It was the treatment of French Africans that, in 1925, turned André Gide communist. The Portuguese in Africa, who do not mind blending their blood with that of the blacks and then giving them European status, also have forced labour. The Belgian Africans suffer a social, if not an economic, colour bar; they are not, except to become Catholic priests, allowed to attend universities; and so shocking was the scandal of the treatment of natives by the Congo Free State that now there are a *Charte Coloniale* and a Protective Commission to guard their full rights as Belgian citizens.

The British hold before their black colonials the vision of Self-Government. But, in 1945, a Government Welfare Report said of Kenya that "poverty of a massive and grinding nature, assessed by modern standards, is at present the outstanding feature of African society everywhere in the Colony." British Trusteeship in Tanganyika has had a bad report from a UN mission. Rhodesia has the maximum fixed price of twenty-two and six for a beginning black labourer and forty-five shillings for an experienced black labourer (unskilled); and if the experienced black labourer stays at home for more than six months he starts again at twenty-two and six. Wages no higher are paid in Nyasaland.

There is a thing in South Africa, stranger than any. The greatest oppressors of African natives are the descendants of the freed Negro slaves, now running the Negro Republic of Liberia. No one despises what they call "Bush" people as they do.

Who can deny that black men are exploited throughout Africa? Who can believe white men came to Africa out of simple love of black men? Of all African countries, South Africa, with most to fear, has done the black man the least hurt. Her social services for Africans cost more than those in the rest of Africa together. Her African population has doubled in the last forty years. The Director-General of the United Nations Food and Agricultural Organization said, in March 1950: "I still wonder . . . that such a small European population can do so much for the natives in South Africa. . . ."

But what is the cause of it all? What makes decent people lose their humanity in Africa? Is it only the question of skin? Then where is the answer to Liberia?

There is a deeper cause than colour. There is a terrible answer. It is that human beings have it in them to kick those that are down. What does the saying mean about not kicking those that are down except that the impulse is to do it?

The Africans are kicked because they are down.

But will they always stay down?

In the year 1949, there were native riots in Kenya. Over Kenya flew Lancaster bombers; European and Asian members of the Kenya police reserve were mobilized. One saw that, if the Africans spread riot over Africa, the Asians would stand with the Europeans: as one saw, through the Durban native riots against the Indians in January 1949, that if the Asians advanced down Africa the Africans would stand with the Europeans—though who would eventually dominate one could not tell, except that it would not be Europeans. . . .

There have been riots in Uganda; again civilians mobilized. They guarded planes, halting for the night, on the journey north. There are fears in Tanganyika. Black talk down the east coast is of driving Europeans into the Indian Ocean.

In 1948 a commission enquiring into native disturbances on the Gold Coast found a leading cause to be the Communism learnt by Africans in England. They had evidence of a secret society, the Circle, whose watchword was "service, sacrifice, suffering"; whose aim was a Union of African Socialist Republics, who had a shadow government ready to displace the white government and drive out the Europeans.

They say in Rhodesia and Nyasaland that the Russian consulate in Abyssinia is sending black Communists to excite their natives. Talk about Communists is generally exaggerated; but it is a fact that, in the 1920's, the Colonial Department of the Comintern, acting in Moscow, instructed Communists in South Africa to work for a Black Republic, with a guarantee of minority rights for Europeans. Communists or not, today in South Africa there is talk of strikes which may ruin the country.

One can see what may happen in African territories by looking, not only at Asia, but, more appositely, at Trinidad.

Here were Indians, despoiled in turn by the Spanish, British, Dutch, and French; taken by the British in 1797 and remaining with them after the Treaty of Amiens. Here came Negro slaves and indentured Indian labourers from the East.

Today one may enter a law court in Port of Spain and find only the judge—a British official—white. Lawyers, litigants, witnesses, spectators are all, from yellow to black, dark men. One may see a procession of schoolchildren of whom only two are white. Englishmen of good class are happy to be invited to the homes of coloured dignitaries who maybe have British titles. The white man is on his way out. . . .

Now what, thinking of all these things, is the South African who, alone of white men in Africa, has no other home —what is he to do?

He can withhold the vote, the essence of democracy, from the black man.

He can give the educated black man the vote. If he also gives the black man education, then all educated black men will have the vote, and the white man will in time be enormously outvoted.

He can be utterly just and give the black man the same voting rights as the white man. The white man needs only to be twenty-one to have the vote. If the black man too, at twenty-one, gets the vote then the white man will immediately be outvoted by people four times as many as himself and mostly barbaric. There is the fact of the four million whites in Africa and the hundred and sixty million blacks. His position, under absolute justice, would be that of the

American if the American had five or six hundred million
Negroes, nearly all raw men, within his country, and nine
thousand million Negroes, rawer still, outside his country.
The South African smiles at the fuss Americans make about
their tenth of Negroes.

Even J. H. Hofmeyr, Deputy Prime Minister in General
Smuts's last government, South Africa's wonder-boy, as
General Smuts called him on his death, the greatest brain
(sheer genius apart) South Africa has known—even Jan
Hofmeyr, who died, blamed by supporters no less than opponents, while fighting for their rights, could not think of
giving the natives absolute equality, absolute justice. He
was not a Hofmeyr for nothing. He could stop where reason
overcame feeling.

Abraham Lincoln did not understand the Declaration of
Independence to mean that all men are in all ways equal.
"Certainly the Negro is not," he said, "our equal in colour."

Judging by the preponderance of dark-skinned people in
the world one might think the Creator preferred the coloured to the white people. Their preponderating representatives at the UN begin to think so too. South Africans look
at the equal vote they have at the UN with almost the
dread they have of an equal vote in South Africa. The UN,
indeed, points to their own dilemma. How, under it, they
ask in despair, can they have justice? How can the *white*
man have justice?

We are indeed past the stage where Lincoln may further
be quoted on the Negro: "If God gave him little, that little
let him enjoy.". . . They say at the UN: "Why little?"

The South African, in his fear, withholds this, withholds
that, from the black man. The black man knows the deprivation of the day. His millennium is not yet here.

Against that time, there are in South Africa Negrophilists
who offer the native what they call Christian Trusteeship.
This is a smug and unpronounceable term and likely to be

suspect by people who see how often in our world the name
of Christ is attached to works directly against His teaching.

All, however, that the apostles of this creed mean (Hofmeyr belonged to it) is that they wish, for those that need
it, a measure of humanity. They stand with Dickens.

"Did you hear him say that he could have shed his blood
for me?"

"Do you want any blood shed for you? . . . Does he
shed anything for you that you do want? Does he shed employment for you, instruction for you, pocket money for
you? Does he shed even legs of mutton for you?"

VI

From the lands that were the reserves of native self-rule,
but yet the reservoirs of forced native labour, the natives
came to the farms and mines.

Before Rhodes's day, before the Kimberley mines were
discovered, and after too, there were those derelict natives
working for white masters on the diamond diggings on the
Vaal, who were not any particular sort of people—any tribe
or part of a tribe—but a mixture of the defeated and abandoned peoples that had fled to the Vaal to escape their
servitude to the whites or their destruction by the blacks.

There were the Griquas and Bastaards and Hottentots
running away from the Cape and pursuing the Bushmen
running before them. There were the Hottentot brigands
from Namaqualand under the Afrikaner family. There were
the fugitives from Chaka, Mantatisi, Moselikatze, the
Voortrekkers. There were Xosas escaped from other Xosas.
Zulus, Bechuanas, Basutos, Hottentots, Griquas, Bastaards
fought one another until the end was starvation, the eating
of other human beings—death.

All were against the Bushmen, living with the monkeys
on the hills, in caves or under rocks; against the Bergenaars,
living there too, the People of the Bergs—brown, yellow and

white confused—creeping down to rob, mutilate, kill or be killed.

White men found diamonds, and came too.

And all bred together, and in the end there was a meagre, diseased, feeble assembly of people living on the Vaal that, because of the Griqua, Bastaard, and pure white in them, had yet a something more civilized in their blood than could be found among the great fighting tribes in their own lands. Like the Griquas and Bastaards, they wore European clothes, and they scornfully refused to call the conquering Matabele of Moselikatze other than Kaal Kaffirs—Naked Kaffirs. Most of them spoke one or two native languages, and also Dutch. They were, because of the original London Missionaries on the Vaal, Christians. By the time, however, that the white men were coming for diamonds, the Berlin Missionaries had all but mineral rights on the alluvial diggings that they called Pniel; they collected dues from the natives to send to the Fatherland; but what spiritual or human good they did the natives was not obvious. If Trollope needed a proof of his words that "nothing is done by religion and very little by philanthropy. But love of money works very fast," he should have gone from Kimberley to the diggings, thirty miles away, and seen the contrast between the enlivened natives on the Kimberley mines and the degenerating natives on the River Diggings. Why were the River natives not in Kimberley? To begin with, they had their homes on the river. But also, they were so feeble, the Kimberley mines could not use them.

In the beginning, the River natives, like all natives, had owned cattle and sheep and planted some mealies, and later they had worked for the diggers, and their women had lived with the diggers.

Then, in the year of the Jameson Raid, there fell on the land the great cattle pest, the rinderpest, and the cattle of the River natives died. The Boer War broke out; diamonds dropped to two or three pounds a carat; the diggers gave up both work and workers.

The natives had no cattle left, and they ate their sheep and goats. They gave up planting. They wore, against cold, sacks over their shoulders. The children's legs were like sticks and their stomachs were swollen through the eating of wild berries and roots. There was no longer any question of lobola, and the women came to the men as animals to their mates; and, in between bearing black children, they sometimes bore yellow ones to the white men to whom they also went.

Nearly all the natives had syphilis (which the women gave the white men) and many people went about with rags over their sunken noses or across their lost eyes. The children's faces grew swollen and pimpled. Any little illness that came along was enough to make dust of them. One day a man would be walking about. The next day he was dead. "His head, it was troubling him." "His stomach, it was drawing." "He had the bad sickness."

From the rinderpest and the Boer War the natives on the River Diggings never recovered. A few of them were able to go "on the join" in the two World Wars. The diggings yielded less and less; De Beers controlled the new ones in the Transvaal; Afrikaners and returned soldiers began to farm on the River. The alluvial diamond diggings of the Barkly West District died one by one.

In Kimberley the mines, recruiting their natives from far away, barely troubled to look for workers among the feeble River natives. The De Beers diamond mines, like the Rand gold mines, brought, housed, fed, guarded, tended, and amused their workers. None but the mines had any connection with them. But the diamond mines had a work to do the gold mines had not. Through the theft of diamonds, which might be hidden between toes, in hair, mouths, noses, ears, and also stomachs, the diamond mines had, in the beginning, lost every year hundreds of thousands of pounds. People said that buckets of diamonds were brought as tribute to native chiefs. But in eighty years no native chiefs have sold diamonds or shown any evidence of possessing diamonds. Still, the diamonds that disappeared were never—could never be—found. A part of the process of searching natives, about to return home from the Kimberley mines, was the administering of strong purgatives.

There are today over three hundred thousand natives working in the Rand gold mines, and there have been more. South Africa's new industries get many of the natives the mines used to get, and, on the whole, the civilized ones.

The mine natives are recruited from various parts of the Union—chiefly the Reserves—from the British Protectorates; from Portuguese territory; from the tropics. They may not stay less than ten and a half to twelve and a half months. The Portuguese do not let them stay longer than eighteen months. The Union and other natives stay as long as they like. Most of the Union, Protectorate, and Portuguese natives come several times. Only a third of the Tropical men come back again. The natives represent scores of tribes with scores of languages.

The black miners that the mines like best are those from the East Coast—the Portuguese. Unlike the Union natives, they establish themselves with hearty good will in the compounds. They take more pleasure in keeping themselves clean. They rub their heads with a paste of used carbide until their brushed-out peppercorns become rusty and make a handsome coiffure. Some dance wild and rhythmic dances to the tune of their Kaffir pianos. Others strut and quiver and charge to the accompaniment of a clapping chorus dressed as maidens. The Union natives too have their particular dances.

There are two reasons that make the natives come to the mines. One is to see life—every self-respecting native feels he ought to come to "Josaberg." The other is to earn money. If a family could earn more (on an average) than eleven or twelve pounds a year in the Reserves, the meagre food apart, or more than nine or ten pounds a year in the Protectorates, not many natives would be eager to give up their ease in the sun to go down a shaft in a dark skip at half past three in the morning, to creep about, sweating, on underground stopes.

However, they do not, all of them, all the time, begin work at half past three in the morning. They have their eight-hour shifts, like the white miners.

And there are consolations.

To begin with, the food. What native in a Reserve, Protectorate, or Territory gets (as the Union government decrees) nearly twenty-four pounds of meat a month; thirteen pounds of vegeables; twelve pounds of dried maize or lentils; twelve pounds of bread; four and a half pounds of sugar; peanuts or fat; coffee or cocoa; a slightly alcoholic drink of meal and malt always on tap; and a gallon and a half of beer? For that matter, what Asiatic gets it? How many Europeans?

The calories a native mine-worker has are nearly thrice as many daily as the British got in the years after the war. And sometimes, in those years, when one saw the British agitating themselves over the starved, kicked, baked, or frozen natives in the mines, one had to be sadly amused.

The mines, whether through humanity or self-interest, treasure their natives. The mines, some of them nearly two miles deep, must be properly ventilated. Water must wash down the mine dust. Under the surface there are trains, rest-rooms, first-aid stations, bright lights. After shifts underground, the natives are required to take hot showers. They sleep in dormitories that are heated in winter. They are cared for if they are sick; they have games, cinemas, tribal dances, night schools, Red Cross lessons, and any religion they wish. A sixth as many have tuberculosis as in the reserves.

The only thing they have not much of is money. They get about three pounds ten a month (up to ten pounds if they have special competence) against the white miners' fifty pounds a month; against the higher wages of industrial workers, against the much higher wages of house-workers. And, though they are savages compared, not only with white men, but also with native house-workers, and though their food is worth five pounds a month (the mines get it for less) and they are also housed, cared for, and entertained, they begin to ask why, if the white miner gets two pounds a shift, they may not have ten shillings a shift; and it is hard to explain to them that, if they got even five shillings a shift, a great many mines, new devaluation and all, could not persist. Ignoring dreams of ten shillings a shift (which are put down to Communist tales, though they asked for ten shillings twenty-eight years ago), it is expected that natives will be much encouraged by the promise of an extra twopence a shift upon the completion of two hundred and seventy shifts. And there is always the thought that, little as their wages are on the Rand, they remain the best for unskilled workers in any English-speaking territory.

Now some of the great mining companies have the idea of building houses for their natives on the new Free State mines, and so bringing the families to the men instead of taking the men from the families.

VII

Is there a reason why South Africa's prosperity—indeed, its civilized existence—depends on cheap black labour?

There is a reason embracing many reasons.

The Cape began in 1652 as a wayside station for a trading company whose dealings in the East were dependent on cheap Eastern labour. The Dutch East India's first governor had not been in the Cape two years when he was importing Eastern convicts to help his few Dutchmen who were growing food for the Company's ships.

Four years later he sent for West African slaves. He needed this aid from abroad because the Hottentots were, as yet, not only too inimical, but too savage to do what Eastern convicts or West African slaves would do. The question was also not settled whether the Hottentots would destroy the white men and their cattle or the white men overcome the Hottentots and theirs. South Africa's first piece of Apartheid was the digging of the ditch between the Dutch and the Hottentots.

In the end, the white men overcame the Hottentots. Within the next fifty years Hottentots were working beside slaves and convicts.

They none of them, Hottentots, slaves, or convicts, worked well. Even today, a white people seeing natives eat their lumps of boiled mealie-meal think it is the right food for them. But the mines know it is not—that men cannot work well on such food. The industries know it is not. Only the farms haven't yet made the discovery, and so they cannot get labour, and have now begun to build government-controlled jails in order to get convict labour—just as was done by the Dutch East India Company, when they sent all the way to the East for convicts.

The Hottentots were, in any event, a naturally lazy people, much devoted to drink. "Arré!" they cried, as they drank the fiery stuff, "if only one had the neck of an ostrich!" But the food they got was a little mealie-meal or a bit of pumpkin a day, and they were probably as much exhausted as lazy.

In 1716, the Dutch East India Company asked the Council of Policy at the Cape "whether it would be more advan-

tageous to employ European slaves." Only two men voted
for European labour.

One, von Imhoff, said:

"Having imported slaves, every common or ordinary European becomes a gentleman and prefers to be served rather
than to serve. We have, in addition, the fact that the majority of farmers in this Colony are not farmers in the real sense
of the word, but plantation owners, and many of them consider it a shame to work with their hands."

Yet so it had been instituted from the beginning: when
van Riebeeck brought in slaves, when Hottentots were set
to work. The shame of their overlords was only relatively a
shame. The distance between "a common or ordinary European" and the slaves and Hottentots was, in those days,
hardly greater than the distance of the common or ordinary
European and a man entitled to call himself Von. Even
now, in Socialist England, how many Members of the
House of Lords work in the fields? . . .

But there was another aspect to the Company's question
about whether they should send to the Cape Europeans or
slaves—an aspect they themselves could not foresee. They
did not know, in 1716, about the real natives of Africa,
those hordes of black men that Time had in reserve for the
white men. If it had been decided in 1716 to bring more
Europeans to South Africa; if the burghers of those days had
laid down a tradition of opening the door of one's land, as
one opened the doors of one's house; if they had offered to
share their earthly paradise with others, and not brought in
only a few thousand here and there just to help against the
blacks; if they had craved freedom, not for themselves alone,
but all humanity, South Africa would not today be a country with under two and a half million whites to face a continent of a hundred and sixty million blacks and Asiatics
coming in besides.

South Africa was discovered at the same time as America.

Had its ideas in 1716—before 1716—after 1716—been different, South Africa might have had a white population—never as large as America's since it has not America's waters and rich earth, but still nearer the black population of Africa which America's white population can almost, man for man, match; it might have been a greater South Africa; it might have been the heart of a United States of Africa proudly declaring its mind, and giving its help, to the Old Bad World.

There are Americans who, looking at their vanished chances in the East, say that the only place on earth left to exploit is Africa. Let them come. Let them come to Africa, not only to exploit it, but, if they are not too tired of trying to save the world, through Africa to save it.

Well, one did not know or one would not know.

Does it lie in the heart of the land that its destiny was set the day the Lord filled Africa with Africans and not Europeans? Is it bound to happen that the white man, being first deluded into ease by the service of millions of black men, will in the end find these millions of black men too much for them? Dare they feel themselves so safe—shall they feel themselves so doomed—as not to attempt to enlarge themselves, late as the time is, in order to save their heritage?

For South Africa is surely the white people's heritage. The black people laboured with their hands, that is true. But ownership is to the deviser, not to the means of the fulfilment of his device.

This can be easily seen when one thinks of the men that have been displaced by machines. What rights do the machines take over from the men? None. They had none. Ownership remained where it was.

Men have not even—not any men—the rights they assert, and that are asserted for them, to Life, Liberty, and the

Pursuit of Happiness. Who gives human beings birthrights? Who makes contracts with them, saying: "If you will consent to enter this world, you shall in return have long, free, and happy years"?

Nature gives them no rights. Men merely do for others what their heads and hearts approve or what other men can enforce.

It is the fundamental error of rule by peasants or labourers that they are replaceable by machines and machines cannot rule—they need only, like machines, to be well kept to do their work. Men have just this advantage over machines: they can rise by "the labour that is in wisdom and in knowledge and in equity."

Nor should birth in a land create rights in it. The thing is not only that, as Pope Leo XIII (a Socialist really by disposition) said: "God granted the earth to mankind in general. . . . No part of it has been assigned to anyone in particular"—what claim should a man rightly have to share in a common property if he wantonly damages it? His fellows have indeed a claim *against* him.

So here is the claim civilized men have to lands of savages—but only to the extent to which they themselves maintain and embellish these lands. This planet is all humanity can live on. No people, merely because they have been spawned on a part of it, have planetary rights to utter possession.

It took the white men a hundred years to conquer, in their thousands, the black men in their millions. But, throughout these hundred years, the black men were fighting among themselves, and, by the time the white men overcame them, they were begging the white men for their help. Far, far more than the white men ever did to the black men, the black men did to one another. . . .

At just this time the diamond mines were discovered.

Hundreds of thousands of tons of earth had urgently to be moved. Hundreds of thousands of black men, deprived, as Rhodes said, of their old "interesting employment" of fighting, were thus available to move the hundreds of thousands of tons of earth.

The gold fields were discovered. Millions of tons of earth this time. Tunnels under the earth that would come to pierce more miles of earth than lay between Cape Town and Khartoum. The black men of South Africa were no longer enough for all the tons of earth to be moved. They had to be brought from outside South Africa.

Could the few proud white men of South Africa wish to work side by side with these hordes of wild Africans?

Presently, even if they wished, they might not. Skin and pride apart, the law forbade it. A Colour Bar prevented black men from doing white men's work. A Minimum Wage Act prevented the white men from taking a wage low enough to be offered to black men.

One began almost to fear that presently white South Africans would lose the faculty of labouring when, in a curious way, the contrary was proved. A number of young Jews—boys unaccustomed to wielding anything nearer a spade than a cricket bat, the descendants of men who, for two thousand years, had not had a land of their own to dig in—went from South Africa to become workers in the land of Israel. And what they could do, any white man could do, if the claim were made upon them. White South Africans, white immigrants to South Africa, could do it.

But another thing is being done.

When, in 1716, the Cape Council of Policy laid down their policy of black labour for South Africa, the sole thought was cheap labour; and cheap labour is what all Africa stands for today. The very countries whose people read with abhorrence of this cheap African labour, and that are themselves developed on dear labour, are intent now on coming to Africa for cheap labour.

There was an affair that, in the nineteenth century, was called the Scramble for Africa.

The Portuguese, British, Dutch, Belgians, French got there in good time, but the Germans did not come until, in the eighteen-eighties, H. M. Stanley, the discoverer of Livingstone, went to lecture in Germany and fired them to join in the rush. Then all they could get was German East Africa and German South-West Africa where, in spite of nearly destroying the native populations and setting the Boers against the British, they could not achieve their dreams of a Mittel-Afrika. After the First World War the British got the mandate over German East Africa and South Africa got the mandate over German South-West Africa; and when the League and the UN would not let South Africa make a fifth province of South-West Africa, the new Nationalist government simply offered the South-West Africans representation in the Union Parliament, and so here they are with (or it may be in) South Africa and General Smuts and his followers are very pleased too.

Talking of lands that do not fringe the Mediterranean, there are then these owners of Africa already mentioned; there are the Negro Republic of Liberia and the Lion of Judah in Abyssinia.

Well, now we are in the middle of the twentieth century, and, things having gone as they have gone in the world, and particularly in the East, there is a new kind of scramble for Africa; a conquest through kindness; a taking through giving; a trade-through-aid—America has come to Africa, the New World has come at last to the oldest continent; and high time too.

For only Africa is left to give to and get from. Africa is going to sand because the time is past when religion could leisurely follow the flag, and business, religion. Let business come in quickly on Rhodes's terms of "any flag, any rag," for one cannot live on fried flag or chewed rag.

Into South Africa America has already put much money. She is in the diamond mines of Kimberley, the gold mines of the Rand, the boreholes of the Free State, the copper mines of Namaqualand that the Dutch East India's men found nearly three hundred years ago, the copper mines of South-West Africa, the chrome and manganese and other base metals. She is in enterprises connected with the great companies of the Rand. She sells to South Africa her cars, clothes, and machinery.

Shortly before General Smuts's defeat in 1948, twenty American journalists came to look at South Africa. They called it the place for "venture capital," "risk capital." They expected that American capital would be entering South Africa in "a big stream." They spoke of South Africa's "terrific potential." At the same time, a great American banker said privately that South Africa had a drawback. "The people hate too much," he said.

Now American aid is to go to Africa's undeveloped areas. She is building a great harbour in Liberia. She is arranging with the British to put her money into Africa. The British Colonial Office has invited sixty-odd American experts to survey Africa's neglected earth.

The special thing about Africa's neglected earth is its neglected African. When the American journalists went on to say that South Africa had greater opportunities than Canada, Australia, or New Zealand they meant that these had "reached a social equality before reaching the right stage of development"—they meant, in fact, that in South Africa one still had the cheap African. They advised South Africans not to be concerned with what sentimentalists in the States might say. If you told people in Kansas that there was a terrible racial problem in Natal, they would ask:

"Where's Natal?" And, though they may have heard where
it was at the time the Zulus attacked the Indians of Durban, they have probably forgotten again.

And, if the people of Kansas do not know about Natal,
what can the whole dark continent of Africa be to America but the reverse of the moon? Novelists, journalists, and
propagandists have told how far below the European's
standard of living in South Africa is the Africans', but do
they know how far it is above the African's standard outside South Africa?

With all this new development, we shall now be able
to see whether Americans will pay Africans in Africa what
they pay Africans in America, whether Europeans will pay
them according to the standards of their trade unions. The
world has never rejected the works of Indians or Chinese
getting a penny a day; of children in Madeira getting twopence a day. Even South Africa's Negrophilists do not reject shares in the mines, goods from the industries, the
ease of life that comes from paying the black man a tenth
or fifteenth as much as the white man. The secret heart
says: "Be not righteous overmuch, neither make thyself
overwise: why shouldest thou destroy thyself?"

VIII

As the South African native, seeking work in the homes or
businesses of Johannesburg, is a superior man (an individual rather than a mass man) to the man recruited for the
mines, so he expects a superior life. Like most people in the
world, the African prefers the town to the land, and in
the end the unrecruited worker often settles in the town
where the mineworker can do nothing but go home. In the
last ten years, the native population in the towns of the Union has nearly doubled, and in Durban it has risen by sixty-
four per cent.

Now, when carrying a travelling pass from his commissioner, the native leaves his reserve for Johannesburg, when he stands at a back door facing a smart and civilized Ntaka who is called Charlie, or a Mkubeni who has been renamed Scotchman, or a Mahlohlane who answers to Napoleon, when he utters what is sometimes his only word, "job," when, degraded by his disgusting clothes, he clutches his filthy cap in incompetent supplication, there is little in him to remind one of Chaka's warriors. Who gives these natives their first employment is the mystery.

However, work the native must get, or he may not—the law forbids it—remain in the city. And so he walks the streets of Johannesburg, looking for work.

When he gets it, he is taken to a pass-office to be examined by a doctor and get a pass, which must be renewed monthly at a premium of two shillings, legally payable by his employer. The employer keeps this permanent pass; the servant keeps a copy of it; he gets a special pass if he wishes to stay out after eleven at night. There is the travelling pass. But, again, if he has been in the same work for three years, has no criminal record, can read and write, and is commended by his chief and employer, he can get an Exemption Pass. This is, as it were, a life-pass that exempts him from needing other passes.

There is talk of Europeans getting Identity Cards. This will be chiefly in order to declare their race and citizenship. But it will leave the Exempted natives without the grievance that, unlike Europeans, they have to carry a pass at all.

Any day in the pass-office a concourse of natives may be seen. . . .

Now humanity in the mass—unless it partakes of the quality of the individual: is dressed in uniform, marches in step, sings in harmony, is excited as one, or is blurred into unity by dimness or distance—an assembled humanity is always offensive to the sense and spirit.

But it is never so offensive to either as when it takes the

grub-form preceding civilization, as when it presents itself in the shape of a swarm of dirty, dusty-haired natives, dressed in the discarded clothing of the European—the unrelated, the filthy, the unsightly rags that not the most degraded of white men would wear. There are circumstances in which dirt and tatters are held to be picturesque. Yet no artist would wish to express his realism in the drabness and dirt of a group of natives waiting outside a pass-office.

So here the first member of a kraal has got his foot into a town.

He goes to work in a house, office, or store. He works for a tradesman.

If he is a storeboy, he begins by sweeping floors and cleaning windows and delivering and depositing packing-cases or packages. He gets seven or eight pounds a month, and sleeps on the floor of a room in a yard and finds his own food. He cleans offices and makes tea for officeworkers.

No white tradesman works without his native. Certain tradesmen bring two natives. Caliban digs the ground, mixes the concrete, melts the solder, stirs the paint, holds the bucket, fetches the tool, clears the mess.

After a while he unofficially helps with the work and sometimes becomes so competent that he ventures to break away and work for himself. He then charges from ten shillings to a pound a day; is often quite able; is seldom to be relied on. He does not come when he says he will come; stays away in the middle of the work; leaves it uncompleted in order not to lose something else that offers at the particular moment; is yet so much cheaper than the white tradesman who charges for an hour what the black man charges for a day and ten shillings a day for the black man besides, that he is forgiven all his derelictions if only he will come.

If the native is a houseboy, he begins as a general servant in a small house; is next a garden or kitchen boy in a bigger house; is presently a table and upper houseboy; watches the cook; does the cook's work on the cook's day out; occasionally displays a faculty for cooking; becomes a cook. The gardener-kitchen boy gets four or five pounds a month; the houseboy six to eight pounds a month; the cook nine or ten pounds a month. They have their own quarters. They buy their own blankets. On their walls hang photographs of themselves or their friends, with the faces a ghostly white, yet clearly Bantu faces. Sometimes they put flowers in their rooms. Sometimes they have gramophones. They frequently have visitors; and it may happen that, although to harbour strange natives is against the law, a householder will unwittingly be entertaining for weeks, with bed and board, friends of his servants, and occasionally these friends are women.

The food natives get in what they call "decent" houses (and their pride is greatly involved in the sort of house they work in and their employer's status) is, daily, a half-pound of meat, a half-pound of sugar, a pound of bread, a half-pint of milk, vegetables, jam or syrup, incredible quantities of maize, oats, dried beans or peas; potfuls of tea—coffee, when tea is very dear. They refuse the bush-tea poor Europeans take.

In the days of rationing, they said nothing when sometimes there was no meat; they agreed to take coffee alternately with tea; but they regarded it as a malevolence if they got less than their daily half-pound of sugar. Even if they got most of the household's ration as well as their own, they said where black-market sugar might be had, and, if it was not provided for them, bought it for themselves, but remained somewhat resentful.

There are natives who will accept dismissal rather than do what they were not told they would have to do the day they arrived. There are others who will stay for years, and bring their relations, so that, in the end, all the people in the household come from one kraal. If the Zulus are not as clever as the Shangaans, they identify themselves more with their employers; the homes they serve in become their homes, not only in practice, but as of right: so that they may bring a substitute; go back to the kraal for a year; return, without question, to their job. The Zulus and Shangaans do not regard the Basutos or Bechuanas as their equals, but in these days they tolerate them. Men of different tribes seldom, now, fight one another.

To the family at home, the natives at work in town will not only send money regularly, but also, now and then, a sack of mealie-meal—maize-meal. For, while there is mealie-meal, the family, even in a drought, will not starve.

Mealie-meal is the staple of the Africans' food. If the maize crop fails, they can hardly be induced to eat potatoes instead. And, when they go home, they forget about the daily meat, bread, sugar, jam, vegetables of the town; they eat what their wives cook in a tripod pot outside their huts: and this will be a stiff mealie-meal porridge, with sugar if there is any, and no nonsense if there is not.

Once a year an old cow may be slaughtered; some of the meat is then eaten immediately, the rest is salted and dried in strips to be eaten later on. Occasionally, there may be a sheep or goat.

One talks of men, rather than maid, servants for the reason that natives of good class try to keep their women at home, and also householders prefer men to women. They can work harder, they carry passes.

Women do not carry passes; they are thus not medically examined at pass-offices; they are liable to disappear with one's goods, or have syphilis, or be liquor queens. The men themselves may, in due course, get syphilis. Three hundred thousand natives are yearly treated for venereal diseases at

the Union's hospitals and clinics. Forty per cent of native
women going to prenatal clinics have it. There are others,
naturally, who do not go to clinics, or who become infected
or re-infected after being medically examined. The difficulty
is the nurses, for when they are found to be in a contagious
state, not only are they sent to lazarettos, but the children
they have tended, and also their mothers, have to undergo
Wassermann tests.

It is not true, as is sometimes thought, that the decent
kraal natives are infected by the dissolute town natives. The
natives on the River Diggings, who work where they live,
nearly all have it. Some years ago an official report found
that over ninety per cent of the natives of Northern Rhodesia (which has not much in the way of towns) were venere-
ally diseased; anyone who has lived on the land knows that
kraal people, living together as amiably as the cattle Walt
Whitman so much respected, share their diseases as they
share their blankets, their blood, and their other sad possessions.

At the same time, there is a native social life going on in
the towns that is only in degree different from the social
life of Europeans.

The people have their sets and standards. They live in
brick houses with streets at their doors. They save, incred-
ibly, from low wages. They love the particular church
among the eleven hundred Christian creeds they have developed, though, for purposes of grants and so on, the government acknowledges only seventy. They reverence not only
their white, but their ineffably churchy native ministers.
They marry as Christians, not like the natives who have
still connections with the kraal, with lobola. They have
English or Afrikaans Christian names, and call one another
Mr., Mrs., Miss, Olifant, Selebane, Itumeleng. Though advanced natives go to the Bantu Social Centre to dance and

act and sing there, the conservative ones go, with avidity, from youth through maturity into senility, to Sunday School. For anything connected with the Church is their club, and they sing hymns in their Bantu voices; and the hymns get a strange African quality in the singing—wildness penerates the meek words and notes of the music.

The children go to school. They play football and cricket and tennis. They grow up to dance. They pass examinations and become clerks, or go round on bicycles selling their own goods, or open shops, or learn trades.

They love letter-writing. "I take this short delightful," they write in English, "to acknowledge to you my life on earth." Or: "Just a few lines as to let you know for I am still under Power of God hoping to hear the very same from you." Or: "I am asking £8 because next month my sister is going married. She asks me that she wants everything for married. . . . My wedding has took place on the 20/7/49. Pass my best regards to the boys. I understand about £5. Present is £3. £2 only to paid back. . . ."

The older ones are greatly comforted by insurances of various kinds—particularly insurances that will give them a good funeral. There are some who "keep themselves high" against others—for much the same reasons as Europeans keep themselves high against others: they have a larger house; it is square and not round; it has a pitched, and not a flat, roof; there is a practically complete dinner service; the wife does not work; their minister often visits them; a brother is a teacher; no children in the family are unsanctioned by wedlock—still more, no children have yellow instead of black, skins; despite the temptation of the liquor queens' houses, no son or daughter of the house is in jail.

The black liquor-queens are the people who have replaced the white liquor-kings.

Twenty or thirty years ago, since in the Transvaal intoxi-

cating liquor might not legally be sold or even given to a
non-European, great fortunes were made by white liquor-
kings. The police seldom reached the kings. A desperate,
pathetic person, who had made a shilling or two selling a
native a bottle of bad wine, might be sentenced to a fine; a
too-dark man might try to explain to a sceptical magistrate
that he had a Spanish or Portuguese mother; an Indian or
Chinese might seek to prove how, only by some strange accident, a cask of innocent-seeming liquor had acquired a
high percentage of alcohol; a doctor might be questioned
about the number of his patients that needed brandy.

Much of this business has now disappeared before the
dominance of the black liquor-queens.

The Municipality of Johannesburg, considering it natural
for natives to drink beer, sells them a mild beer at a mild
profit. But they cannot compete against the stronger brew
—not always beer, and sometimes drugs—of the queens; the
beer the mines give their natives can equally not satisfy a
hearty taste. In European homes so imposing that the servants' quarters are far from the main house the business goes
on of illicit beer brewing to which is sometimes added the
business of receiving stolen goods.

And then, of course, the business goes on in homes in native townships.

For this and that reason, native crime has greatly grown
in Johannesburg. In the year 1948, well over two thousand
Union natives were convicted of murder or of crimes caus-
ing death. Over a hundred thousand natives were convicted
of assault. Over two thousand were, in the first half of the
year, found with stolen firearms—generally used in connection with burglary. The increase of serious native crime is
such that many householders keep revolvers and bar their
windows, and judges say native crime has so proliferated, it
is beyond the control of justice.

There is also much crime that has not to do with anger

and danger: card-swindling, pickpocketing, the cheating by experienced town natives of inexperienced kraal natives.

There are some who say that the drink, like the crime, of the natives is the white man's fault: that the cause is the black man's misery in the face of the white man's hostility.

This is partly true. A native has much to gain for the little he has to lose by committing a crime. There are also the two Great Wars which he did not create, but which fed him on the sight and knowledge of killing and killing. There are (elderly natives say) the films that excite the young. . . .

But there is another cause too for these things: the natives of South Africa are not a soft race. Before ever the white man met the black man, the black man was a killer. No Europeans or Asiatics in South Africa would do what the Zulus did to the Indians of Durban at the beginning of 1949. . . .

The thing the white man may blame himself for is the way natives die of tuberculosis. Though one reason for this is that natives do not take much trouble not to die—one's time has come, so one dies—a greater reason is that tuberculosis has to do with lack of proper food and shelter; that white people think it somehow natural for black men to go cold in foul rags and hungry with lumps of meal; that some even think it an offence against their white superiority when a black man is decently dressed.

So Europeans once passed by their own starvelings and hanged children for crimes of hunger.

And if today workmen are better fed in Europe than they used to be, is it all because of sudden virtue?

"Oftentimes," says Thomas a Kempis, "that seemeth charity which is rather of the flesh. . . . Study of one's own interest will seldom be absent."

Still, good is good.

Let the thing come of the flesh if not from charity. It does not pay a land for its people to go hungry.

IX

There is the trouble in South Africa that people call the whole mass of African conflicts simply the Native Problem, as if it were only one problem needing only one solution.

Natives are not merely natives. They are peoples, nations, groups, tribes, communities, kraals, locations, congregations, classes, sets, individuals. Over a hundred years ago, Robert Moffat wrote of a Bechuana aristocrat who, being degraded for a misdemeanour to poverty, killed himself rather than live like the despised poor. One may as well try to use the same formula for a Turk, an Englishman, a Spanish grandee, a Russian peasant, as for a kraal dweller, an immigrant miner, a Tembu medical student, a Zulu driving a taxi, a Christian Basuto in a Bloemfontein location, a Shangaan cook letting his property with some slight evasion of rent control, a Bechuana chief educated in England and married to an English typist. . . .

Yet there is one thing, the darkness of the skin apart, that applies to all South African natives. They are changing; they are rapidly changing. This change may be seen not over ten years, over five years, but in a single year.

By nature, the African, like all primitive people, is lazy. Gibbon's words concerning the ancestors of the industrious Teutons describe also the African: "The care of the house and family, the management of the land and cattle, were delegated to the old and infirm. The lazy warrior, destitute of every art that might employ his leisure hours, consumed his days and nights in the carnal gratifications of sleep and food."

Until just yesterday the African's dream was to buy a few wives and breed up sons to labour for him and daughters to bring him a lobola of cattle. Or, if he could not help himself, he would work a few months, and then idle until he had eaten up his savings. The life bequeathed to him by his forefathers was a large, easy life.

Now Emerson has said that the ultimate end of all social intercourse is a little high conversation. But, nearer the beginnings of social intercourse, a little low conversation may be just as agreeable. To lie naked under a mimosa tree discussing the making of rain is probably quite a good substitute for walking in the garden of Epicurus cogitating on the destiny of man. And the native, untouched by the European, was able to achieve the first. But the day he put on his earliest bead at the instance of that same European, he entered upon a new scheme of existence.

Now, whether he wishes it or not, whether the white man wishes it or not, he has started behind his master on the long road whose end—a little good talk—is but the artificial form of its beginning. While white men are discussing with one another whether they shall or shall not educate the native and civilize him, Nature is laughing at them. "You began this business," she says. "But can you not see I have taken it out of your hands now? For better or worse, this thing is going on, and you won't stop it. You have lost control."

The young Africans, walking about the streets of Johannesburg on a Sunday, sometimes a little drunk, sometimes clasping hands with one another, sometimes in the company of smart young spectacled girls who are in Johannesburg not necessarily to work, make the white South Africans thoughtful and nervous.

The young Africans are dressed very like their masters. They are natty and rollicking. They have ideas in their heads. They write English. They meet members of other tribes than their own, and think increasingly that the chief thing about an African is not that he belongs to this or that nation, but that he has a black skin (one calls it a black skin) and a European has a white skin (one calls it a white skin) and that the issue is not between African and African, but between African and European.

It is chiefly on the Rand—in the streets, mines, factories, shops, and houses of the Johannesburg—that the native is learning to develop a self-consciousness, a race consciousness, an economic and social consciousness. And the more he is differentiated from the white people, the more he has this consciousness. He questions at last whether the white people can do no wrong, and whether a black man may not use the white man's physical and moral weapons against the white man himself; and a quarter of a century after he follows the First World War with strikes, he follows the Second World War with strikes—and he knows better why.

But a stranger thing than strikes happened among the black people of South Africa in the strike-year of 1920.

About thirty years before there had been created in America a Negro organization called the Church of God and Saints of Christ. It had a prophet and its followers adopted a mixture of Hebrew and Christian ritual, conformed to the Jewish calendar, regarded Saturday as the Sabbath and observed the Jewish Passover.

A South African native, a Wesleyan Methodist preacher, dismissed from his Church, visited America; became an adherent of the Church of God and Saints of Christ; in due course returned to South Africa—a Bishop now—to spread the new faith.

It became popular. It had everything, from baptism by total immersion at midnight and a kiss of peace, to a revelation of the rise of the black people.

But then the Bishop died, and was succeeded by one
Enoch, and presently the sect was split in two.

Now every year, for three years, Enoch and his followers
met, by official permission, at a place called Bullhoek, to
celebrate the Passover. They feasted for a few weeks and
dispersed.

But early in the year 1920 they met and did not disperse.
They pleaded special services, sickness, and inability to pay
their train fares. The months ran on, and still they were
there, calling themselves now Israelites and their leader a
prophet. In a newspaper in Italy appeared the information
that the Jews were making trouble in South Africa.

The police ordered them at last to go home. But they had
learned lessons from Asiatics as well as from ancient He-
brews and Greeks and modern Americans. They adopted a
policy of Passive Resistance. They offered no violence, but
they obeyed no orders. They isolated themselves, refused to
give their names, would allow no white interference, placed
a guard at their entrance, posted notices in English and
Xosa: "Halt!—No Admittance."

In December they were still there. The non-Israelite natives protested that their wives and children were being
lured away. The Israelites were beginning to starve and
steal and the white people near them grew more and more
alarmed. The Israelites were offered free railage and rations
if only they would go home. The Israelites, however, declared that they had a Pact with God, and refused to go.

A force of police came and was ordered to leave by the
prophet of the Israelites. The force left, withdrew to a
neighbouring farm, remained on guard, but took no action.

April of 1921 arrived. To save the white man's face, the
government offered, on certain conditions, to allow the Israelites to remain at Bullhoek.

The Israelites' answer was that they dealt only with, and

through, God, whose prophet was Enoch; that God wished them to remain there; that the Scriptures contained God's promise to gather his people together; that, deeply as they desired to obey the law of the land and injure no one, Jehovah was above the law of the land and they dared not disobey Jehovah; that they would go when they received their instructions from above; and that the punishment of Jehovah would surely fall on unbelievers, for the end of the world was at hand, and, for their part, divinely instructed, they were here to await it. . . .

They refused further discussion. The matter was very simple. The issue was between God and the government, and they were with God.

A month had passed in parleyings. Now force was used. The troops of the government advanced upon the resisting legions of God, clad in holy white, led by their prophet in a cloak of scarlet. They cried: "God will not let you burn our huts. If there is a fight, He will fight with us."

But it was artillery and a machine-gun against swords and assegais. On God's side, nearly three hundred Africans were killed and wounded, and seventy-five were taken prisoner. On the government's side, a European was stabbed and a horse killed.

From a neighbouring town members of the Automobile Club came to search out the dead and dying; a hospital made ready to receive them. But yet there were South Africans who wondered if this bloodshed of half-savages, yielding themselves too utterly to the faith of conquering civilization, could not have been avoided. . . .

Not very far from Bullhoek there had perished, sixty-five years before, tens of thousands of black people who also had believed in a Kaffir millennium. Their descendants were inspired by a different creed, but the faith in their hearts was the same.

X

All around the black man there are new, strange, terrible forces. To these he still submits himself because they are the forces of the white man, his master, teacher, and conqueror. He believes in the white man's God. He does the white man's work. He wears the white man's clothes. He learns the white man's language, his skill, and his wisdom.

Well, where is he? At Bullhoek he relies on this God, and he is slaughtered. To the mines he is lured to this work, and the white miners rise in bitterness against him. From small shops, from second-hand-clothes men, at back doors, he buys the clothes of civilization, and the better he dresses the more he is sneered at and disliked. He attends government and mission schools and colleges and thinks, like a child, how he will please by his decency, his industry, and his progress, and hostile tongues declaim: "A native educated is a native spoilt. . . ."

And spoilt, he begins to feel, he is—though not in the white man's sense. For to the white man it merely seems as if a useful cart-horse has been turned into a circus-horse. He cannot carry a load, he cannot draw a vehicle, he can only uselessly and showily run round a ring, a freak, unsuited henceforth, to nature's purposes.

As for what then has nature devised him? Why, obviously, to serve the white man. And, so considered, a native educated is a native spoilt.

But, from the native's point of view—things being what they are today—he is also spoilt. He cannot return to his kraal life any more than an adult can return to his childhood. The native leader who writes of "the more decent native" having to sit with "the blanketed heathen" and "annex his vermin" is bitter not only against the white man who has awakened longings in his heart that may not be satisfied, but also against the black man who, not having

similar longings, shames him with an exposure of his beginnings. And no man so hates the black man as that one
with both white and black in him, who can only rise towards the white by rejecting the black. "Kaffir!" he cries,
with a passion a man cannot know who has not to suffer
for his blood. "Kaffir!" his heart feels of the blood in his
veins that gives him such anguish. . . .

Now the educated black cannot but make distinctions between "the blanketed heathen" and the "more decent native." Now his tastes are delicate: his skin may be dark, but
he is shocked by the vermin of other dark-skinned men.
Now he has ideas of comfort: he does not, in the aboriginal
way, bear with equanimity, as a matter of fate, the affronts
of the weather. Now he has a sense of his rights: he raises
his voice against the indignities and injustice to which he is
subjected. . . . And yet, at the same time, the fact remains
that he prefers the scorn of the white man, for the sake of
his civilization, to the society of the black man, who can
only drag him back. The educated native trembles at the
thought of a country of his own—separation of black from
white—segregation.

As things are, then, what is the maturity of the black man
to him but a tragedy: a ripeness unused, souring, ferment-
ing? What can he do with his training and education? He
can teach other Africans to be as himself. And that is all.
He may not try to rise. He may not, even if his intelligence
and capacity are of the highest, aspire to mount beside a
European whose intelligence and capacity are of the lowest.
And all the laws of nature would seem to stop and planets
would crash wildly into one another and the universe
would come to an end if ever the black man were lifted to
a position of command over the white man.

That is the feeling of the white South African. And it
slumbers in the hearts of otherwise just and temperate men.

However they may wish the happiness of the native, and strive for it, and demand his rights, there is something which prevents them from making an equal of him, except spiritually, except theoretically; and still less a superior. They would feel their forefathers and their race degraded and the flag of civilization in the dust if they saw a white man taking an order from a black man. Nor can they easily —here and now—bring themselves to touch his skin. They might do it, but they would feel it. Men who have given their lives towards bettering the African's condition cannot, without a certain self-consciousness (they confess it with shame), take the hand of a native, or wear clothes he has worn, or sleep in a bed he has used.

There are a few who maintain that they positively have no colour sense; but they are, biologically speaking, sports, or they have overcome traditional weakness, or they are nobly deceiving themselves.

There seems to be only one thing that can, to any noticeable extent, override this profound feeling which physically divides white from black: and that is the force of sex. A white man who would not touch a black man will take to himself the black man's sister, and make her the vehicle for perpetuating his being, and give his children the blood he abhors.

CALIBAN

. . . I am all the subjects that you have,
Which first was mine own king: and here you sty me. . . .

PROSPERO

. . . Thy vile race,
*Though thou didst learn, had that in't which good **natures***
Could not abide to be with; therefore wast thou
Deservedly confined. . . .

CALIBAN

You taught me language; and my profit on't
Is, I know how to curse.

Now here we are. The white man has awakened the native, and, like a dream, the old savage life is ended. He has been called. He has risen. He is on the road—travelling in the shadow of the white man, carrying his chattels.

The white man looks around at this being he has himself aroused, who is following him; who is serving him; who is dependent on him; for whom, on the journey, he must provide. And he thinks how good it is that someone else's back shall be bowed under his burden while he is free to exult in the air and sun of Africa.

The native follows. Now it is time to take food. The white man throws the native a scrap. They go on again. The native is useful to the white man, but also he makes demands on the white man's resources. The master begins to wonder, a little resentfully, if he would not, on the whole, have been happier without his servant.

The journey is an arduous one. The white man opens up again his bundle of food, and thinks that, really, he cannot afford to give any more away, that he needs it all himself. He begins to be unpleasingly conscious of this creature that makes demands on him. If only he could shake him off, he thinks to himself. He begins to feel he is being dogged. He begins to suspect the native is not keeping a decent distance. He begins to distrust him, to fear him. The native, he knows, is not getting enough to eat. What if he were suddenly to take it into his head to spring upon him, and rob him of his means of subsistence, and run away ahead of him, and leave him there to starve?

How can he get rid of the native? How can he get rid of him—yet have him?

He makes suggestion to the native that he should retrace his steps, return to his beginnings.

"Look," he says, "this journey of ours has been a mistake. You and I can't do it together."

"It is hard for both of us," agrees the native.

"You'd better leave me," says the white man. "You'd better go back home."

"Go back?" says the native. "Home? . . . But the road has fallen in behind us. And my home is broken up. How can I go home now?"

"You are taking the bread out of my mouth," says the white man.

"But I am carrying your load."

"I could have carried it myself. It would have been better."

As easy too?

The black man looks at him through his sweat.

"Then why did you call me?"

They face one another, unable to move forward, unable to move back.

And: "I wish to God I never had called you," mutters the white man.

Yet, does he?

XI

This strong thick river that is called the Vaal River and runs through the lands of gold and diamonds and shines molten under a burning sun has a black, rocky bed which lies under the moving waters like a dark secret under a pleasant life. At the bottom of existence, as it flows onward in South Africa, is always the black man.

Why is there a poor-white problem? Why do white boys leave school without hope of employment? Why, with a population of five white people to the square mile, is immigration restrained?

The answer to these questions and a hundred others is the Black Man.

Take the Poor-White Problem. It manifests itself as soon as high prosperity goes. Then one notices that the black man is working where the unskilled white man ought to be working—he is working for this, for that, for all but nothing, because the white man must be an aristocrat. He cannot work beside the black man, he cannot work like the black man, for he has a certain lack of pigment that—whatever his antecedents, whatever his character, whatever his standing—makes him Baas to every black soul in the land.

Take the boy leaving school. He cannot begin at the bottom of the ladder. He cannot shoulder a burden or make a road or till the earth or use a jackhammer or fetch and carry in a business. He can learn a trade, he can go into an office or shop, he can study a profession.

But there is no labouring class with the means to set the social machine going full speed. In South Africa there is not plenty of room on the top because the foundation is not strong enough to support a high structure, and yet, such room as exists has to be high up.

Take the immigrant. Disregarding that one who, after the Second World War, the destruction in Europe, the Socialism in England, sought refuge for his money, the immigrant is the man with no place in the Old White World.

There is this land South Africa, a dozen times as large as England and Ireland together, with so few whites and so many black. Must South Africa not want more white men, must it not be the very place for an immigrant?

Yet what shall he do in South Africa, this immigrant? Work in an industry, help on a farm? The black man does it at the black man's wages.

Only the special sort of man, the sort who, in fact, has small need to be an immigrant, is wanted in South Africa.

. . .

Well, a smallness is imposed on South Africa that, for the white person, is very sweet. Life is lovely. All the unpleasant work is done by the black man. No white woman need scrub a floor. No white man need move the garbage. The digger does not dig, and the farmer does not hoe and the miner does not break the rock or coal. The black man, with his tradition that work is only for women, suffers the indignity of toiling for the white man who talks of the dignity of labour.

For fifty-six years now there has been talk of the urgent need of separating black from white: for the good of the black, for the good of the white.

It began, in modern times, with Rhodes.

But will the white housewife live like her sister overseas —a domestic slave? Will the white labouring man bend his back? Will the white farmer himself till the stony earth through the droughts that come thrice in five years? Will the manufacturer bring himself to depend on an arduous efficiency? Will the gold and coal and diamonds and copper and chrome and manganese of their own volition rise to the astonished surface?

Will the white man of South Africa truly *like* to live without the black man? Will he feel that discomfort and discomfiture are truly for the good of the white man?

What if the *black* chooses to make a spiritual Great Fish River—that boundary separating black and white when they first met two centuries ago—between himself and the white man?

There is the dilemma: If the black man is repressed, kept poor, ignorant, and uncivilized, it is not humane, it is not well for the land, it may be dangerous.

If he is not repressed, kept poor, ignorant, and uncivilized, South Africa faces what England has come to face, now that she has taught the world her skill, and especially the world of her Empire; now that she has not the mastery her particular knowledge gave her.

Some rise above the dilemma. They hold that the white man must do his duty, without regard to his own sole well-being, since, not by the colour of his skin, but by the colour of his conscience, does man find salvation. They believe that even the desire for good is a good—radiating a magnetic field for good which draws good and where good may live and grow, so that the result must be good.

Only does good indeed prevail? In every land on earth, there are a few virtuous people who strive to draw the multitude to good. In vain.

But let a Hitler arise, and a thousand million people are wildly inspired towards evil. It is as if the soul of man, like his body, can be infected not at all by health but only by sickness.

However, good or evil, the question still remains of how far the African can accompany the European on the advance towards civilization. The other question—whether he should be allowed to make the attempt—no longer arises. The thing is finished. The black man has been started on the road and will not go back.

Now what are his hopes in the world? Has the African the same capacities as the European? Can the two establish brotherhood? Will the time ever come when each will consider the presence of the other a blessing? Is it destined that white shall finally overcome black from the south of Africa as in thousands of years it has not succeeded in doing from the north? Or has it already happened once in South Africa, and do the Zimbabwe Ruins and their own faces stand witness to it, that the black people of the country have absorbed a higher civilization, and must white South Africa

have a care lest some day, in General Smuts's words, "little
brown children play among the ruins of the Union Government Buildings"?

Well, people have the naïve and pathetic idea that their
own concerns are of universal moment. The hawker sees
life in terms of penny packets. The lover thinks the gods
are solely absorbed in his heart-throbs. The dying Basuto,
with his fading eyes on his helpless dependants, whispers:
"I don't know what will happen to the world when I am
gone." A million people at any given time are imagining
that the laws of nature are directed to their especial discomfiture.

The South African thinks it a malevolence of other nations not to feel for his plight. Here he is, standing like a
thin dyke against an ocean of blackness, facing such a problem as Balfour said had never before presented itself in the
history of mankind, and the world can only blame him for
not letting the floods through.

The problem, indeed, is even greater than Balfour conceived, for he was thinking of South Africa alone, and the
question is of the Continent of Africa. The question is (the
figures have been given before, but they need emphasis) as
if white Americans were facing five or six hundred million
Negroes in their midst and another nine thousand million
beyond their borders. Perhaps the Lord (South Africans
think), having created black and white, knows how to do
justice to all: the white man fearing for his civilization; the
black man menacing, even while he craves it. The white
South African, without a revelation, goes fumbling along.

It is seventy-three years since Anthony Trollope said:
"South Africa is a country of black men—and not of white
men. It has been so; it is so; and it will be so."

If the thought is abhorrent, it no longer seems strange.

There are even a few hundred Africans to whom it no longer seems strange. When Arnold Toynbee says that, after an Atom Bomb war, civilization, as like as not, will start again from the Negritos—an advance really on our previous beginnings—he cannot make it seem strange.

Yet does not the world's future depend on how far we can see our present life as strange? . . .

And still, none will be as wise as Destiny.

INDEX

aboriginals, 7, 14, 277
Abyssinia, 186, 312
African, use of term, 9–10
African Empire, plan for, 130–1, 151
African Mine Workers' Union, 99
African Pact, 196
Afrikaans language, 106, 115–16, 120, 123, 181, 209–11, 266
Afrikaner Party, 83, 190
Afrikaners, 9, 17, 203–24
Aliens Act, 236–7
AmaXosa, 45, 278
AmaZulu, 278
America: production of war weapons, 188; interests in Africa, 309, 312–14
Apartheid, 4, 130, 193, 222, 307; meaning of word, 4
Arabs, 7, 10, 12, 240, 276
architecture, 117–18
art, 114, 117–18, 211, 265
Asiatics, 242–4, 247, 249, 298, 308. See also Indians
Assembly, House of, 168, 171
Atlantic Pact, 196–7

baas, 214–15
Baca, 278
backvelders, 213–15, 217

Baker, Sir Herbert, 59, 77, 117
Bakwena, 275
Bamangwato, 126–7
Bantu states, 28, 39
Bantus, 3, 7, 9, 169–70, 207, 263–4, 274–8, 281, 286. See also Kaffirs and natives
Barend, 47
Barkly West, 64, 303
Barnato, Barney, 70–3
Barotse, 274
Barotseland, 54
Bastaards, 6, 16, 42, 46–7, 53, 66, 207, 263
Basuto-Bechuanas, 277–9
Basutoland, 124–5, 128–9, 292
Basutos, 34–5, 42, 47, 66, 278, 287, 318
Batavian Republic, 17, 20, 26
Batlapis, 35, 38
Batlokwa, 33–4
Bechuanaland, 58, 59, 87, 124–8, 131, 287, 292–3
Bechuanas, 35, 47, 66, 126–8, 203, 278–9, 318
Beit, Alfred, 73
Belgian Africans, 296
Bergenaars, 47, 53, 66, 301–2
Beyers, General, 92
Bezeidenhout, 25
Bill for Africa, see Glen Grey Act

Blaauwberg, battle of, 20

Black Circuit, 24–5

black man, use of term, 9

Bloemfontein, 106, 109–10, 124; Convention, 42

Blood River, 38, 39, 41, 56

Boer Mine-Workers' Union, 206

Boer Rebellion, 135, 148, 173, 180

Boer War, 69, 87–9, 100, 142, 206, 208–9, 242

Boers: Dutch settlers, 12–13, 15–16; grievances, 17–20, 23, 27–9; first rebellion against British rule, 25–6; blamed for Kaffir wars, 28; settle in Natal, 37–9; barrier between English and Boer, 49, 94, 122, 146, 203, 208–9, 226–7; English push out the Boers, 53, 55–6; independence regained, 56; Kaiser's guarantee of Boer Republic, 135, 173; conciliation with British, 142–3, 146–7; their politics, 145–51, 204–10; Hertzog and Boer Republic, 180; growth of nationalism, 210–11; characteristics, 212–15; backvelders, 213–15, 217; poor whites, 215–17; well-to-do and professional classes, 217–20; their hospitality, 220–1; attitude towards the Kaffir, 221–4; wars against natives, 286–7. *See also* Trekkers

Booth, General, 61

Botha, General, 4, 124, 230; on the Boer War, 88; and Rand strikers, 91, 92; on victory in South-West Africa, 135; first

Botha, General (*continued*) Union Prime Minister, 137; his association with General Smuts, 137–41; his conciliation policy towards England, 143–4, 146; defeated at provincial elections, 145; forms new ministry, 148; and native reserves, 292; his death, 144, 194

British: early settlers, 16, 23–4; present-day immigrants, 16; the Cape ceded to England, 19–20, 24; barrier between English and Boer, 45, 94, 122, 146, 203, 208–9, 226–7; acquire Griqualand West, 55; Rhodes's idea of a world under British rule, 133–4; the Englishman in South Africa, 225–30

Broederband, 180–5

Bulawayo, 33, 58

Bullhoek, 45, 326–7

Bunga, 295–6

Burgers, President, 56

Bushmen, 10, 13–15, 47, 48, 66, 264–5, 301

Buys, Coenraad de, 23, 46–7, 271

Cape-Cairo All-Red route, 4, 58, 73, 125, 130–1

Cape Colony: English ships call, 11–12; history, 17–20; ceded to England, 19–20, 24; boundary between blacks and whites, 22; British settlers, 23–4; Boers and British in, 40; acquires Constitution, 42; its politics, 145–7, 168–70;

Cape Colony (*continued*)
Indians in, 241; imported labour, 306–7
Cape People, 9, 14, 16, 204, 207, 263–9
Cape Town, 18, 106–9, 142, 234; population, 25, 62, 265; legislative capital, 106–7, 124
Cape Town Agreement, 250, 251
Carnegie Commission on white population, 215
Chaka, 30–4, 36, 37, 38, 270, 275–9, 287
Chamber of Mines, 96, 97, 99
Chamberlain, Joseph, 87
children, 281–3, 303
Chinese labour, 90, 122
Christian National Education, 181–2
Chudeep, 53
Chudoo, 53
Church of God and Saints of Christ, 325–7
Churchill, Winston, 248
cinema, 114–15
citizenship, 167, 192, 240, 296
classes of people, 112–13
clergy, 219
climate, 103–4, 113, 151
Clu-Clu, 38
coal miners, 96
Coalition, 163–4, 228
Colonial Development Corporation, 130
colour bar, 94, 112, 241–2, 244, 271–2, 295–7, 311
"coloured," use of term, 263
Commonwealth of Nations, 196–7, 207

Communism, 93, 99–100, 193, 196–7, 205–6, 298–9
compounding of natives, 68, 70
controls, 111–12
crime, 250, 321–2
Cripps, Sir Stafford, 83
cultural life, 114–15
Curzon, Lord, 123

De Beer, 50–1
De Beer Mines, 51, 57, 62, 63, 70–3, 132, 288
Defence Act, 179
de la Rey, Groot Adrian, 59
devaluation of sterling, 83–4, 159–60
De Villiers, Baron, 84, 122
diamonds: in bed of Vaal River, 6; Griqualand fields, 47; discoveries, 48–50; amalgamation of companies and mines, 57, 58, 63, 70–1; native labour, 61–2, 65–70, 301–4; diggers and diggings, 61–7, 71–3; production control and trade, 63, 73; alluvial and mine, 64–5; "rush" described, 64–5; illicit selling and buying, 66–9, 303–4
Diaz, Bartholomew, 10
Dingaan, 36–9, 277, 284
Dingaan's Day, 39, 56, 228
Dingiswayo, 31, 33
discovery of South Africa, 10–12
Dominion Party, 166
Drakensbergen, 33, 37, 40, 46, 287
Drakenstein Valley, 58
drought, 152–3, 154
Duncan, Sir Patrick, 145

Dunn, of Natal, 271
Durban, 62, 90, 106, 107, 109, 234; population, 109, 314; Indians in, 109, 250, 251, 256-7; Zulu-Indian riots (1949), 255-61, 298, 314, 322
Dutch, *see* Boers
Dutch East India Company, 11-13, 15-19, 29, 203, 216, 307-8
Dutch language, 123
Dutch Reformed Churches, 168, 181, 215, 231
du Toit, Rev. S. J., 50, 73

East London, 109
education, 118-19, 181-2
emigrants, British, *see* immigration
English, *see* British
English East India Company, 11
English language, 24, 120
Enoch, 326-7
Enscombe, Sir Harry, 241-2

farming, 216, 218, 233
Fengus, 33, 69, 278
flag, South African, 151
food, 111-12, 305, 317, 318
forces, South African: employment overseas, 179, 185-6, 187, 188; demobilization and resettlement, 190
Fort Hare Native College, 9
franchise, 168-9, 296, 299-300; native, 124, 168-9
"Free Burghers," 15, 17
French, 16-20, 48; colonials, 295, 296
Froude, J. A., 26

fruit, 111-12
furniture, 108, 118

Gaika, 22, 23, 42-3
Galekas, 5
Gama, Vasco de, 10, 11
Gandhi, Mohandas Karamchand, 90, 240, 242, 243-7, 248, 252, 254
Germans, 4, 16, 45-6, 48-9
Germany, 183; South African sympathizers, 84, 134-5; Kaiser and South Africa, 89, 135, 173; colonies in Africa, 132-7, 312; plans for Africa, 132-7, 312; collaboration with Boers, 173
Gide, André, 296
Gij Gariep, 5
Gladstone, Lord, 148
Gladstone, William Ewart, 56
Glen Gray Act (Bill for Africa), 4, 58, 288, 289-90, 292
Goering, Hermann, 132
Gold Coast, 298
gold standard, 83, 152, 154-6, 162
goldfields: and industry, 74, 80-1; in Lydenberg, 54; illicit buying of, 67-9; labour, 81, 90-1, 96, 99, 303-6; taxation, 81-2, 83; profits, 82; price, 83, 159-60; threat to destroy mines, 89; in Free State, 110, 160, 306; boom of 1933, 156-9
government, 167-72
Governor-General-in-Council, 168, 171
Great Fish River, 22, 28, 41, 287

Great Trek, 29, 37–9, 174–6, 203, 228–9
greatness, 57
Greeks, 236
Griqualand East, 46, 53
Griqualand West, 46, 47, 53, 55
Griquas, 6, 34, 35, 43, 46–7, 54, 66, 269

Haggard, Sir Henry Rider, 55
half-castes, 262–73
Havenga, N. C., 83–4
Hereros, 136
Hertzog, General, 4, 100; and the Boer War, 143–4; Minister of Justice, 146; his attitude to the British, 146–8, 174; his relations with Botha, 146–8; leads the government, 150; his policy, 151, 152, 162–3; on independence, 165; and the franchise, 169–70; and the First World War, 173–4; and the Second World War, 176–80, 182–3; his resignation, 178; and the Boer Republic, 180; founds Afrikaner Party, 183; and the Broederband, 182–3; on Indians, 248–9; native policy, 262–3; death, 185
High Commissioners, 172
Hitler, Adolf, 133, 134, 135, 183, 185, 186
Hobhouse, Miss, 138
Hofmeyr, Jan, 60
Hofmeyr, J. H., 119, 140–1, 145, 163, 168, 221, 230; his colour policy, 193, 194; and Indians, 251; death, 300

Hofmeyr, Mrs. J. H., 175
Holland, 18, 212
Holmes, Oliver Wendell, 108
Hottentots, 9, 10, 13–15, 24–5, 42, 207, 264–5, 277, 279; regiment formed, 19, 20; in South-West Africa, 132–3, 136; use of word, 207, 263–4; slaves, 307–8
houses, 78
Huguenots, 16–17, 23, 203

Imhoff, von, 308
immigration, 16, 105, 190–2, 332–3; of Jews, 149, 204, 236–7; of Indians, 148, 242–4, 247
Imperial Conferences, 174
indentured labour, 204, 240, 241
independence question, 165–6; autonomy granted, 166–7
India: position in the Commonwealth, 167, 195–6, 244, 252–3, 263; disabilities for South Africans in, 252
Indian Ocean, 187
Indians in South Africa, 15, 16, 90, 109, 196, 204, 207, 239–61, 262–3, 275; status reduced, 148; Zulu attacks on, in Durban, 255–60, 298, 314, 322
industrial progress, 191
Isaacs, Barnett, *see* Barnato, Barney
Israel, 193–4, 238, 311
Israelites, 326–7

Jameson, Sir Starr, 72, 122, 145, 173
Jameson Raid, 84, 87, 89, 135

Japanese, 130

Jews, 16, 105, 149, 193–4, 204, 207, 230, 231–8; Nazi persecution, 189, 231, 234, 236; at first welcomed by the Boers, 232; as professional men and farmers, 233; percentage of population, 234; in politics, 233–4; present position, 234–8; effect of Quota Act, 236–7; settlement in Israel, 237–8, 311

Joel, Woolf, 73

Johannesburg, 75–81, 104–8, 145; population, 62; suburbs, 78–9; mines, 79, 81; Chinese labour, 90; strikes, 90–3, 95–100; boom, 158–60; Jews in, 233, 234; native labour, 314–15; native crime, 321–2

Kaffir Wars, 7, 22–3, 28, 287

Kaffirs, 18, 276, 302; use of word, 4, 7–8, 9, 263–4; the Kaffir millennium, 31–2; labour and labourers, 50, 52, 68, 205; Boer attitude to, 221–3

Kaffraria, 7, 8

Kaiser, *see* William II, Kaiser

Kenya, 297, 298

Khama, 126

Kimberley, 51–2, 58, 69–70; diamond mines, 57, 61–4, 72, 73–4, 302, 303–4; population, 62

Kleurlinge, 207, 263

Kok, Adam, 47, 53, 55

Koranna, 47, 66

Kottler, Moses, 117

kraals, 283–6

Kreli, 5

Kruger, Paul, 30, 84–9, 106, 125, 153, 173, 242; alleged hidden gold, 68–9; Kaiser's telegram to, 135, 173

Labour Party, 149, 150, 151, 152, 206

land: diamond fields, 50–2; owning and selling, 53–4; Indian-owned, 249; for native use, 292–3

Langa, 23

languages, 120, 123, 209–11, 304

law, 24, 172, 219

Lemba, 278

Leo XIII, Pope, 310

Liberia, 297, 312, 313

Lincoln, Abraham, 300

liquor traffic, 320–1

literature, 115–17

Lobengula, 54, 57, 68–70, 287

lobola, 279–82, 287, 303

locusts, 149, 151

London Missionary Society, 14

Lydenberg, 54

Madagascar slaves, 15

magistrates, 172

Majuba, battle of, 56, 88, 89, 184

Makalangas, 11, 276

Makana, 43

Malan, Dr., 169, 175, 192, 195; Apartheid policy, 4, 222; and South-West Africa, 136–7, 199; and National Party, 147, 166, 183; returned to Parliament, 164; and independence, 164–5; and the Ossewa

Malan, Dr. (*continued*)
Brandwag, 176, 184–5, 190;
and the Second World War,
177, 179–80, 186; member of
Broederband, 182; wins election, 194; on future, 195–6;
on Communism, 196–7;
tribute to Smuts, 199; on the
Great Trek, 228
Manicaland, 54
Mantati, 34–5
Mantatisi, Queen, 6, 33–4, 37,
270, 275, 277, 287
marriage between white and
black, 14–15, 24–5, 127,
265–6, 267–8, 271, 330
Mashonaland, 59, 69, 274, 287
Matabele, 33, 42, 54, 59–60,
126
Matabeleland, 36, 69–70, 287
Matoppo Hills, 36, 60, 61, 277
millionaires, 110
Milner, Lord (Alfred), 19, 77,
84, 87–8, 145, 242, 248, 262
Minimum Wage Act, 311
Mining Board, 72
missionaries, 14–15, 20, 24–5,
28, 29, 38–9, 302
Mist, Abraham de, 26
Mittel-Afrika plan, 133–4, 312
mixed breeds, 264, 269
Moffat, Robert, 38–9, 282, 323
Moffat, Thomas, 25, 34, 35
Mokotsho, 33
Monomotapa, 11, 12, 18, 276–8
Moselikatze, 32–3, 35–6, 39, 40,
42, 54, 270, 276–7, 279, 282,
287, 301, 302
Moshesh, 34–5, 42, 44, 46,
85–6, 125, 277
Motsholi, 33–4, 37

Mountain Schools, 280
Mozambique, 187
music, 117

Namaqualand, 63, 313
Namaquas, 47
Napoleon, 20, 203
Natal: named, 10; Zulus in, 12,
240, 278, 284; Indians in, 16,
240, 241, 247, 250–1; Boers
settle in, 37–40; end of black
power, 38; declared a British
colony, 40; parts from Cape
Colony, 42; and the Union,
123, 124; its politics, 145–7;
franchise, 168
National Convention, 122–3,
134
National Party, 147–50, 163–4,
165, 183, 196, 210
Nationalists, 97–8, 149, 189,
192, 206
nationality, *see* citizenship
Native Affairs Commission, 290
Native Problem, 58, 287–310,
323–5, 331–7
Native Representative Council,
100, 170
natives, 274–337; use of term,
8–9; racial consciousness, 149;
representation in Parliament,
169–70, 262–3; attitude to
Indians, 255–61; groups and
divisions, 277–9; tribal life,
280–6; history, 286–8; intellectuals, 293–4; education,
295–6, 328–9; labour, 296–7,
301–8, 311–12, 314, 334;
treatment of, 297–306, 317;
town dwellers, 314–22; wom-
en, 318–19; social life, 319–

natives (*continued*)
20; crime, 321–2; developing
a self-consciousness, 324–5;
religion, 319–20, 325–7; divi-
sion of white and black, 330–
2, 333–7; prospects, 335–7
Nazi activities, 135, 184, 185
Ndlambe, 22, 23, 28, 42–3
Negroes, American, 7, 8, 170,
171, 224, 263, 271, 272–3,
300
Nehru, Pandit, 196, 250, 261
Nguni, 278
Njubi, 69–70, 128
Nongkwase, 43–4
North Africa landings, 188
Ntsikana, 42–3
Nyasaland, 120, 297

Ophir, 276
Oppenheimer, Sir Ernest, 63
Orange, Prince of, 18, 19, 94
Orange Free State, 41, 42, 53,
55, 106, 198; bankrupt, 109–
10, 153; gold discoveries, 110,
160, 306; its politics, 145; Indians in, 241
Orange River Sovereignty, 41,
46
Ossewa Brandwag, 176, 179,
184–5, 190

Panda, 38
Pandit, Mrs., 253
Parker, Stafford, 64
Parliament, 167–72
passes for natives, 105, 314–15,
318
Passive Resistance, 244, 245–7,
252, 306

Peace Conference (Paris), 174
Pegging Act, 251
Philip, Dr., 28, 39
Phœnicians, 12, 14, 240, 275
Pienaar, General, 188
Pietermaritzburg, 106
platinum, 54, 151, 152
polygamy, 282–3
Pondos, 278
poor whites, 65, 79–80, 105,
119, 215–17, 333
population, 3, 4, 62, 170–1,
212, 234, 264–5, 297
Port Elizabeth, 93, 109
Portuguese, 10–11, 272, 276,
296, 304
Portuguese discovery of South
Africa, 10–11
Prester John, 11
Pretoria, 35, 55, 62, 106–7, 108,
117, 142; Kruger's house, 85;
administrative capital, 106–7,
124; Jews in, 234
Pretorius, Andries, 36, 40, 41
Prime Ministers' Conferences,
167, 195–6, 225
Prime Ministers' houses, 107,
142
Pringle, Thomas, 24
professions, 118–19
profits tax, 157
property laws and Indians,
249
protectorates, British, 124–30,
292–3, 304, 305
Provincial Administrators and
Councils, 171–2
Purified National Party, 147,
166, 178

Quota Act, 236–7

racial problems, 15–17; English and Boer, 49, 94, 122, 146–7, 203, 208–9, 226–7; the Jews, 231–8; the Indians, 239–61; the natives, 58, 288–311, 323–5, 331–7

Rand mines, 57, 75, 77, 81–2, 93, 98, 99, 304; revolt of 1922, 97–100, 149, 204–5

Rarabe, 22, 23

Read, missionary, 24

Reitz, Deneys, 88, 145

Reitz, F. W., 76–7, 148

reserves, 289–93, 301, 305

Responsible Government granted, 122

Retief, Peter, 37–9, 41, 56

Reunited National Party, 147, 178, 183

Rhodes, Cecil John: Bill for Africa, 3–4, 58, 288–90, 292; house in Cape Town, 19, 107, 142; his burial place, 36, 59, 61; and the diamond trade, 51, 52, 56–7, 58, 63, 70–3; acquires Rhodesia, Barotseland, and Manicaland, 54–5; and Lobengula, 54, 68–70; career, character, and influence, 56–61; founds De Beers Company, 56, 70–1; establishes Goldfields Company, 57; his constituency, 64; on the Rand, 75; desire for united Africa, 84, 125, 131; and Jameson Raid, 87; encourages South African products, 118; his idea of world under British rule, 133–4; and the natives, 287–9

Rhodes Scholarships, 134, 140

Rhodesia, 33, 36, 54, 237, 274–6, 297; natives move to the Union, 105; proposed federation, 120–1, 130–1; and the Union, 120–1, 130–1

Richardson, Henry Handel, 116

rinderpest, 302

River Diamond Diggings, 302–3, 319

Robinson, 74

Roman-Dutch law, 24, 219

Roos, Tielman, 85, 148, 153–5, 161–4

Roos, Tielman, teacher of Kruger, 85, 153

royalty tax, 116–17

Salt-pan Mountains, 278

Sand River Convention, 42

Sandile, 44–5

segregation of natives, 148, 290–3, 329, 334

Selous, Frederick C., 274

Senate, 168, 171

Senzagakone, 30

Seretse Khama, 126, 127–8

Shangaans, 33, 279, 318

Shangana-Thonga, 278, 279

Sheba, Queen of, 275–6, 283

Shepstone, Sir Theophilus, 5, 56, 61, 84, 284

Sikonyela, 37

Slachter's Neck, 26

slaves, 15, 307–8; slavery abolished, 15, 26–7; compensation of owners, 27, 28

Smuts, General: quoted, 104, 120; *A Century of Wrong*, 19, 88; and the Boer War, 69, 89, 100–1, 208–9; and the strikes, 90–4, 96–100; de-

Smuts, General (*continued*)
ports strike leaders, 92; "Union of Brothers," 92–3, 94,
124, 146, 166, 180, 228; and
a united South Africa, 122,
123, 124–5; his visit to Rhodesia, 130–1; and South-West
Africa, 134–5, 136–7, 173;
his association with Botha,
137–41; his character and political ability, 137–44; his association with Hofmeyr, 140–
1, 193–4, 300; becomes
Prime Minister, 142, 149,
178–9; his conciliation policy
towards British, 143, 146; attitude to Hertzog, 146, 152;
his party defeated at elections, 149–50, 151–2; and
the gold standard, 152, 154–
5; invited by Roos to join in
coalition, 161–3; links up in
coalition with Hertzog, 163;
defeated at elections, 164; on
independence, 165–6; and the
Second World War, 177–80,
186–7, 189; his life threatened, 184; becomes British
Field Marshal, 186; wins
1943 elections, 190; defeated
in 1948 elections, 101, 193–
4; stands by the Jews, 193,
234–5, 236, 237; on the future, 195; his eightieth birthday, 197–8; on the Commonwealth, 206–7, 228; his hospitality, 220–1; attends opening of Voortrekker Monu-
ment, 228–30; and Indians,
243–4, 246–8, 251–4; on native question, 288; his last ill-

Smuts, General (*continued*)
ness and death, 198–9; Ma-
lan's tribute, 199
Smuts, Mrs., 175, 186, 221
Sobuza, 130
social life, 110–11, 112–14
Socialists, 204–6
Sofala, 12, 276
Soga, Tiyo, 8
Solomon, 283
Sotho, 278
South Africa Act, 123, 165,
167
South African, use of term,
207
South African Party, 147, 149,
152, 163
South African Republic, 41, 55,
56
South African War, *see* Boer
War
South-West Africa, 62–3, 132–
7, 173, 176, 178, 199, 312;
UN mission, 136
Speed, John, 276
sports, 113, 220
Stanley, Sir H. M., 132, 312
Status Act, 165–7
Statute of Westminster, 164,
166–7, 228
Steyn, ex-President, 123, 134–6,
148
Steyn, Colin, 145, 198
stinkwood, 118
strikes, 90–4, 95–100, 148, 325
sugar farming, 218, 240
Sumptuary Laws, 112
Swaziland, 124–5, 129–30, 292
Swazis, 33, 38, 54
Syndicalism, 90, 92, 93, 94, 99
syphilis, *see* venereal diseases

Tanganyika, 297, 298
taxation, double, 116–17
Tembus, 22, 278, 287
Tetwa, 30–1
theatres, 114
Tixo, 42
Tobruk, 187
Toynbee, Arnold, 104, 337
Transvaal, 40–2, 87; Trollope's visit, 5; first white settler, 46–7; annexed by England, 53, 55–6, 84; Boers proclaim their Republic, 56; diamond diggings, 62, 63; political, 124, 145, 148; and Indians, 241, 242–3, 246–7, 249
Trekkers, 18, 20–2, 26–30, 40, 41, 216. *See also* Great Trek
Trinidad, 299
Trollope, Anthony, 4–5, 40, 52, 68, 69, 302, 336
Trotha, General von, 132–3
Tshekedi, 126–8
Tswana, 277
tuberculosis, 306, 322

Uganda, 120
Uitlanders or Outlanders, 77, 84, 226
Unandi, 30, 32
Union of African Socialist Republics, 298
"Union of Brothers," *see under* Smuts, General
Union of South Africa, 3, 42, 90, 101; peoples and races, 15–17; Rhodesia and, 120, 130–1; established, 123–4; constitution, 123; provinces within the Union, 145; relations with British Crown,

Union of South Africa (*continued*)
165, 166; suggested division into three Dominions, 253
Unionists, 146, 149
United Nations, 196, 300; South-West African mission, 136; Indian case before, 253–5, 259; Tanganyika mission, 297
United Party, 147
United South African National Party, 147
universities, 118–19, 210
Uplift Clause, 250, 251

Vaal River, 5–6, 15, 34, 40, 41, 263, 301, 302, 332; diamond diggings, 64, 66
van der Bijl, Hendrik Johannes, 189, 194
van der Kemp, Johannes Theodorus, 14–15, 24, 25, 42, 43
van Riebeeck, Jan, 12, 212, 277, 308
Venda, 278
venereal diseases, 303, 318–19
Vienna, Congress of, 20
Voortrekkers, 30, 35, 36, 87, 118, 175–6, 203, 232, 287; Monument, 39, 175, 228

Wag-'n-bietjie (wait-a-bit), 6
Waterboer, Nicolaas, 47, 53, 55
Weenen, 38, 40
White Kaffir, 271
Whitman, Walt, 286, 319
Wilberforce, William, 26
William II, Kaiser, 89, 134, 135, 173

Witwatersrand, 74
women: franchise, 168–9; native women, 318–19
World War, First, 89, 92, 134, 135, 148, 173–4
World War, Second, 89, 109, 111, 133, 136–7, 140, 176–90, 212

Xosas, 20, 22–3, 33, 42–5, 47, 66, 277–9, 287

Yellow River, 5

Zimbabwe, 274–6, 335
Zoutpansberg, 278
Zulu-Xosas, 12–13, 31, 277–9
Zululand, 32, 37, 38, 129
Zulus, 12, 30–3, 93, 277–9, 284, 287; attack Dutch in Natal, 37–8; attack Indians in Durban, 255–61, 298, 314, 322; labour, 318

DATE DUE	
MAR 9 1995	
NOV 3 0 1997	
DEC 1 4 1997	
NOV 1 9 1998	
DEC 1 3 2003	
MAY 02 2011	